THE RESTRICTIVE COVENANT IN THE CONTROL
OF LAND USE

The Restrictive Covenant in the Control of Land Use

DONALD L. SABEY
BSc LLB PhD FRICS FRTPI
Latterly, One of the Lord Chancellor's Independent Inspectors
Formerly, County Planning Officer of Leicestershire

ANN R. EVERTON
LLM PhD of Lincoln's Inn, Barrister
Professor, Department of Built Environment
University of Central Lancashire

Ashgate

DARTMOUTH

Aldershot • Brookfield USA • Singapore • Sydney

Published by
Dartmouth Publishing Company Ltd
Ashgate Publishing Ltd
Gower House
Croft Road
Aldershot
Hants GU11 3HR
England

Ashgate Publishing Company
Old Post Road
Brookfield
Vermont 05036
USA

KD
954
S23
1999

Ashgate website: http://www.ashgate.com

British Library Cataloguing in Publication Data
Sabey, Donald L.
    The restrictive covenant in the control of land use
    1.Land use - Law and legislation - England 2.Land use - Law
    and legislation - Wales 3.Real covenants - England 4.Real
    covenants - Wales
    I.Title II.Everton, Ann R. (Ann Rosemarie)
    346.4'2'045

Library of Congress Cataloging-in-Publication Data
Sabey, Donald L.
    The restrictive covenant in the control of land use / Donald L. Sabey, Ann R. Everton
        p. cm.
    ISBN 1-84014-482-3
    1.Real covenants--Great Britain. 2. Land use--Law and legislation--Great
    Britain. I. Everton, Ann R. (Ann Rosemarie) II. Title.
    KD954.S23 1999
    346.4104'5--dc21

                                                                99-45178

ISBN 1 84014 482 3

Printed in Great Britain by
Antony Rowe Ltd, Chippenham, Wiltshire

Contents

Preface   *vii*
Table of Cases   *ix*

Foreword   1

PART I: THE EVOLUTION OF THE LAW OF RESTRICTIVE
        COVENANTS

1 The Restrictive Covenant before 1926   7
2 The Restrictive Covenant after 1925   45

PART II: THE DISCHARGE OR MODIFICATION OF RESTRICTIVE
         COVENANTS

3 Discharge or Modification and the Official Arbitrator   81
4 Discharge or Modification and the Lands Tribunal before 1970   121
5 Discharge or Modification and the Lands Tribunal after 1969   141

PART III: THE FUTURE FOR RESTRICTIVE COVENANTS

6 The Restrictive Covenant and Law Reform   183
7 The Restrictive Covenant and Planning Control   193

Appendices   213

Preface

The current law relating to the restrictive covenant is treated from the academic viewpoint in the standard textbooks on the Law of Property, notably Cheshire & Burn, Gray and Megarry & Wade, and for practitioners in the invaluable and unique Preston & Newsom. It is our belief, however, that no one has attempted an in depth historical account of the evolution of the law of the restrictive covenant and the operation of the discharge or modification mechanism with the express intention of showing how the restrictive covenant has been adapted to operate in the control of land use and development, firstly on its own and later alongside planning control. We hope that this excursion into its history and progress, and not least the operation of section 84 of the Law of Property Act, 1925, will assist an understanding of the importance of the restrictive covenant both in the past and for the future. By concentrating on its operation in an area increasingly dominated by planning and environmental issues it should be of interest to lawyers, surveyors, planners and others involved in the profession of the land who from time to time encounter its rôle and effect.

We finalised the main body of the text on 22 December 1998 - 150 years to the day of the judgment by the Lord Chancellor in *Tulk v Moxhay* - and presume to dedicate this small work to celebrate the sesquicentenary of that memorable decision.

Donald L Sabey
Ann R Everton

March 1999

Table of Cases

Cases heard by the Official Arbitrator were the subject of 'unofficial' reports in the Estates Gazette by non-legal reporters and are not included in this Table of Cases but are, for reference, listed on pages 85-6 and 101-2 of the text. References from Notes are indicated by 'n' after page reference.

Abbey Homesteads (Developments) Ltd's Application, Re (1984)
    49 P & CR 263   169
Abbey Homesteads (Developments) Ltd v Northamptonshire CC (1986)
    53 P & CR 1, (1990) 61 P & CR 295, (1992) 64 P & CR 377   169, 170
Aldred's Case (1610) 9 Co Rep 57b   72n
Alexander v Mansions Proprietary Ltd (1900) 16 TLR 431   37
Alliance Economic Investment Co. v Berton and Others(1923) 92 LJKB 750   38
Allnatt (London) Ltd's Application, Re (1959) 12 P & CR 256   126
Associated Property Owners Ltd's Application, Re (1964) 16 P & CR 89   137
Austerberry v Corporation of Oldham (1885) 29 Ch D 750   27, 65, 188n

Ballard's Conveyance, In re [1937] 1 Ch 743   47
Barclays Bank plc's Application, Re (1990) 60 P & CR 354   159
Bass Ltd's Application, Re (1973) 26 P & CR 156   160, 163
Baxter and Others v Four Oaks Properties Ltd [1965] 1 Ch 816   54, 66
Beardsley's Application, Re (1972) 25 P & CR 233   145
Beecham Groups Ltd's Application, Re (1980) 41 P & CR 369   171
Bell v Norman C. Ashton Ltd. (1956) 7 P & CR 359   124
Bhavnani (K & C) (Holdings) Ltd's Application, Re (1960) 12 P & CR 269   130
Bradley Clare Estates Ltd's Application, Re (1987) 55 P & CR 126   167
Briarwood Estates Ltd's Application, Re (1979) 39 P & CR 419   167
Brierfield's Application, Re (1976) 35 P & CR 124   149
Bristow v Wood (1844) 1 Coll CC 480   13
Brown v Heathlands Mental Health NHS Trust [1996] 1 All ER 133   61n
Brunner and Another v Greenslade [1971] 1 Ch 993   66, 67
Bushell's Application, Re (1987) 54 P & CR 386   156
Byrom's Application, Re (1960) 12 P & CR 273   126

Carshalton Urban District Council's Application, Re (1963) 16 P & CR 68   127
Catt v Tourle (1869) 4 Ch App 654   19n, 23, 24, 25
Chapman's Application, Re (1980) 42 P & CR 114   150
Chatsworth Estates Co v Fewell [1931] 1 Ch 224   49
Child v Douglas (1854) Kay 560   21
Coles v Sims (1853) Kay 56, (1854) 5 De GM & G 1   22, 23
Collett's Application, Re (1963) 15 P & CR 106   133
Collins' & Others' Application, Re (1974) 30 P & CR 527   146
Cook (James T) & Son's Application, Re (1957) 8 P & CR 460   125
Cooke v Chilcott (1876) 3 Ch D 694   24
Cornick's Application, Re (1994) 68 P & CR 372   168
Cowderoy's Application, Re (1955) 7 P & CR 184,*
    (1957) 9 P & CR 522   129, 130
Cresswell v Proctor [1968] 1 WLR 906, (1968) 19 P & CR 516   69, 158

Da Costa's Application, Re (1986) 52 P & CR 99   164
Darvill (S & K) Ltd's Application, Re (1955) 7 P & CR 212   135
Davies' Application, Re (1971) 25 P & CR 115   144
Davis' Application, Re (1950) 7 P & CR 1   123, 134, 138
De Mattos v Gibson (1858) 4 De G & J 276   19n, 25
Dr Barnardo's Homes' Application, Re (1955) 7 P & CR 176   21n, 156n
Doe v Keeling (1813) 1 Man & Selw 95   21
Dolphin's Conveyance, In re [1970] 1 Ch 654   66
Driscoll v Church Commissioners for England [1957] 1 QB 330,
    (1956) 7 P & CR 371   56, 135
Dyce v Hay (1852) 1 Macq 305   27n

Eagling and Another v Gardner [1970] 2 All ER 838   66
Eastwood v Lever (1863) 4 De GJ & S 114   22
Ecclesiastical Commissioners for England's Conveyance, In re
    [1936] 1 Ch 430   47
Edwards' Application, Re (1983) 47 P & CR 458   167
Elliston v Reacher [1908] 2 Ch 374   20, 24, 36, 54, 66
Emery's Application, Re (1956) 8 P & CR 113   125, 130
Esso Petroleum Co Ltd v Harper's Garage (Stourport) Ltd [1968] AC 269   51

Farmiloe's Application, Re (1983) 48 P & CR 317   150
Federated Homes Ltd v Mill Lodge Properties Ltd [1980] 1 WLR 594   62
Fisher & Gimson (Builders) Ltd's Application, Re (1992) 65 P & CR 312   168
Fisher's Application, Re (1954) 7 P & CR 153   136
Forestmere Properties Ltd's Application, Re (1980) 41 P & CR 390   154
Formby v Barker [1903] 2 Ch 539   24n, 32
Freeman - Thomas Indenture, Re [1957] 1 All ER 532   58

Gaffney's Application, Re (1974) 35 P & CR 440 — 164
Gaskin v Balls (1879) 13 Ch D 324 — 28
Gedge v Bartlett (1900) 17 TLR 43 — 37
Gee v The National Trust for Places of Historic Interest or Natural Beauty
   [1966] 1 WLR 170 — 58
Ghey and Galton's Application, In re [1957] 2 QB 650 — 56n
Gilbert v Spoor [1983] 1 Ch 27, (1982) 44 P & CR 239 — 70, 72, 155
Goodman's Application, Re (1970) 23 P & CR 110 — 157
Greaves' Application, Re (1965) 17 P & CR 57 — 127

Hall & Co Ltd's Application, Re (1955) 7 P & CR 159 — 129
Harlow v Hartog (1977) 245 EG 140 — 67
Harper's Application, Re (1986) 52 P & CR 104 — 167
Hathway's Application, Re (1968) 20 P & CR 505 — 127
Haywood v The Brunswick Permanent Building Society (1881)
   8 QBD 403 — 25, 26
Hedges' Application, Re (1956) 7 P & CR 270 — 123, 134
Henderson's Conveyance, In re [1940] 1 Ch 835 — 56, 116
Henman's Application, Re (1970) 23 P & CR 102 — 144
Hickman & Sons Ltd's Application, Re (1951) 7 P & CR 33 — 123
Hobbs' & Marshall's Application, Re (1951) 7 P & CR 25 — 136
Hopcraft's Application, Re (1993) 66 P & CR 475 — 173
Houdret & Co's. Application, Re (1989) 58 P & CR 310 — 172
Howard (M) (Mitchum) Ltd's Application, Re (1956) 7 P & CR 219 — 123
Hunt's Application, Re (1997) 73 P & CR 126 — 68, 161

Independent Television Authority's Application, Re The (1961)
   13 P & CR 222 — 131

Jackson v Winnifrith (1882) 47 LT 243 — 28
Jaggard v Sawyer and Another [1995] 1 WLR 269 — 168n
Jamaica Mutual Life Assurance Society v Hillsborough Ltd and Others
   [1989] 1 WLR 1101 — 67
Jamelson Property Co Ltd's Application, Re (1956) 7 P & CR 253 — 129
Jones & Another v Rhys-Jones (1974) 30 P & CR 451 — 69, 158
Jones' & White & Co.'s Application, Re (1989) 58 P & CR 512 — 173
Joyce (F & H) Ltd's Application, Re (1956) 7 P & CR 245 — 134

Kelsey v Dodd (1881) 52 LJ Ch 34 — 28
Kemp v Sober (1851) 1 Sim NS 517 — 20
Kennet Properties' Application, Re (1996) 72 P & CR 353 — 160
Keppell v Bailey (1834) 2 My & K 517 — 11, 17
Kershaw's Application, Re (1975) 31 P & CR 187 — 166

Kimber v Admans [1900] 1 Ch 412   37
Knight v Simmons [1896] 1 Ch 653, [1896] 2 Ch 294   30
Knott's Application, Re (1953) 7 P & CR 100   134

Lee's Application, Re (1996) 72 P & CR 439   68, 160
Leicester (Earl of) v Wells-next-the-sea UDC [1973] 1 Ch 110   62
Lloyd's & Lloyd's Application, Re (1993) 66 P & CR 112   156
London County Council v Allen [1914] 3 KB 642 CA   18, 24n, 33, 34, 52
London & South Western Railway Co. v Gomm (1882) 20 Ch D 562   26, 27
Love's & Love's Application, Re (1993) 67 P & CR 101   150
Luker v Dennis (1877) 7 Ch D 227   24
Lund v Taylor (1975) 31 P & CR 167   67
Luton Trade Unionist Club & Institute Ltd's Application, Re The (1969)
   20 P & CR 1131   135

MacKenzie v Childers (1889) 43 Ch D 265   28, 199n
Mann v Stephens (1846) 15 Sim 377   13, 15, 17
Manners (Lord) v Johnson (1875) I Ch D 673   29
Mansfield District Council's Application, Re (1976) 33 P & CR 141   147
Margate Corporation's Application, Re (1969) 21 P & CR 669   133
Marten and Another v Flight Refuelling Ltd and Another [1962] 1 Ch 115   48
Martin's Application, Re (1986) 53 P & CR 146,
   (1988) 57 P & CR 119   171 172, 173
Mawdit Harris's Application, Re (1966) 18 P & CR 138   133
Mercian Housing Society Ltd's Application, Re (1971) 23 P & CR 116   153
Mitchell v Steward (1866) LR Eq 541   22n
Morland v Cook (1868) LR 6 Eq 252   19n
Murray's Application, Re (1962) 14 P & CR 63   136

New Ideal Homes Ltd's Application, Re (1978) 36 P & CR 476   167
Newman v Real Estate Debenture Corporation Ltd [1939] 1 All ER 131   54
Newton Abbott Co-operative Society Ltd v Williamson & Treadgold Ltd
   [1952] 1 Ch 286   48
Nisbet & Potts' Contract, In re [1906] 1 Ch 386 CA   35
North's Application, Re (1998) 75 P & CR 117   160
Northbourne (Lord) v Johnston & Son [1922] 2 Ch 309   37

Osborn's & Easton's Application, Re (1978) 38 P & CR 251   149
Osborne v Bradley [1903] 2 Ch 446   37

Page's Application, Re (1996) 71 P & CR 440   150, 159
Patten Ltd's Application, Re (1975) 31 P & CR 180   146
Peacock v Penson (1848) 11 Beav 355   14

Pearce v Maryon-Wilson [1935] 1 Ch 188   53
Pearson's Application, Re (1978) 36 P & CR 285   158
Peek v Matthews (1867) LR Eq 515   22
Peyton's Application, Re (1959) 12 P & CR 263   132
Pinewood Estate, Farnborough, In re [1958] 1 Ch 280   55
Pointe Gourde Quarrying & Transport Co Ltd v Sub-Intendent
    of Crown Lands [1947] AC 565 PC   170n
Potter's Application, Re (1958) 10 P & CR 68   125
Price v Easton (1833) 4 B & Ad 433   7
Prior's or Pakenham's Case, The (1369) YB 42 Edw 111, pl 14, fol 3a   8n, 9n
Purkiss' Application, In re [1962] 1 WLR 902   58

Quaffers Ltd's Application, Re (1988) 56 P & CR 142   159

R v Plymouth City Council, ex parte Plymouth & South Devon
    Co-operative Society [1993] JPL 1099   200n
R v Westminster City Council & The London Electricity Board, ex parte
    Leicester Square Coventry Street Association Ltd (1989) 59 P & CR 51   64n
Reid v Bickerstaff [1909] 2 Ch 305   37
Reid's Application, Re (1955) 7 P & CR 165   129
Renals v Cowlishaw (1878) 9 Ch D 125, (1879) 11 Ch D 866   25
Rhone and Another v Stephens [1994] 2 All ER HL 65   64, 188n
Richards' Application, Re (1983) 47 P & CR 467   167
Roake and Others v Chadha and Another [1984] 1 WLR 40   63
Robins v Berkeley Homes (Kent) Ltd [1996] EGCS 75 (Ch D)   63
Rogers v Hosegood [1900] 2 Ch 388 CA   32n, 34n, 62
Roper v Williams (1822) T & R 18   13
Runnymede District Council v Harwood [1994] JPL 724   198n

S.J.C. Construction Co. Ltd's Application, Re (1974)
    28 P & CR 200   145, 164, 166
S.J.C. Construction Co. Ltd v Sutton London Borough Council
    (1975) 29 P & CR 322   165, 166
Saddington's Application, Re (1964) 16 P & CR 81   133
Sainsbury (J) plc and Another v Enfield BC [1989] 2 All ER 817   64
St. Albans Investments Ltd's Application, Re (1958) 9 P & CR 536   132
Saviker's Application (No. 2), Re (1973) 26 P & CR 441   158
Sayers v Collyer (1884) 28 Ch D 103   28
Schreiber v Creed (1839) 10 Sim 9   14
Seven Trent Water Ltd's Application, Re (1993) 67 P & CR 236   151
Shah & Shah's Application, Re (1991) 62 P & CR 450   156
Sharp v Waterhouse (1857) 7 E & B 816   20
Shaw's Application, Re (1966) 18 P & CR 144   127

Shelley v Kraemer (1948) 334 US 1, 62 SCt 836, 92:1161   195n
Shepherd Homes Ltd v Sandham (No. 2) [1971] 1 WLR 1062   69
Sheppard v Gilmore (1887) 57 LJ Ch 6   29, 33
Smith & Snipes Hall Farm Ltd v River Douglas Catchment Board
    [1949] 2 KB 500   20n, 48n
Sobey v Sainsbury [1913] 2 Ch 513   37
Solarfilms (Sales) Ltd's Application, Re (1993) 67 P & CR 110   151
Solihull District Council's Application, Re (1953) 7 P & CR 97   128
Spencer's Case (1583) 5 Co Rep 16a   8n, 9n, 27, 33, 189, 208
Spicer v Martin (1889) 14 App Cas 12   30
Stephens' Application, Re (1962) 14 P & CR 59   131
Stokes v Cambridge (1962) 13 P & CR 77   164, 166
Surrey County Council v Bredero Homes [1992] 3 All ER 302   168n

Teagle's & Sparks' Application, Re (1962) 14 P & CR 68   137
Tesco Stores Ltd v Secretary of State for the Environment and Others
    [1995] 1 WLR 759   200n
Texaco Antilles Ltd v Kernochan and Another [1973] AC 609   68
Tiltwood, Sussex, In re [1978] 1 Ch 269   68
Tophams Ltd v Earl of Sefton [1967] AC 50   51
Torbay Hotel Ltd v Jenkins & Lawley [1927] 2 Ch 225   53
Towner's & Goddard's Application, Re (1989) 58 P & CR 316   172
Trollope's & Andrew's Application, Re (1962) 14 P & CR 80   131
Truman, Hanbury, Buxton & Co Ltd's Application, In re [1956] 1 QB 261   56
Tucker v Voles [1893] 1 Ch 195   29
Tulk v Metropolitan Board of Works (1868) 16 WR 212   20
Tulk v Moxhay (1848) 2 Ph 774, 1 H & Tw 105,
    11 Beav 571   7, 8, 11, 13, 15, 17, 18, 32, 183, 204
Twiname (John) Ltd's Application, Re (1971) 23 P & CR 413   163

Union of London & Smith's Bank Ltd's Conveyance, In re, Miles v Easter
    [1933] 1 Ch 611   46
University of Westminster v President of the Lands Tribunal, In re
    University of Westminster [1998] 3 All ER 1014 (CA)   135n

Vaizey's Application, Re (1974) 28 P & CR 517   166

Wakeham v Wood (1981) 43 P & CR 40   155, 198n
Wallace & Co's Application, Re (1993) 66 P & CR 124   173
Wards Construction (Medway) Ltd's Application, Re (1973) 25 P & CR 223   154
Watson's Application, Re (1966) 17 P & CR 176   138
Westminster City Council v Jones [1981] JPL 750   198n
Westripp v Baldock [1939] 1 All ER 279   50

Whatman v Gibson (1838) 9 Sim 196   13, 17, 22
White v Bijou Mansions Ltd [1937] 1 Ch 610, [1938] 1 Ch 351 CA   47, 50
Whiting's Application, Re (1988) 58 P & CR 321   172
Wickin's Application, Re (1961) 13 P & CR 227   135
Wilkes v Spooner and Another [1911] 2 KB 473 CA   35
William's Application, Re (1987) 55 P & CR 400   156
Williamson's Application, Re (1994) 68 P & CR 384   174
Willis's Application, Re (1998) 76 P & CR 97   172
Winship's Application, Re (1954) 7 P & CR 151   136
Wrighton's Application, Re (1961) 13 P & CR 189   135
Wrotham Park Estate Co v Parkside Homes Ltd and Others
    [1974] 2 All ER 321   60, 198n, 200
Wynyates Smith Ltd's Application, Re (1963) 15 P & CR 85   135

Zetland (Marquess of) v Driver [1939] 1 Ch 1   47
Zopat Developments' Application, Re (1966) 18 P & CR 156   132

Foreword

The year was 1848. On the 31st August the Royal Assent was given to 11 & 12 Vict. c. 63 and on the 22nd December the Lord Chancellor, affirming the decision of the Master of the Rolls, granted an injunction to a Mr Tulk.

These two events were to have far-reaching implications for the control of the use and development of land. The former, known by its 'short title' as the Public Health Act, 1848, was the instigator of statutory control in the public interest, to be achieved through a series of Acts dealing with health, housing, planning and the environment. The latter, the seminal case of *Tulk v Moxhay*, was the genesis of a long line of 'celebrated' cases giving form to the Restrictive Covenant and its 'composite identity' in the building or development scheme.

Until 1848 control had depended on 'ownership' of the freehold in possession or in reversion (leasehold control), with such minor exceptions as the rarely invoked power of the state in respect of compulsory acquisition or requisition, strictly limited statutory control in respect of 'health and safety', and certain specific rights of the individual 'landowner' such as the natural right of support of land and the easements of light and way. It is no exaggeration to assert that the events of 1848 were, each in their own way, a 'watershed'. However, it is with the 'private' control of land use by means of the restrictive covenant and the building scheme that we are here primarily concerned, although we shall turn to the matter of 'public' control when considering the future for the restrictive covenant in a world of increasing public control through planning and environmental legislation and regulation.

Both from a land law and a land management standpoint, the inception of the restrictive covenant has to be seen against the background of the instruments of management that the law had provided for the 'landowner' and his professional advisers to achieve management and control of the use and development of their 'estates'. With increasing population, urbanisation and industrialisation the 'aristocratic' control of vast acres through the medium of the strict settlement and the trust for sale, whilst still an important element and one which would remain so until the end of the 19th century, had already passed the peak of its influence and, in spite

1

of the measures brought in during the 19th century to increase the powers of the tenant for life and thereby enable a more efficient management and control, the concept of settled land was of little relevance in a society which was in the process of becoming the 'world' leader in industry and commerce.

It is in the context of population growth, urbanisation and industrialisation that we see the need for forms of private and public control. It was the scale of change that was so dramatic. In the nineteenth century, despite high infant mortality, especially in the first half of the century, the population of England and Wales nearly quadrupled, doubling in the first half of the century (from 8.9 million in 1801 to around 17 million by the mid century) and nearly doubling yet again in the second half (to 32.5 million in 1901). Whilst population growth was significant in itself, even more was the degree of urbanisation resulting in development of high density housing cheek by jowl with manufacturing. At the beginning of the century the indigenous society was predominantly agrarian (some 80% of the population being classified as rural and 20% as urban) with probably less than 2 million people living in towns and cities. By the middle of the century the proportion as between urban and rural was roughly half and half and by the end of the century the proportion as between urban and rural had virtually reversed the position pertaining at the beginning of the century such that England and Wales could by then truly be described as a predominantly urban society (some 77% of the population being classified as urban and 23% as rural) with more than 25 million living in towns and cities.

Set alongside this dramatic demographic change in society was the decline of the landed estate. The concentration of large areas of land in a few hands had been instrumental in developing the 'leasehold system' as a means of managing and controlling land use and development through the imposition and enforcement of covenants covering all aspects of present and future building form and land use. The break up of the large estates meant that as land holdings became smaller the number of individual 'owners' increased and the pattern of land ownership and use became fragmented and more complex, particularly in those areas where industrialisation was the spur to intensive development of houses and factories.

The 'commercial' instruments of management - the lease, the mortgage, the easement and the rentcharge - were available and were adapted and refined to meet the ever-increasing demand for housing and

industrial development in the expanding urban settlements, market towns
and cities. Apart from the limited range of issues which could be embraced
within the law relating to easements and the control that the rentcharge
afforded - the latter restricted mainly to low-cost high-density
developments of artisans dwellings and confined to a few specific areas of
the country, namely the midlands and the north west - no powers existed
whereby land, the freehold of which had been disposed of to another, could
be controlled in either its use or its development.

Not having the benefit that leasehold control could provide through the
enforceable covenant, owners disposing of the freehold in part of their land
needed some form of protection. The restrictive covenant, through the
good offices of Messrs Tulk and Moxhay, was to provide that protection in
some measure. It may be argued that the requirements of a free market in
land and the increasing commercialisation associated with property
transactions would have necessitated statutory intervention to provide or
facilitate protection if *Tulk v Moxhay* had not intervened.

Although here concerned primarily with the 'private' control of land
use it is important to recognise the distinct connotations ascribed to
'control' when qualified as being either 'private' or 'public'. From the
point of view of the 'landed interest' the history of the use of land is
dominated by the desire of landowners for the power privately to exercise
ever-increasing control. The individual estate owner has sought to extend
his control as far into the future as the law allowed him, as for example by
the strict settlement and the long term lease. He has sought tightly to
control the management and the use of land through covenants in leases
and collateral stipulations in mortgages. He has striven to achieve control
over the land of others through the acquisition of easements and,
eventually, by the imposition of restrictive covenants.

By contrast, the introduction of public control - first health, then
housing, planning and most recently environment - was to be met by
landowners, certainly in the early days, with attitudes varying between
reluctant acceptance and outright hostility to 'outside' interference in the
use and development of their land. Indeed, in the early years, certainly up
to the mid 1870's, the only statutory control was as a direct result of some
real or perceived 'disaster' affecting either 'health' or 'safety'. It is only in
comparatively recent times that landowners have generally acknowledged
(with varying degrees of acceptance) the need for 'planning' and
'environmental' control. But the arrival of 'public' control was not to
eclipse 'private' control. Many forms of 'private' control are as relevant

today as they were a hundred years ago; the lease (and more recently, the licence), the mortgage, the easement and the restrictive covenant are still essential constituents of estate management and development. For more than a century now some 'public' control of land use and development has existed alongside the 'private' control of the estate owner. Sometimes the various controls conflict, sometimes they are complementary, sometimes supplementary. In their myriad potential relationships it is the relationship between the restrictive covenant and town and country planning that is of particular interest. The restrictive covenant may seek to prevent development entirely, to restrict development to a particular use or group of uses, to control the density of development and its size, form and design, all of which matters are the very substance of planning control as it has now been administered in this country for half a century.

On the surface, therefore, whilst the objectives of these two leading forms of land use control may appear very similar, such superficial similarity is misleading. The former being geared to the protection of private property rights, and the latter to the protection and benefit of the public interest and good, each régime has its distinctive and fundamentally different raison d'être. The bearing in mind of this distinction is important particularly when looking at only one system, in our case the restrictive covenant, and this distinction will be reinforced when, in the final chapter, the future of the restrictive covenant is viewed alongside public planning control.

Having introduced the matter of the *Restrictive Covenant in the Control of Land Use* by setting it within its historical context it may be helpful if, to conclude this short introduction, we outline the scope of the book. First, it considers the evolution of the law of restrictive covenants by means of an historical study and analysis of the considerable body of case law which the concept has engendered in the course of its development. Secondly, it considers the operation of section 84 of the Law of Property Act, 1925 in the discharge or modification of restrictive covenants, by means of an analytical examination of, and commentary on, the decisions of the Official Arbitrator and the Lands Tribunal, whereby the restrictive covenant was enabled to retain credibility and utility. And finally, it looks at the future for the restrictive covenant through the possible reform of the law and in its relationship and relevance alongside the 'public' control of land use and development.

PART I

THE EVOLUTION OF THE LAW OF RESTRICTIVE COVENANTS

1 The Restrictive Covenant before 1926

Introduction

The origin, growth and impact of the doctrine of the restrictive covenant has been admirably summarised by A.W.B.Simpson:[1]

> The starting point for the modern development of restrictive covenants is, of course, the case of *Tulk v Moxhay* in 1848; from that decision there has been developed a body of law which proved to be, if not an unmixed blessing, yet of very great importance in regulating the urban development of the country before the introduction of modern planning legislation, for it became possible to impose upon land by private treaty a wide variety of restrictions upon user and development. Today the older system of private regulation continues alongside the modern system of public regulation, and both have their distinctive merits, and their distinctive disadvantages.

With these words Professor Simpson both introduced restrictive covenants and co-incidentally provided an appropriate 'text' for an historical analysis of the evolution of the law relating to restrictive covenants affecting freehold land. As he went on to observe, *Tulk v Moxhay*[2] was not an entirely new departure and 'if we are to understand the history of the equitable doctrine we must...examine not only the doctrines of equity but also the doctrines of law on the running of covenants'.

Indeed, to appreciate fully the significance of the development in the law which would flow from *Tulk v Moxhay* it is necessary to understand first, the influence of Equity upon the rigours of the Common Law doctrine of privity of contract and, second, the position pertaining to covenants immediately prior to the decision - a position that had remained fundamentally unchanged for 300 years.

In the early part of the nineteenth century, 'privity' (the doctrine which in a sense confines the concept of contract) became firmly established in the Common Law. In *Price v Easton*[3] decided in 1833, it was made clear

7

that 'no-one [might] be entitled to or bound by the terms of a contract to which he [was] not an original party'. Although the doctrine survives it has not been unreservedly accepted - its history is obscure, it is subject, *inter alia,* to the well-founded exception of the notion of the undisclosed principal in agency, and (particularly important in the present context) it clashes 'with the needs and concepts of the law of property'.[4]

It had long been appreciated that property rights could not be contained by so restrictive an idea as privity. For centuries the Common Law had facilitated the running with the land of the benefit of a covenant[5] and, likewise, statute and the Common Law had combined in the law of leases to accommodate the running of both the benefit and the burden of covenants.[6] Such principles, however, could not cover the range of situations in which a perceived need for the enforcement by or against a 'non-party' of a land-related covenant might arise. In particular, it did not cover the situation where a purchaser of land had voluntarily accepted a covenant upon purchase, later sold the land to a third party, and the third party then having broken the covenant the original vendor sought to enforce it. Because of the long standing Common Law rule that only the benefit and not the burden might run, the obstacle of privity prevented the enforcement of any such covenant.

It was into this sector of privity's domain that Equity was to make a spectacular incursion, albeit eventually in respect only of negative or restrictive covenants. As will soon emerge more fully, Equity was able via its crucial decision in *Tulk v Moxhay*[7] to distance itself from the stance of the Common Law by granting an injunction to restrain a breach of covenant on the part of a third person into whose hands, with notice of the covenant, affected land had come. In itself, such an effort by Equity to circumvent a Common Law inconvenience was not remarkable. From the 18th century, attempts had been made to limit the impact of privity by resort to the device of the trust, while as far back as the 17th century the Court of Chancery proved itself able to overcome the Common Law view that a right arising under a contract could not be assigned, so as to enable the assignee to seek to enforce the right in his own name. What was to prove remarkable was rather the way in which from humble beginnings Equity's incursion was to blossom. As time went by the doctrine of the restrictive covenant was to develop into one of great import for land management and further, was not only to contribute significantly to private land law but also to influence, if only indirectly, the public law of planning control.

So far as the law of covenants was concerned the position immediately prior to *Tulk v Moxhay* may be briefly outlined, a distinction having to be drawn between leaseholds and freeholds; between the original parties and their successors in title; between 'benefit' and 'burden', and, lastly, between positive and negative covenants.

With regard to *leaseholds*, the position was that as between the original lessor and lessee, both parties were bound by all covenants by virtue of privity of contract; as between the lessor and an assignee of the lessee's term, both the lessor and the assignee of the lessee's term might enforce covenants which touched and concerned the land, both the benefit and the burden running with the land by virtue of privity of estate,[8] and as between the assignee of the lessor's reversion and the lessee, both the assignee of the lessor's reversion and the lessee might enforce covenants which 'touched and concerned' the land, both the benefit and the burden in this situation running with the reversion by virtue of certain statutory provisions.[9]

In the case of *freeholds*, by contrast, the position was that as between the original covenantee and covenantor, both parties were bound by all covenants by virtue of privity of contract, and as between successors in title of the original covenantee and covenantor the *benefit* of covenants (both positive and negative) which 'touched and concerned' the land could run to successors in title of the covenantee,[10] but, and here the distinction is crucial, the *burden* could not run to successors in title of the covenantor.

The problems raised by the obstacle of privity on the one hand and the position regarding freehold covenants on the other, together fashioned the basic contours of the ground which was to host the new equitable doctrine, upon the development of which we now embark. Naturally, the cases soon to be cited relate in the main to covenants affecting freehold land. However, occasional reference will also be made to cases concerning covenants in 'long leases' where a matter of principle is involved which throws light on the way the law relating to covenants affecting freeholds was evolving.[11] Of the numerous cases which have been decided on the restrictive covenant those have been selected for reference which show the evolving state of the law in relation to the different stages in the development of land and land use. They are treated chronologically, in two chapters, the first dealing with the growth of the law up to 1925 and the second with the growth thereafter.[12] The former, the current chapter, is in three parts, namely the period leading up to *Tulk v Moxhay,* the period thence to the end of the 19th century, and the period from the turn of the century to the advent of the Law of Property Act, 1925. The latter chapter comprises two parts, the first embracing the period from 1926 to the end of the 1960's and the second bringing the history up to date.

As these periods are considered certain basic matters need to be borne in mind.

First, the land management background to the analysis imparts objectives which have influenced its form. Through the cases a study will be made of the doctrine's origins, evolution, adoption and adaptation with particular reference to:

(a) the promotion and control of development and use through, in particular, the building scheme;

(b) the evolving importance and influence of planning, amenity and environmental issues, and

(c) the continuing relevance of restrictive covenant control through the medium of the statutory procedure for discharge or modification.[13]

Secondly, there is the importance, peculiarly so in the case of the restrictive covenant, of its socio-economic context. The decades in which the doctrine was formed were years of far-reaching change in that they witnessed:

(a) the rapid growth in the population of England and Wales;

(b) the change from a rural to a primarily urban society with the growth of employment in manufacturing and extractive industries and the decline of employment in agriculture;

(c) the improvement in communications, notably as a result of the development of the railways, affording greater mobility and accessibility;

(d) the break up of the large estates resulting in an increase in the number of "landowners' and a decrease in the size of 'landholdings', and

(e) the sheer volume of urban (town) development leading to the need to control building in the interest of public health.

Here were changes to the national fabric fundamental in character and pursued with unprecedented speed. To them the restrictive covenant made its own distinctive contribution. Although in name it suggested inhibition, in reality it was a facilitative device enabling land, which otherwise might not have been disposed of, to be freed for 'controlled' use and development to meet the escalating demands and needs of the market.

The Period leading up to *Tulk v Moxhay*

The Preceding Cases

If the doctrine in *Tulk v Moxhay*[14] is to be appreciated it is essential to consider certain of the earlier cases, and a useful starting point is *Keppell v Bailey*.[15] The facts may be briefly stated. Certain landowners and owners of ironworks formed a Joint Stock Company and constructed a railroad connecting a lime quarry (Trevil) with several ironworks and with the railroad of a canal company (Monmouthshire Canal Navigation). In the partnership deed the lessees of one of the ironworks (Beaufort) covenanted 'to procure all the limestone used in the said works from the Trevil Quarry, and to convey all such limestone, and also all the ironstone from the mines to the said works along Trevil Railroad'. A bill was later filed by the shareholders of the railroad to enforce the covenant against a purchaser of the Beaufort Works who had notice of the partnership deed. It was held, *inter alia*, that:

> the covenant did not run with the land so as to bind assignees at law; and that a Court of Equity would not, by holding the conscience of the purchaser to be affected by the notice, give the covenant a more extensive operation than the law allowed to it.[16]

Lord Brougham found that the covenant was not repugnant to the rules respecting perpetuity, that it was not in restraint of trade, nor was there 'want of mutuality',[17] and although he considered that there was an objection relating to the parties' statutory powers such as to dispose of the present application for an injunction, he went on even so to consider the nature of the covenant which 'very clearly...does not run with the land, and therefore is not binding upon the assignees'.

He considered some fifteen cases in the course of his learned commentary - cases confirming his instant view that the covenant in question could not run with the land at law and was accordingly not binding upon the assignees. It was purely collateral, it did not inhere in the land, and there was no privity of estate between the estates of the occupiers of the iron works and the estates of those with whom they covenanted. Taking the view that equity should follow the law and only enforce the covenant if it were enforceable in a court of common law he concluded that as the burden of the covenant did not run at law it could not run in equity either.

Prior to his review of the authorities he intimated the problems which would arise if land could be burdened with enforceable covenants:

> [I]t must not...be supposed that incidents of a novel kind can be devised and attached to property at the fancy or caprice of any owner [as] great detriment would arise and much confusion of rights if parties were allowed to invent new modes of holding and enjoying real property, and to impress upon their lands and tenements a peculiar character, which should follow them into all hands, however remote [for] if one man may bind his messuage and land to take lime from a particular kiln, another may bind his to take coals from a certain pit, while a third may load his property with further obligations to employ one blacksmith's forge...besides many other restraints as infinite in variety as the imagination can conceive.[18]

This said, he took pains to emphasise the great difference between:

> such a case as this and the case of covenants in a lease, whereby the demised premises are affected with certain rights in favour of the lessor. The lessor or his assignees continue in the reversion while the term lasts. The estate is not out of them, although the possession is in the lessee or his assigns. It is not at all inconsistent with the nature of property that certain things should be reserved to the reversioners all the while the term continues.[19]

Having made this crucial distinction between freeholds and leaseholds in respect of the running of the burden of a covenant, he then took similar pains to point out that even though (for the reasons given) in the case of leaseholds the burden of a covenant can run, the law is restrictive. Pursuing this equally critical point he observed that:

> the law does not leave the reversioner the absolute licence to invent covenants which shall affect the lands in the hands of those who take by assignment of the term. The covenant must be of such a nature as to inhere in the land [and only then shall it] follow into the hands of persons who are strangers to the contract of lease, and who only become privy to the lessor through the estate which they take by assignment.[20]

The learned judge addressed himself also to the question as to whether the notice which the purchaser had of its existence would, upon an application for an injunction (i.e. an equitable remedy), alter the position. He was of the firm opinion that it certainly would not as otherwise there could be 'wild attempts' to create new devices which, however repugnant to rules of law, would succeed 'because equity would enable their authors to prevail'.[21] Consequently, the Lord Chancellor was not prepared, on the ground of the doctrine of notice, to provide a covenant with a more extensive sphere of operation than the law would afford it.

After the denial of any new equitable doctrine in *Keppell v Bailey*[22] the position was considered undetermined in *Bristow v Wood,*[23] but change was to come with *Mann v Stephens*[24] in 1846 and *Tulk v Moxhay*[25] itself in 1848. Before dealing with these cases, however, attention must be drawn to an event of great potential importance, namely the 'birth of the building scheme' - a concept involving (in general terms) the laying out of an area of land in plots, its development in accordance with a plan, and the maintenance of its character and amenities via a system of interlacing covenants.

The Beginnings of the Building Scheme

One of the earliest references to attempts to control the way in which building development should take place occurred in 1822 in *Roper v Williams.*[26] It concerned a covenant for the erection of buildings according to a 'general plan', to restrain the breach of which an injunction was refused, the covenantee having already acquiesced in a partial deviation from the plan. But one had to wait until 1838 and the case of *Whatman v Gibson*[27] for a clear statement of what was later to become 'the development (or building) scheme'. A, the owner of a piece of land, divided it into lots for building a row of dwelling houses, and a deed was made between him of the one part and X and Y (who had purchased some of the lots from him) and the several persons who should at any time execute the deed of the other parts, thereby creating (and imposing) a network of covenants.

It was expressly declared that it should be a 'general and indispensable condition of the sale of all or any of the lots that the proprietors thereof for the time being should observe and abide by the several stipulations and restrictions thereinafter contained'. A sold and conveyed one of the plots to B, and another to C, both of whom executed the deed of covenant. The plaintiff afterwards purchased B's lot, and the defendant purchased C's lot *with notice* of the deed of covenant. The defendant, intending to use the house on his lot as a family hotel, a use which would be in breach of a restriction, was restrained from so doing by an injunction.[28]

The issues of both 'notice' and 'community of interest' featured in the judgment of Sir Lancelot Shadwell, Vice-Chancellor, who observed:

> It is quite clear that all the parties who executed this deed were bound by it: and the only question is whether, there being an agreement, all persons who come in as devisees or assignees under those who took with notice of the deed are not bound by it. I see no reason why such an agreement should not be binding in equity on the parties so coming in with notice. Each proprietor is manifestly interested in having all the neighbouring houses used in such a way as to preserve the general uniformity and respectability of the row, and, consequently, in preventing any of the houses from being converted into shops or taverns, which would lessen the respectability and value of the other houses.[29]

The extent to which the courts would take cognisance of plans purporting to control (or at least influence) the form of development was again considered in the following year in *Schreiber v Creed*.[30] Here, the owners of certain land, being minded to erect a pump room and to lay out the rest for buildings, pleasure-grounds, roads etc., had a plan drawn up. Under it the mode in which the lands were intended to be laid out and the purposes for which they were intended to be converted and used were described, in order that 'the beauty and regularity of the whole of the design might be for ever thereafter preserved, subject only to such alterations as should be made or approved of by [the vendor] his heirs or assigns and as should not destroy the general beauty of the same design'. Each of the other parties to the deed had purchased or agreed to purchase one or more of the pieces of land described in the plan as set out for building.

Following sales of lots for building, a subsequent purchaser of one of the lots began to build a house some 12 feet in advance of the plaintiff's house. The latter contended that this would be a nuisance, would lessen the value of his house and be a violation of the covenant under the scheme. His argument foundered, it being held that the plan was but a 'general plan' and its detail susceptible of variation.

Rather, by contrast, may be noted *Peacock v Penson*.[31] In this case the vendor of land in lots for the purpose of building accompanied his conditions of sale with a map delineating the intended divisions of the property by new roads. In doing so it was held that 'he must be understood to hold out expectations that the lots would be so divided, and it would not be competent to him to divide the land in a different manner, so as to attract an occupancy and population entirely different from that which would have been produced by acting on the plan proposed and held out at the sale'.

Thus, in the first half of the 19th century were the seeds sown for a concept which was to develop so greatly in the latter half of that century and into the 20th. This was occurring at the same time as the restrictive covenant was gestating and it is to the birth of the restrictive covenant that attention is now directed.

The Birth of the Restrictive Covenant

The watershed in the law came, in fact, in the case of *Mann v Stephens*.[32] This case paved the way for *Tulk v Moxhay*,[33] the case which was to give its name to the new equitable doctrine. In *Mann v Stephens*, upon the division of an area of land, the vendor covenanted on behalf of himself, his heirs and assigns, with the purchaser, his heirs and assigns, that the land retained should remain as a shrubbery or garden, and that no house or other building should be erected thereon, except a private house or ornamental cottage, and *that* only on a certain part of it, and so as to be an ornament, rather than otherwise, to the surrounding property. The two parcels of land having thereafter passed from the original parties, a purchaser of one parcel, though having notice of the covenant, nevertheless began to build in breach of the covenant and an injunction was sought.

Counsel moved for the injunction on the ground that the defendant purchased the piece of land with notice of the covenant; against which it was argued that there was no privity between the plaintiff and the defendant and that the burden of the covenant did not run with the land. The Vice-Chancellor, Sir Lancelot Shadwell, was of the opinion that the erection of a beer-shop and brewery was a 'gross violation of the covenant' and accordingly granted an injunction. Further, the Lord Chancellor, Lord Cottenham, upheld the injunction on appeal, but excluded, as being too indefinite, that element of the covenant which required that any private house or ornamental cottage erected should be an ornament to surrounding property.

Two years later, with a remedy already having been successfully sought against a purchaser with notice, *Tulk v Moxhay*[34] emerged. The facts may be briefly stated. In 1808, the Plaintiff had conveyed a vacant piece of land in Leicester Square to Elms, who had entered into a covenant on behalf of himself, his heirs and assigns. The covenant was to the effect that, *inter alia,* the land, with its surrounding iron railing, should be maintained 'in its present form and in sufficient and proper repair as a square garden or pleasure-ground, in an open state, uncovered with any buildings, in a neat ornamental order'.

For some while the ground remained in conformity therewith. Eventually, however, it came into the hands of the defendant (who derived title from Elms) and he made a scheme to erect certain shops and buildings on the square. The plaintiff objected on the ground that it was contrary to the covenant and would injure his (the plaintiff's) houses in the square. Nevertheless, the defendant proceeded to cut down trees and shrubs, to pull down part of the railings and to erect boards across the ground.

To restrain this activity an injunction was sought, and with success. Lord Langdale, MR, though not ready to go so far as to require that the land be kept 'in a neat ornamental order', was willing to restrain the defendant from using the land in a manner 'inconsistent with the use of it as open garden and pleasure ground'.[35]

The decision to grant the plaintiff the relief which he had sought was upheld by the Lord Chancellor, Lord Cottenham, on appeal. In his view, where, upon the sale of land, the purchaser covenanted on behalf of himself and his assigns to use or refrain from using the land in a particular way, Equity would enforce that covenant against all subsequent purchasers who took the land with notice of the covenant, and this quite apart from the question as to whether it was one which would run with the land at law.

Rather than any issue of whether the burden of a restrictive covenant could run at law (or, for that matter, in equity) the heart of the question for Lord Cottenham was:

> whether a party [should] be permitted to use the land in a manner inconsistent with the contract entered into by his vendor, and with notice of which he purchased. Of course, the price would be affected by the covenant, and nothing could be more inequitable than that the original purchaser should be able to sell the property next day for a greater price, in consideration of the assignee being allowed to escape from the liability which he had himself undertaken.[36]

For a practical viewpoint of Lord Cottenham's decision in *Tulk v Moxhay* one can do no better than advert to Professor Simpson's[37] summary of that judgment, which may be paraphrased thus:

> Whilst not disputing Lord Brougham's view that the burden of covenants did

not run with the land *at law*, Lord Cottenham decided that an injunction could be obtained in a *court of equity* (quite unrelated to any doctrine about the running of covenants with land) on the basis of the 'peculiar equitable doctrine of notice'. He took the view that it would be inequitable to allow a purchaser of land who bought it with express notice of the covenant to act in defiance of it. Furthermore, if a landowner could, by selling his land convert it from burdened land to unburdened land, he would transfer something he had never himself owned; 'if an equity is attached to the property by the owner no one purchasing with notice of that equity can stand in a different situation from the party from whom he purchased'.[38]

What can be said about the status of the 'restrictive' covenant immediately following the decision in *Tulk v Moxhay*, a decision which tended to favour *Mann v Stephens*[39] over and above an albeit significant dictum of Lord Brougham in *Keppell v Bailey*?[40] First, it seems to be immaterial whether or not the covenant is of a kind which is capable of running with land, although incidentally in *Tulk v Moxhay* it probably would have done so.[41] Secondly, no specific mention was made of the necessity of retaining land which could benefit from the covenant, although incidentally in *Tulk v Moxhay* there was such land. Thirdly, the question of 'notice' was at the root of the decision; the absence of a 'purchaser for value with notice' would have been a fatal 'flaw'. Fourthly, the eventually crucial issue of the extent of Equity's willingness to intervene in the sense of whether it should enforce both negative and positive covenants was not expressly raised; what may be noted at this point is that the covenant in question involved both kinds of obligation and that whereas Lord Longdale was prepared to restrain inconsistent user, he was not ready to enjoin maintenance 'in a neat ornamental order'.

The speed with which this new concept of Equity came into being is all the more surprising considering the conservative nature of the law and the lawyers of the time and the inbred and resolute resistance to change. In 1834 Lord Brougham in *Keppell v Bailey*[42] 'was not at liberty to create a new interest in land'. Four years later in 1838, by which time Lord Cottenham held the office of Chancellor, Sir Lancelot Shadwell, V-C in *Whatman v Gibson*[43] held that the burden of a covenant could run in equity in a 'building scheme' case. In 1846 a decision to similar effect by Sir Lancelot Shadwell, V-C was upheld by Lord Cottenham in *Mann v Stephens*.[44] Two years later in 1848 the same point was decided in the same way and upheld by Lord Cottenham in *Tulk v Moxhay*.[45]

It is suggested that the decision reached in 1848 would provide a sound basis for not only 'controlling' development and use but also for commercial transactions in land and property which depend on confidence in the 'degree of certainty' that can be placed on the value of realty. But, as will be demonstrated, it would be many years before the boundaries of this 'new interest in land' would be defined authoritatively. As Wade[46] has observed:

> The invention of a new proprietary interest is bound to unsettle the law of property for many years. For example, it took over sixty years to settle the principle that restrictive covenants will not bind third parties unless taken for the benefit of other land belonging to the covenantee.

Challis[47] predicted that the new doctrine, resting upon 'dubious grounds of equity', would be due to have 'its wings clipped when it [came] before the House of Lords', although it would in fact be the Court of Appeal in *London County Council v Allen*[48] in 1914 that finally decided that the 'new doctrine' was confined to covenants restricting the use of one piece of land for the benefit of another.

The way in which the new doctrine evolved, and the further development of the concept of the building scheme, form the subject-matter of the next periods to be considered.

The Period from 1848 to the End of the Century

Tulk v Moxhay - the Early Years

For the lawyer, the immediate effect of the doctrine in *Tulk v Moxhay* was felt both in the law of contract and in the law of property as has been made clear by Gray:[49]

> The covenantee was widely regarded as having not merely a contractual interest in the performance of the covenant...but also a *proprietary* interest in the land of the covenantor [which] could run with the land of the covenantor, so as to bind those into whose hands that land came, until [it] was conveyed to a bona fide purchaser of a legal estate for value without notice...The covenantee was thus given a contractual right to control activities on the land of the covenantor and, by virtue of the equitable doctrine, that contractual right enlarged into...a proprietary right in land.

Furthermore, the broad base of the decision in *Tulk v Moxhay* and Equity's willingness to intervene in restraint of wrongdoers with notice suggested an approach capable of wide application. The ruling in *Tulk v Moxhay* was applied enthusiastically in the years immediately following to, for example, both positive and negative covenants,[50] on behalf of litigants who held no estate in the land benefited by the covenant[51] and even outside the realm of real property.[52]

On a practical note, the decision reflects the perennial dilemma involved in attempting to achieve a proper balance between freedom of contract (to control) and freedom of alienability (to dispose). Lord Brougham in *Keppell v Bailey* had refused to allow the attaching of incidents of a novel kind to land at the 'fancy and caprice' of an owner as it would 'fetter the use and development of the land in perpetuity'.[53] But Lord Cottenham's view, as adopted in *Tulk v Moxhay* was the opposite, namely that far from leading to sterilisation of land use, such an 'incident of a novel kind' could be seen as promoting the commerciability of land. He appreciated and expressly noted that unless restrictive covenants could be enforced against the covenantor's successors 'it would be impossible for an owner of land to sell part of it without incurring the risk of rendering what he retains worthless'.[54]

Whereas a favourable and general consequence of Lord Cottenham's decision was the implicit facilitation of development, in another narrower sense, the inherent limitations of the injunction granted made for a less successful outcome. Lord Langdale, MR had been prepared to restrain inconsistent user but not to require a keeping of the land in good order. Thus, with the negative but not the positive element of the injunction achieved, the development of land in Leicester Square was prevented but its maintenance was not secured.

Leicester Square, as Charles Dickens writing in the 1850's vividly described it, was:

a centre of attraction to indifferent foreign hotels and indifferent foreigners, racket-courts, fightingmen, swordsmen, footguards, old china, gaming-houses, exhibitions, and a large medley of shabbiness and shrinking out of sight.[55]

The historian, Arthur Bryant, writing of the early 1850's, describes the Square equally graphically as:

formerly the home of great artists, [it] was a 'dreary abomination of desolation'. In its centre a headless statue, perpetually bombarded by ragged urchins with brickbats, stood in a wilderness of weeds frequented by starved and half-savage cats.[56]

And it must have remained for some years in this sad condition for, from the case of *Tulk v The Metropolitan Board of Works*,[57] we learn that in 1865, the garden (Leicester Square) being in a neglected and dilapidated state, the Metropolitan Board of Works sought, albeit unsuccessfully on an issue other than the state of the land, to take possession of it under an Act for the Protection of Garden or Ornamental Grounds in Cities and Boroughs.

The newly born 'equity' was destined to reach great heights but not without setback. From a lusty infancy the restrictive covenant would eventually be refined to a more circumspect youth. The doctrine would be modified, clarified and limited, although this would not be for some while. Indeed, it would next be the turn of the Common Law to focus on covenants, taking the opportunity to clarify its position regarding the 'running of the benefit' in *Sharp v Waterhouse*.[58]

The Growth of the Building Scheme

The period between *Tulk v Moxhay* in 1848 and the Judicature Acts, 1873-75 was characterised by the ever-increasing rate of urban expansion and with it the development and adaptation of the concept of the 'restrictive covenant' to 'estate development' and the requirements for the building (or development) scheme, which paved the way for the authoritative statement on the latter finally to be laid down in *Elliston v Reacher*.[59] From a series of cases of those times we glean not only the extent of Equity's readiness (or otherwise) to afford plaintiffs the 'protection' sought but also an insight into the kinds of tension existing between the differing aspirations for the use and development of land.

These cases exhibit a broad and practical approach to issues arising from covenants in a 'building scheme' setting. On the one hand there is shown a plain desire to do all possible to foster the advantages of a 'planned environment'. On the other hand there is an equally plain recognition of the realities of a situation in which changed environmental circumstances (for whatever reason) make superfluous the enforcement of a covenant and where an injunction is accordingly refused.

The former point springs clearly from one of the earliest of the cases, *Kemp v Sober*.[60] Here, the owner of an estate had developed it with houses and sold some of them subject to a covenant not to carry on any trade, business or calling to the 'annoyance, nuisance or injury of any of the houses' on the estate. It was held that the carrying on of a girls' school in one of the houses was a breach of the covenant, (it having previously been decided in *Doe v Keeling*[61] that the keeping of a boys' school was a business within the meaning of the covenant in that case). The Vice-Chancellor, Lord Cranworth, was of the opinion that 'the keeping of a girls' school is [*pari passu*] a business or calling within the meaning of the covenant in this case'. Referring to the argument that the case came within the principle of those cases in which the Court has refused to interfere because no damage has actually been sustained, he went on to state that 'a person who stipulates that her neighbour shall not keep a school stipulates that she shall be relieved from all anxiety arising from a school being kept; and the feeling of anxiety is damage'. Furthermore, 'neighbours will suffer annoyance not only from their [20 young ladies] practising music and dancing, but from their relations and friends continually calling upon them'. Thus, although no damage had been actually sustained and indeed might never be sustained, the 'feeling of anxiety is damage'[62] and the contemplation thereof is sufficient ground to grant an injunction.

The decision reached some three years later in *Child v Douglas*[63] reveals a simple 'commonsense' attitude, owing more to matters of general environment and health than to pure legal construction. In this case, land having been laid out for building a row of houses on a general plan, and the defendant having covenanted that he would not erect any building on the plot purchased within the distance of six feet from a certain intended street, it was held that 'the erection of a wall fifteen feet high, at right angles to the principal street, and extending quite up to it, was an infringement of this covenant'.

The Vice-Chancellor, Sir W. Page Wood, had no doubt that the covenant would preclude the erection of the whole extent of the wall being built to the height of 15 feet; whether the covenant would extend to prevent the erection of such a wall 5 feet high was doubtful, but he did not think it would prevent the building of such a wall to the height of two feet or putting an iron railing thereon, nor did he think that the projection of a brick-built porch one foot beyond the prescribed limit would be an infringement of the covenant:

> [T]he object being to have one uniform range of buildings, I am of the opinion that the Defendant cannot be allowed to erect this wall, as he is now doing, to the height of fifteen feet, quite up to the road. Suppose that every individual

who has bought land along this street did the same, the character of the row would be much altered, and the light and air and general comfort of the houses would be considerably interfered with by the walls of this kind, which I have no doubt are buildings within the meaning of the covenant'.[64]

The case is also noteworthy for the liberal attitude taken to covenant enforcement in a 'scheme' situation. It mattered not, in the view of the court, that (unlike in *Whatman v Gibson*[65]) the *vendors* had entered into no reciprocal covenants. Sir W. Page Wood was of the opinion that:

> The reciprocal advantage here obtained [by the defendant] is really the conveyance of the land; and it cannot be said that, for want of a reciprocal benefit which he did not stipulate for, he cannot be compelled to perform that which he has expressly covenanted to do.[66]

The judges' recognition of reality, in terms of refusing to enjoin breach where circumstances had changed, was made clear in, for instance, *Eastwood v Lever*.[67] Here, property vested in the trustees of a building society had been laid out to a plan and allotted or sold in lots to members or purchasers (aware of the existence of the plan) subject to certain restrictive covenants preserving residential quality. An action for an injunction was brought in respect of certain building infringements but did not succeed, it being found that the plaintiff had acquiesced in the breach. However, whereas the claim for an injunction failed, it was thought that there might be an entitlement to damages under Lord Cairns's Act, 1858, an aspect echoed a few years later in *Peek v Matthews*,[68] from which likewise emerged equity's insistence that damages at law can be the plaintiff's only remedy if, by permitting material breaches of the covenant by some purchasers, he himself has failed to preserve a common building scheme.[69]

While considering the building scheme aspects of mid-nineteenth century litigation attention has necessarily to be drawn to the central concept of 'notice' - a key issue for the Chancery judges being whether or not the defendant had notice of the covenants.

The point was taken in *Coles v Sims*,[70] where land was sold in lots for building purposes and covenants imposed specifying the positioning of houses and forbidding the erection of buildings on the piece of ground in front of each house. Portions of the land, having eventually come into newcomers' hands, and building having been carried out in contravention of the scheme, an effort was made to restrain the same via an injunction.

The action succeeded, it being held that whether the covenants did or did not run with the land, the defendants had notice of them and should be restrained from building in a manner contrary to the general scheme for the benefit of all the original parties.

An appeal from the order of the Vice-Chancellor was later heard before the Lords Justices of Appeal,[71] who upheld the granting of an injunction on a base expressly confirming the *Tulk v Moxhay* approach. In the opinion of Lord Justice Knight Bruce it was quite clear that 'the contract...was intended by the parties ...to bind the land into whatsoever hands it might come'. In his view the question was whether, as the present defendants were not parties to the agreement, they were entitled to stand in a better position than the person under whom they claimed, who was a party to the agreement. The learned judge was in no doubt that the defendants had notice of the covenants and opined that:

> *Tulk v Moxhay* was not the first nor the last case which decided that in a Court of Equity it may be 'competent to any person to bind land perpetually in the sense and manner in which the land here is affected to be bound'; whatever the state of the law with regard to covenants running with the land 'the course of this court is now clearly understood to be to maintain such a covenant - such an agreement'.[72]

From the foregoing it will be noted that the law is responding to the needs of a society undergoing accelerating change in the sphere of land use and development. On the one hand the idea of a binding building scheme was fully recognised and facilitated. On the other hand the doctrine of *Tulk v Moxhay* was confirmed on the simple basis of the taking of land with notice of a covenant earlier entered into.

The very simplicity of this basis is highlighted in *Catt v Tourle*.[73] In this case, it was held that a covenant in favour of a brewer (in respect of land sold by him) giving him the exclusive right of supplying beer to any public house erected on that land was not void for, *inter alia*, either uncertainly or mutuality, and that though in terms positive it was in substance negative. Accordingly the defendant, having taken the land with notice of the covenant, might be restrained by means of an injunction from acting in contravention of it.

Not only does this case show that equity was ready to look to the substance of a covenant when determining its negative or positive quality, it also shows that in this period, unlike in later years, it did not matter that the covenant was personal in nature, i.e. that it was not taken to protect other land. As would emerge later, this important tolerance was to disappear and with it the whole course of the restrictive covenant would change when it became settled that equity would only enforce a restrictive covenant if it was made to benefit other land, i.e. if there were, in the language of easements, a 'dominant tenement'.[74]

In a sense, the third quarter of the century had been years of consolidation but significant refinements were to come.

Development of the Law in the Last Quarter of the Century

In the years immediately following the Judicature Acts (1873-5) a number of important decisions were arrived at by the courts which helped more precisely to shape and give substance to the concept of the restrictive covenant whilst at the same time there was an ever-increasing number of cases dealing with the 'building scheme' (resulting no doubt from the ever-increasing level of building activity to meet the needs of a growing urban population) and which themselves were significant in laying the foundation for the judgment in the leading case of *Elliston v Reacher*.[75] It may be more helpful to an understanding of what was taking place to deal first with the leading cases 'shaping' the law and then consider the ways in which the courts were dealing with the concept of the building scheme.

The first case of significance was that of *Cooke v Chilcott*,[76] which raised the important matter of the distinction between restrictive and positive covenants. A covenant by a purchaser of land to construct a pump and reservoir to supply water to houses to be built on land retained by the vendor, was held to be one that ran, not only as regards the benefit but, importantly, as regards the burden, and it was so held despite the fact that it was not a negative covenant. Further, it was held that a person who took with notice of the covenant was bound by it.

A year after *Cooke v Chilcott* had thus signalled the court's willingness to permit the burden of a positive covenant to run on the basis of none other than notice, there emerged a further case likewise indicating the court's tolerance in the arena of the restrictive covenant. This was *Luker v Dennis*[77] in 1877 which showed clearly, as had *Catt v Tourle*,[78] that the judges were still not requiring (as later they would) that nearby land be kept to benefit from the restrictive covenants.[79] Rather, at this stage, reliance was being placed on notions of contract, notice and natural justice.

Briefly the facts of *Luker v Dennis* were that the lease of a public house contained a covenant by the publican (lessee) to purchase from the brewer (lessor) all the beer consumed at that public house and also at another public house of which the publican held a lease under a different landlord. It was held that the covenant was binding in equity upon an assignee at the second public house who had notice of the covenant.

Fry, J appears to have been influenced by the judgment of the Court of Appeal in *Catt v Tourle,*[80] which itself had relied on the observations of Lord Justice Knight Bruce in *De Mattos v Gibson,*[81] in which he had laid down the general proposition:

> Reason and justice seem to prescribe that, at least as a general rule, where a man, by gift or purchase, acquires property from another, with knowledge of a previous contract, lawfully and for valuable consideration made by him with a third person, to use and employ the property for a particular purpose in a specified manner, the acquirer shall not, to the material damage of the third person, in opposition to the contract and inconsistently with it, use and employ the property in a manner not allowable to the giver or seller.

In contrast to the tolerance shown in the two aforementioned cases, the 1870's concluded with a case in which the law took a more rigorous stance. This was the case of *Renals v Cowlishaw,*[82] which was concerned, however, not with the running of the burden of a restrictive covenant but with the benefit and, more particularly, with the annexation to land of the benefit of a restrictive covenant. The owners in fee of a residential estate and adjoining lands sold part of the adjoining lands to the defendants' predecessors in title who entered into covenants with the vendors, their heirs and assigns restricting their right to build on and use the purchased land. The same vendors afterwards sold the residential estate to the plaintiffs' predecessors in title, the conveyance containing no reference to the restrictive covenants nor was there any contract or representation that the purchasers of the residential estate were to have the benefit of them. When an action was brought by the plaintiffs to restrain the defendants (who had purchased the land with notice of the restrictive covenants) from building in contravention of those covenants it failed, it being held that although the plaintiffs were 'assigns' of the original covenantees they were not entitled to sue on the original covenants. Because there was no reference to the existence of such covenants the plaintiffs could not be treated as being entitled to the benefit of them. The decision was upheld by the Court of Appeal.[83]

With the turn of the decade appeared the landmark case of *Haywood v The Brunswick Permanent Building Society*[84] in 1881. It was in this case that the Court of Appeal demonstrated that the doctrine of *Tulk v Moxhay* was not to be deployed for other than negative covenants. Land had been granted in fee in consideration of a rentcharge and a covenant to build and repair buildings. The assignee of the grantee of the land was held not liable, either at law or in equity on the ground of notice, to the assignee of the grantee of the rentcharge on the covenant to repair.

Brett, LJ, having observed that the action could not be maintained at common law (noting that 'a covenant to build does not run with the rent in the hands of an assignee'), then considered the position in equity. He was of the view that *Tulk v Moxhay* decided that 'an assignee taking land subject to a certain class of covenants is bound by such covenants if he has notice of them, and that the class of covenants comprehended within the rule is that covenants restricting the mode of using the land only will be enforced'.[85] Cotton and Lindley, LJJ were of the same opinion, the latter explaining that 'it is enough to say that in the present case we have been asked to extend *Tulk v Moxhay* as it has never been extended before, and we decline to do so'.[86] For Brett, LJ, to enlarge the rule would be to create 'a new equity', and this they could not do.

Another case underlining the 'nervousness' of the courts that the principles of *Tulk v Moxhay* might be extended too far came before the Court of Appeal in 1882 in *London & South Western Railway Company v Gomm*.[87] This case dealt primarily with questions of *ultra vires* and the rule against perpetuities but Kay, J, in the court of first instance, had held that specific performance must be decreed, a certain covenant being binding on an alienee with notice on the principle of *Tulk v Moxhay*. The covenant in respect of which Kay, J had decreed specific performance was one requiring the re-conveyance of land to the Railway Company should it at some time in the future be required by them for 'operational' purposes and drew from the Court of Appeal acquiescence in the view that 'the doctrine of *Tulk v Moxhay* only applies to restrictive covenants and not to covenants to do acts related to the land'.

In the Court of Appeal, Lindley, LJ, commenting on the broad proposition that there is a general assumption that every purchaser of land with notice of covenants into which his vendor has entered with reference to the land is bound in equity by all those covenants, drew particular attention to the fact that that proposition had been considered in *Haywood v Brunswick Permanent Building Society*[88] and 'because it was sought there to extend the doctrine of *Tulk v Moxhay* to a degree which was thought dangerous, considerable pains were taken by the Court to point out the limits of that doctrine'. He went on to say 'it was contended, on the authority of *Tulk v Moxhay*, that in as much as the defendants took the land with notice of the covenants that they were bound by them in equity. The Court of Appeal declined so to extend the doctrine of *Tulk v Moxhay* and their reasons will be found very carefully stated by Lord Justice Cotton in his judgment'.[89]

It was in the case of *London & South Western Railway Co. v Gomm* that Sir George Jessel, MR sought to justify the doctrine of *Tulk v Moxhay* as being 'either an extension in equity of the doctrine of *Spencer's Case* to another line of cases, or else an extension in equity of the doctrine of negative easements; such for instance, as a right to the access of light, which prevents the owner of the servient tenement from building so as to obstruct the light'.[90] This view has been the subject of much critical commentary, perhaps most trenchantly and clearly expressed by J.C.V. Behan[91] who distinguished *Spencer's Case* which was based on privity of estate - there being no privity of estate in *Tulk v Moxhay* - and departed from the theory of the negative easement on grounds, *inter alia*, that a common law easement is a *jus in rem* of a strictly limited subject matter whereas a restrictive covenant is not a genuine *jus in rem*, being subject to the caveat of notice and not restricted to one or other of the six categories of accepted easements.[92]

The idea that the burden of a positive covenant should be able to run was not one which would readily be subdued. In *Austerberry v Corporation of Oldham*[93] a further (albeit abortive) attempt was made to extend the doctrine in *Tulk v Moxhay* to enforce a covenant to expend money to make, and keep in repair, a road. The report of the case opens thus:

> The doctrine in *Tulk v Moxhay* is limited to restrictive stipulations, and will not be extended so as to bind in equity a purchaser taking with notice of a covenant to expend money on repairs or otherwise which does not run with the land at law.

In an unequivocal and clear statement Cotton, LJ said, *inter alia*:

> In my opinion, if this is not a covenant running at law, there can be no relief in respect of it in equity; it is not a restrictive covenant; it is not a covenant restraining the corporation or the trustees from using the land in any particular way ...[The] covenant which is attempted to be insisted upon is a covenant to lay out money in doing certain work upon this land...[A] Court of

> Equity…will not enforce a covenant not running at law when it is sought to enforce that covenant in such a way as to require the successors in title of the covenantor to spend money and in that way to undertake a burden upon themselves.[94]

The Building Scheme in the Last Quarter of the Century

Turning to the building scheme cases, the unprecedented level of development in this period assured a steady flow of litigation yielding an array of issues.

Acquiescence, the passage of time, and changes in the area were matters which exercised the courts with some frequency. For instance, in *Gaskin v Balls*[95] the Court of Appeal held that an injunction ought not to extend to the removal of a building which had been allowed to remain for five years without complaint. Likewise, in *Kelsey v Dodd*,[96] long acquiescence in breaches of covenants prohibiting the conduct of offensive businesses caused the plaintiffs to lose their rights to an injunction. In *Sayers v Collyer*[97] an attempt to enjoin breaches of covenant restraining use for trade failed on the ground of acquiescence, though the view was taken that change in the character of the neighbourhood was not *in itself* a ground for refusing the plaintiff relief as the change was not caused by his conduct. From *Jackson v Winnifrith*[98] comes the interesting point that a minor breach by the plaintiff himself would not be regarded as a bar to a successful action for an injunction.

In the same decade, *MacKenzie v Childers*[99] underlined the forcefulness of arrangements made in connection with such schemes. In this case a building estate was offered for sale by auction, in plots according to a plan and particulars and conditions of sale referring to a deed of mutual restrictive covenants to be executed by the vendors and each of the purchasers. The deed contained a recital that it was intended to be a part of all future contracts for sale of the plots, that the several purchasers should be bound by its stipulations and that each purchaser covenanted with the vendors and with the other purchasers to conform with certain conditions restrictive of building, but there was no express similar covenant entered into by the vendors.

For years the stipulations were observed but then the trustees sought to sell part of the estate under conditions allowing non-conforming buildings and an effort was made to restrain such a sale. It was held that an injunction should be granted. The view (as explained in the headnote to the case) was that 'the recital in the deed was not a mere expression of intention which the vendors were at liberty to change, but the effect of the deed was that the vendors thereby entered into a covenant not to authorise the use of the unsold plots in a manner inconsistent with the conditions of the building scheme'. Even though there was no express covenant made by the vendors they were 'bound by a contract, implied from the whole transaction, restricting their dealing with the land in violation of the building scheme'.

The extent of enjoyment of amenity which an enforceable building scheme affords had been brought to the fore a few years earlier by the decision in *Lord Manners v Johnson*.[100] Here, an injunction was awarded to restrain building in contravention of a residential scheme, it being held, *inter alia*, that *invasion of privacy* constituted damage and, moreover, that the covenatees might claim an injunction without any need to show *actual* damage.

Such a measure of willingness on the part of the judges to aid the affording of intended protection was not, however, accompanied by any undue readiness to imply the actual *existence* of a scheme. Caution was exercised in the interpretation of the relevant circumstances, as witnessed by *Tucker v Voles*.[101] In this case an intending purchaser of land was shown a plan indicating lots with houses marked thereon and later sought to restrain the erection of certain buildings on the ground that they were in breach of restrictive covenants the subject of a building scheme. The action failed, the plaintiffs being unable to satisfy the judge that a definite, binding scheme existed. Romer, J noted, *inter alia*, that the plots were not put up together as a whole, there were no printed conditions held out as applicable to the whole estate, and no representations that the plots were to be bound by any conditions.[102] The learned judge thought there was no doubt that 'the vendors contemplated the estate being a residential one' but could not conclude that the vendors had 'contemplated that they would never in any respect change [the] plan...or that they were bound by a definite arrangement that each plot should have one house and nothing but a house'.[103]

To similar effect was *Sheppard v Gilmore*,[104] which concerned a restrictive covenant relating to *elevational control*. Several purchasers bought lots of freehold land laid out for building to erect a row of houses thereon each covenanting with the vendor to erect a house according to a plan (signed by the vendor and the purchaser) with a further covenant that 'the front of the house when built should never be altered'. Houses were built and were similar in appearance (but no plan was produced in evidence). It was held that the covenant not to alter the front of the house was not enforceable by one purchaser against another. The decision seems to have been influenced by the absence of the plan and the absence of evidence that each purchaser had signed the same plan and that therefore it was held to be inconclusive as to whether the restrictive covenants were intended to be for the benefit of the purchasers or solely for the benefit of the vendor.

An interesting and instructive case in land management terms was *Knight v Simmonds*,[105] which involved two schemes. The first was a building scheme imposing conditions prohibiting the conduct of trade and requiring on certain lots that houses be not built of less than a specified value. The second was a sub-scheme with modified conditions that no trade be carried on of a noisy, dangerous or offensive character.

In due course injunctions were sought to restrain the carrying on of a laundry and to restrain a breach of the covenant relating to the value of property to be erected. One plaintiff was found able to insist on the original conditions, inasmuch as he had not acquiesced in the contraventions committed and, further, there had not been any such change in the original residential nature of the estate as to make it inequitable for him to succeed. A second plaintiff was held in theory able to enforce the sub-scheme (though not the main scheme), but the laundry business in question had been operated so quietly and unobtrusively that there was no breach of the modified restriction.

It was also held that the condition as to minimum value had not been broken simply by the fact that there had been built to start with one of a pair of semi-detached houses, although there was an obligation to erect its companion within a reasonable time.

For the legal historian a case of particular importance in the period must surely be the House of Lords decision in *Spicer v Martin*.[106] It adds to the law on building schemes by showing that while the concept originated with the building scheme it works equally well where an estate which is already fully developed is disposed of in sections. However, of much greater significance for the history of equity's furtherance of the building scheme was the explanation given for the basis on which such schemes were enforced being, quite simply, that of 'reciprocity'. In the course of his speech, Lord MacNaughton adverted to the existence of a 'community of interest' which, in his view, 'necessarily [required and imported] reciprocity of obligation'.[107]

The basis of enforcement would eventually become more intricate and then later more relaxed but, as Gray[108] observes:

> In the 19th century...it was...more generally recognised that the authentic basis for the enforcement of 'schemes of development' was the idea of community of interest.

Thus, despite the breadth of practical matters with which the judges were required to contend, at the very heart of the subject there lay, at this time in its growth, an unsophisticated notion, namely that of obligations of conscience stemming from mutuality of interest.

The last decades of the century were a period of intensive litigation. One explanation is surely to be found in the fact that in the whole course of English history no other period had (or even since) experienced a growth of building activity (especially housing) so prolific and so intense.

The situation at the turn of the century has been admirably summarised by the Law Commission:[109]

> By the beginning of this century the courts were thus able to uphold the validity and enforce the observance of restrictive covenants arising both from private contracts between individuals and from large schemes of estate development. Nor did they show any reluctance to do so; for, until the comparatively recent advent of planning control exercisable in the public interest by the local authority, this was the only method of controlling undesirable development and preserving the character of a neighbourhood in the interests of its inhabitants.

The Period from 1900 to 1925

The period from the turn of the century to the 'reforming' property legislation of 1925 witnessed a continuation of the 'building boom' which had already by the end of the first decade of the 20th century started to slow down - a process which was to be accelerated by the outbreak of the 1914-18 Great War and which, as far as house building was concerned, was not to recover (and then nothing to the same or like extent) until the era of the 'great council housing estates' of the late 1920's and the 1930's. It was a period of burgeoning social awareness, albeit tentative, but one in which building controls and standards were no longer restricted to those required to meet the twin needs of health and safety. Standards relating to 'general amenity' such as, for example, density, air, light and space about buildings, the provision of open space, the protection of the 'character of the neighbourhood', the exclusion of obnoxious uses (abattoirs, gasworks and public houses), were more and more commonly becoming controlled features of housing estate development. As such they were increasingly embraced within the régime of the restrictive covenant. Many of these issues had formed the subject of restrictive covenants during the 19th century but it was only towards the end of that century and during the early years of the 20th century that their use became more universal[110] and their application, content and intent more refined.[111]

The first quarter of the twentieth century was to prove, moreover, to be a period especially important in the evolution of the concept of the restrictive covenant, as well as in the development of an understanding of the building scheme. In considering the growth of the law during this period we follow the format already used, dealing first with the cases concerned with general principles and then proceeding to consider those cases concerning the building scheme.

General Principles - LCC v Allen

The early nineteen hundreds were to prove a critical time for the direction of the restrictive covenant inasmuch as it was then that a crucial question came to be addressed. Should Equity be prepared to enforce against a third person covenants taken for the personal benefit of the covenantee (i.e. covenants in gross) or should it only enforce against such a person covenants taken for the protection of land retained by the covenantee?

Soon after the turn of the century the question arose in *Formby v Barker*,[112] the decision in which indicates that if the burden of a restrictive covenant is to run, the covenantee must keep nearby land for the protection and benefit of which the covenant is taken. Here, crucially, the covenant (essentially, not to carry on any noxious industry) into which the purchaser entered was upon a sale to him of the *whole* of the vendor's land, and a later action upon the covenant against a successor of the covenantor was hence doomed to fail. Vaughan Williams, LJ, intimating that the covenant had not been entered into for the benefit of any land of the vendor, explained that there was 'no relation of 'dominancy' and 'serviency' of lands which [would] enable an action to be brought against a person not a party to the original contract'.[113] In the view of the learned judge the covenant was 'merely personal and collateral' and not within the doctrine of *Tulk v Moxhay.*[114]

Not many years passed before there came from the Court of Appeal the landmark decision on the matter in *London County Council v Allen*.[115] This case decided categorically in the affirmative the even yet 'lingering question' as to whether or not it was indeed necessary for a covenantee to possess land which the restrictive covenant sought to benefit. In the headnote the crucial conclusion is set out thus:

> An owner of land, deriving title under a person who has entered into a restrictive covenant concerning the land, which covenant does not run with the land at law, is not bound in equity by the covenant even if he took the land with notice of its existence, if the covenantee is not in possession of or interested in land for the benefit of which the covenant was entered into. In such a case the doctrine of *Tulk v Moxhay*...does not apply.

A builder had entered into a covenant with the London County Council under which he promised not to build on a piece of land which lay across the end of a street which he proposed to make. In due course the land was sold to Mrs Allen who, though having notice of he covenant, nevertheless proceeded to build houses on it. An action by the County Council for, *inter alia*, an injunction failed. The Council had not retained any interest in adjoining or affected land and therefore, in the view of the Court of Appeal, the restrictive covenant was not binding on Mrs Allen even though she had taken the land with notice of it.

Buckley, LJ reviewed the authorities and came to the conclusion that:

> the doctrine in *Tulk v Moxhay* does not extend to the case in which the covenantee had no land capable of enjoying, as against the land of the covenantor, the benefit of the restrictive covenant...Where the covenantee has no land, the derivative owner claiming under the covenantor is bound neither in contract nor by the equitable doctrine which attaches in the case where there is land capable of enjoying the restrictive covenant.[116]

In the view of the learned Lord Justice the doctrine of *Tulk v Moxhay* was:

> either an extension in equity of the doctrine in *Spencer's Case*[117] (in which ownership of land by both covenantor and covenantee is essential) or an extension in equity of the doctrine of negative easements, a doctrine applicable not to the case of easements in gross, but to an easement enjoyed by one land upon another land.[118]

Scrutton, J, rather less happily, drew the same conclusion. He explored the growth of the doctrine in *Tulk v Moxhay* and, though he found in that case that adjacent land was held, he could detect no trace in Lord Cottenham's judgment of any requirement for the covenantee to have held and continue to hold land to be benefited by the covenant. However, later cases impelled him to the opinion that here the plaintiffs must fail on the ground that they had never had any land for the benefit of which this 'equitable interest analogous to a negative easement' could be created.[119]

That Scrutton, J was not at ease with the decision to which he was a party can be gauged from certain comments that he made by way of conclusion. He regarded it:

> as very regrettable that a public body [as here involved] should be prevented from enforcing a restriction on the use of property imposed for the public benefit against persons who bought the property knowing of the restriction, by the apparently immaterial circumstance that the public body did not own any land in the immediate neighbourhood.[120]

Behan,[121] commenting upon the views of Scrutton, J, concludes, regarding the issue of 'public interest' as follows:

> The implied proposition that Courts of Equity should endeavour to mould doctrines which refer exclusively to matters of private right in a manner calculated to promote some supposed interest of the public, is as novel and startling as it is indefensible. It may, with all respect, be suggested that it should be the sole aim of the Courts to function in a manner which tends least to the disturbance of individual interests, that the redress of public ills should be left to legislative action.

Scrutton, J wondered whether, if the matter were to be considered by a higher tribunal, that tribunal might revert to the simple ground of notice, but it was not to be. The decision in *London County Council v Allen*[122] has survived intact in that, save for the 'building scheme' and certain statutory exceptions, the enforcement of a restrictive covenant depends on the possession of land which can benefit. The concern of Scrutton, J, for the 'public interest' has been taken care of (as Behan suggested) by Parliament giving to specified public authorities the power to enforce restrictive covenants in gross, even though they are not possessed of any dominant land which could benefit therefrom.[123]

At the same time as the courts were engaged in the refinement of *Tulk v Moxhay*,[124] so also were they emphasising the fact that it was a creation not of the Common Law but of Equity. Because of its 'equitable' character it was an inescapable feature of the doctrine that the burden of the covenant would run (provided the required conditions were satisfied) until such time as the burdened land came into the hands of a *bona fide* purchaser for value without notice. If such a purchaser acquired the property he would take free of the restriction[125] and the interest enjoyed by the covenantee and his successors, being an equitable interest, would thereupon cease.[126]

The confined scope of the '*bona fide* purchaser defence' on the one hand and the absolute quality of the defence (where applicable) on the other, were respectively manifested in two cases of the time. The former aspect was revealed in the case of *In re Nisbet and Pott's Contract*,[127] where an action to enforce a restrictive covenant against a squatter met with success. The court, being of the view that such a covenant would bind land in the hands of anyone other than a *bona fide* purchaser, so would it bind land to which a squatter had subsequently acquired the statutory title by adverse possession. The statutory 'extinguishment' of the title of the dispossessed owner of the land had not the effect of destroying the covenant and the covenantee could enforce the covenant against the squatter both before and after he had acquired his possessory title and also against any subsequent owner of the land not being a *bona fide* purchaser for value without notice. Thus, even though a squatter gained a new title, and might accordingly be thought to stand clear of a restrictive covenant, he was not a *bona fide* purchaser and was, of necessity, bound.

The latter aspect (i.e. the absolute character of the *bona fide* purchaser defence where applicable) emerged from the equally well known case of *Wilkes v Spooner*.[128] Highlighting the strength of the barrier which the defence erects, the Court of Appeal held that 'the purchaser of land from one who has purchased it for value, without notice, either actual or constructive, of a restrictive covenant, is not bound by the covenant, although he himself had notice of it'. Vaughan Williams, LJ quoted with approval from Ashburner's Principles of Equity that a 'purchaser for valuable consideration without notice can give a good title to a purchaser from him with notice'.[129] Farwell, LJ, endorsing the respectable antiquity of the equitable doctrine, agreed that it 'is impossible for us or any Court to upset law which has been settled for so many years'.[130]

The Building Scheme - Elliston v Reacher

Turning from general principles to the building scheme, this was a period in which the historic judgment in *London County Council v Allen* was matched by the equally important decision in *Elliston v Reacher*,[131] where the plaintiff was able to satisfy both Parker, J and the Court of Appeal that a building scheme was in existence and that the use of certain premises as a hotel should be restrained by injunction as being in contravention thereof. The particular importance of the case lies in the way in whch Parker, J set out the conditions to be met for a building scheme to be brought into existence.

In the view of the learned judge a scheme would exist and purchasers and their successors would be able to enforce the relative restrictive covenants against one another irrespective of the dates of the respective purchases provided that: (i) both the plaintiffs and the defendants derived their title from a common vendor; (ii) prior to selling the lands to which the plaintiffs and the defendants were respectively entitled, the vendor had laid out his estate in lots subject to restrictions to be imposed universally on all the lots; (iii) the restrictions were intended to be and were for the benefit of all the lots, and (iv) the plaintiffs and the defendants, or their predecessors in title, purchased their lots from the common vendor on the basis that the restrictions were to enure for the benefit of the other lots included in the general scheme. He went on to explain, *inter alia*, that regarding the third point, 'the vendor's object in imposing the restrictions must in general be gathered fom all the circumstances of the case',[132] and that if the first three points were established, the fourth might readily be inferred 'provided the purchasers [had] notice of the facts involved in the three first points'.[133]

Parker, J spoke of the existence of a building scheme in terms of purchasers and their successors being able to enforce the relevant covenants against each other irrespective of the dates of the respective purchases. As Megarry and Wade[134] observe, where land is sold or let in lots on the basis of a plan, 'much of the purpose of the covenants given by the purchaser of one lot would be lost if they could not be enforced (i) by those who have previously bought lots and (ii) by those who subsequently buy the unsold lots'. Both these results can 'be achieved without any special rules for schemes of development' so long as precisely worded covenants are employed but 'the special character of schemes of development makes it possible to dispense with these formalities'. Herein lies the critical value of a scheme of development. Where one exists, it creates, by reason of the reciprocity of obligation which is at its heart, a kind of 'local law' for the area it affects.

Cases of the period show the considerable detail ascribed to the concept and content of schemes. For instance, in *Kimber v Admans*[135] the question arose as to whether a building containing several residential flats constituted only one house within the meaning of the word 'house' in a covenant, while in *Alexander v Mansions Proprietary Ltd*[136] the issue was whether there was a departure from a scheme for the management of a building as 'residential flats' if flats were converted into a hotel. In *Gedge v Bartlett*[137] what exercised the court was whether, where a number of lessees of flats covenanted with the defendant lessor to use the flats only for residential purposes, but there was no express corresponding covenant on the part of the lessor, such a covenant might be implied. All these cases in their own small way testified to the intensification of land use particularly in London and south east England.

Parker, J in *Elliston v Reacher* had brought together the requirements for the existence of a building scheme with such clarity that for many years after, in only a handful of cases (it is alleged) was the existence of such a scheme proved. It is suggested that it was perhaps the 'clarity of the requirements' that reduced the need for the intervention of the courts rather than there being any widespread inability to comply with the strictness of the requirements.

The careful attitude displayed at the time to building schemes had been shown a few years earlier in *Osborne v Bradley*,[138] where it was held that no mutual covenants between purchasers would be implied unless both the persons and the plots to be bound were in some way defined. By contrast, a rather more generous attitude prevailed in *Lord Northbourne v Johnston & Son*[139] regarding the precision with which the extent of an intended area of benefit (from certain covenants imposed) had to be shown.

Such painstaking a crystallisation of Equity's conditions was to provide guidance for years to come, its cautious approach being reinforced by the Court of Appeal only a little while later in *Reid v Bickerstaff*.[140] Here the Court affirmed that in order to establish the existence of a building scheme there must be *definite* reciprocal rights and obligations extending over a *defined* area. The plaintiffs failed to establish the essential requisites of a building scheme and so, on this basis, could not succeed, Cozens-Hardy, MR, being of the view that a purchaser must know the extent of both his burden and his benefit.[141]

The desire to circumscribe the notion of the enforceable restriction on land use was similarly displayed (albeit from a different angle) in *Sobey v Sainsbury*.[142] In this case the existence of a building scheme was established but an attempt to enforce certain covenants by means of an injunction failed for two reasons. First, the plaintiff and his predecessors had on occasions refrained from enforcing the restrictions. Secondly, a general change in the character of the neighbourhood had taken place. Neither situation was novel and, in the refusal of an injunction, there can be discerned the continuation of two basic principles of equity at work. It would be inequitable for a person who was himself 'in default' to obtain an injunction and 'Equity does nothing in vain'. Regarding equity's position on building schemes, the latter is of particular interest, the court remaining ever alert to the danger of enforcing covenants which no longer serve any useful purpose. Sargant, J, in referring to his entitlement 'to take into account the general change in the character of the area irrespective of the particular acts and omissions of the plaintiff and his predecessors' pointed out that if it were otherwise, restrictions could become obsolete, stereotyped and perpetuated 'to the prejudice of successive generations [and] far beyond the real intentions of the contracting parties'.[143]

It cannot be gainsaid that it is vital for the law to be able to deal with situations where altered conditions render a restrictive covenant a hindrance. Were it otherwise, such covenants would soon cease to be efficient land management tools.

Before 1925 the effect of 'changes in the character of a neighbourhood' could only be considered in the courts by way of defence to an action for breach of a restrictive covenant. The one exception was that provided by the Housing, Town Planning, etc. Act, 1919, section 27. Under that section an application could be made to the County Court for an order varying a restrictive covenant on the ground that, owing to changes in the character of the neighbourhood a house could not readily be let as a single tenement but could readily be let for occupation if converted into two or more tenements and that by reason of the provisions of the restrictive covenant affecting the house such conversion was prohibited or restricted. The Court could then, if satisfied, vary the terms of the restrictive covenant to enable the house to be so converted.

The need to interpret section 27 of the 1919 Act arose for the Court of Appeal in *Alliance Economic Investment Co. v Berton & Others.*[144] Adverting to the problematic and responsible nature of his task, Bankes, LJ found it hard to establish what exactly constituted 'a change of character' and of what 'a neighbourhood' consisted.

Regarding the first he was of the view that:

[C]hanges in a neighbourhood must not be taken into account unless they are changes which have affected the character of the neighbourhood. Great changes may have taken place in the mode of life of all the inhabitants of a neighbourhood owing to heavy taxation and loss of income. Carriages and motor cars may have had to be given up, women servants substituted for men servants, all entertaining abolished, and though the inhabitants have entirely changed their mode of life, they continue to occupy the same houses, and I do not think that such a change as I have indicated constitutes a change of character of the neighbourhood within the meaning of the section.[145]

Regarding the expression 'neighbourhood' he found it impossible to lay down any general rule. Whereas in country districts people are said to be neighbours who live many miles apart, the same cannot be said of dwellers in a town 'where a single street or a single square may constitute a neighbourhood within the meaning of the section'. Again, physical conditions may determine the boundary or boundaries of a neighbourhood, as, for instance, a range of hills, a river, a railway, or the line which separates a high class residential district from 'a district consisting only of artisans' or workmen's dwellings'. Considering the relevance of changes which may have occurred in the surrounding districts, he expressed the view that:

It seems obvious that changes occurring outside a neighbourhood may materially affect the character of a neighbourhood. For instance, a neighbourhood in a country district may become so surrounded by working class dwellings, factories, tramlines or omnibus routes as to drive all the inhabitants out of the neighbourhood, and to render it uninhabitable by the class of persons who formerly inhabited it.[146]

The interest of the case lies not so much in the decision (the County Court judgment favourable to the appplicants being set aside by the Court of Appeal) as in the exploration of these illusive concepts of 'character' and 'neighbourhood'. Here, in fact, were matters which would exercise the minds of the Official Arbitrator and the Lands Tribunal in the years to come.

Notes

1 A.W.B. Simpson, *A History of the Land Law,* 2nd edition, OUP, 1986, p.256.
2 (1848) 2 Ph 774.

3   (1833) 4B & Ad 433.

4   Cheshire, Fifoot & Furmston, *Law of Contract,*15th edition, p. 463.

5   See *The Prior's or Pakenham's Case* (1369) YB 42 Edw 3, pl 14, fol 3a; Co Litt 385a.

6   Through a body of law with its roots in the Grantees of Reversions Act, 1540 and *Spencer's Case* (1583) 5 Co Rep 16a.

7   (1848) 2 Ph 774.

8   Since *Spencer's case* (1583) 5 Co Rep 16a, which distinguished between covenants referring to a thing in *esse* (e.g. to repair an existing wall) which bound assignees in all cases and covenants referring to a thing in *posse* (e.g. to build a new wall) which bound assignees only where the original lessee covenanted for himself and his assigns: the distinction was abolished by the Law of Property Act, 1925, s.79(1).

9   Since the Grantees of Reversions Act, 1540.

10 Since *The Prior's or Pakenham's Case* (1369) YB 42 Edw 3, pl 14, fol 3a.

11 Again, the inclusion of cases concerning covenants in 'long leases' is further justified when considering the operation of section 84(1) of the Law of Property Act, 1925 which, by section 84(12) as amended, brought covenants in certain leases (leases of over 40 years where 25 years of the term had expired - originally the periods had been 70 and 50 years respectively) into line with restrictive covenants affecting freeholds for purposes of discharge or modification.

12 While any division of a continuum has an inevitable artificiality, 1925 appeared as appropriate as any. With the enactment in section 84 of the Law of Property Act of that year making provision for the discharge or modification of restrictive covenants, the doctrine not only gained its first statutory dimension but its practical future was (albeit indirectly) assured.

13 Confined in these chapters to matters of law and legal interpretation. The practice, first of the Official Arbitrator and later of the Lands Tribunal, is considered separately in the chapters dealing specifically with *The Discharge or Modification of Restrictive Covenants.*

14 (1848) 2 Ph 774, I H & Tw 105, 11 Beav 571.

15 (1834) 2 My & K 517.

16 This last point was to be much criticised by Lord Cottenham in *Tulk v Moxhay* (1848) 2 Ph 774.

17 To the argument that though one party is bound to use the railway, the other is not bound to maintain it, it may be implied that there is an undertaking to keep the railway in repair.

18 *Keppell v Bailey* (1834) 2 My & K 517, at 536.

19 *Ibid.*

20 *Ibid,* at 537. Though, for covenants entered into from 1 January 1996, the Landlord and Tenant (Covenants) Act, 1995 removes the need to consider whether a covenant 'touches and concerns' the land.

21 *Ibid,* at 547.

22 (1834) 2 My & K 517.

23 (1844) 1 Coll CC 480.

24 (1846) 15 Sim 377.

25 (1848) 2 Ph 774, 1 H & Tw 105, 11 Beav 571.

26 (1822) T & R 118.

27 (1838) 9 Sim 196.

28 The plan was very detailed: 'the form of the front building line of [the] intended row of houses was delineated in a ground plan thereof in the margin of the indenture, and did contain, including the curve in length, 400 feet in front towards the south east; and, in order to preserve some degree of similarity and uniformity of appearance in

such intended row of houses...declared, that...the several proprietors of such land respectively for the time being should observe and abide by the several stipulations and restrictions thereinafter contained or expressed in regard to the several houses to be erected thereon'.

29   (1838) 9 Sim 196, at 207.
30   (1839) 10 Sim 9.
31   (1848) 11 Beav 355.
32   (1846) 15 Sim 377.
33   (1848) 2 Ph 774, 1 H & Tw 105, 11 Beav 571.
34   *Ibid.*
35   (1848) 11 Beav 571, at 587.
36   (1848) 2 Ph 774, at 777f.
37   A.W.B. Simpson, *A History of the Land Law,* 2nd edition, OUP, 1986, p. 258.
38   This latter argument assumes that the equity is attached to the property, though this is the very question for decision, and the said argument can equally well be applied to any contract affecting any property, *ibid,* p. 259.
39   (1846) 15 Sim 377.
40   (1834) 2 My & K 517.
41   In as much as it was the kind of covenant which, in a leasehold situation, would (as it appears) have touched and concerned the land.
42   (1834) 2 My & K 517.
43   (1838) 9 Sim 196.
44   (1846) 15 Sim 377.
45   (1848) 2 Ph 774, I H & Tw 105, 11 Beav 571.
46   H.W.R. Wade, *Licences and Third Parties,* (1952) 68 LQR 337, at 349.
47   Challis, *Law of Real Property,* 1911, 3rd edition, p. 185.
48   [1914] 3 KB 642.
49   Gray, *Elements of Land Law*, 1993, 2nd edition, p. 1138.
50   *Morland v Cook* (1868) LR 6 Eq 252.
51   *Catt v Tourle* (1869) 4 Ch App 654.
52   *De Mattos v Gibson* (1858) 4 De G & J 276. Within ten years of *Tulk v Moxhay* the propriety of a similar restriction upon use was canvassed in the case of a ship, but without success - on the facts of the case it was held that no injunction be granted.
53   (1834) 2 My & K 517, at 536.
54   (1848) 2 Ph 774, at 777. It is the case that the same 'restriction' can be both a 'fetter' on the use, development and free alienability of land and a 'form of control' able *positively* to regulate use and development in the commercial interest.
55   Charles Dickens, *Bleak House,* first published 1852-3, Penguin Classics, 1985, p. 356.
56   Arthur Bryant, *English Saga (1840-1940),* Collins, 1940, p.147.
57   (1868) 16 WR 212.
58   (1857) 7 E & B 816. For the benefit to run the covenant must touch and concern the land of the covenantee; there must be an intention that the benefit should run with the land of the covenantee; the covenantee, at the time of making the covenant, must have the legal estate in the land to be benefited, and an assignee must have the same legal estate in the land as the original covenantee. This last requirement was rescinded for covenants made after 1925; see the Law of Property Act,1925, section 78 and *Smith and Snipes Hall Farm Ltd. v River Douglas Catchment Board* [1949] 2 KB 500.
59   [1908] 2 Ch 374, 2 Ch 665 CA.
60   (1851) 1 Sim NS 517.
61   (1813) 1 Mau & Selw 95.

62 This wide interpretation of 'damage' would be again adopted in one of the early cases heard by the Lands Tribunal under the Law of Property Act, 1925, section 84 concerning the discharge or modification of restrictive covenants; see *Re Dr. Barnado's Homes Application* (1955) 7 P & CR 176.
63 (1854) Kay 560.
64 *Ibid*, at 567.
65 (1838) 9 Sim 196.
66 (1854) Kay 560, at 570.
67 (1863) 4 De G J & S 114.
68 (1867) LR 3 Eq 515.
69 On the question as to what kind of conduct might amount to acquiescence see *Mitchell v Steward* (1866) LR Eq 541.
70 (1853) Kay 56.
71 *Coles v Sims* (1854) 5 De G M & G 1.
72 A photographic impression from (sic) the building, which was the subject of complaint, was put in evidence. Surely one of the first, if not the first, examples of 'photographic evidence' being produced in a court of law.
73 (1869) 4 Ch App 654.
74 See Megarry & Wade, *The Law of Real Property*, 5th edition, p. 772: 'For some while the question [of enforceability] was thought to depend on two things only: the character of the covenant, and the fact of notice...On this footing it was immaterial whether the restriction had been imposed to benefit other land or merely the covenantee personally'.
75 [1908] 2 Ch 374, 2 Ch 665 CA.
76 (1876) 3 Ch D 694.
77 (1877) 7 Ch D 227.
78 (1869) 4 Ch App 654.
79 See *post*, per Scrutton, J in *London County Council v Allen* [1914] 3 KB 642: 'The question is whether it is essential to the doctrine of *Tulk v Moxhay* that the covenantee should have...land for the benefit of which the covenant is created'. After reviewing the authorities (including *Luker v Dennis*) he went on to conclude that for many years after *Tulk v Moxhay* it was not essential, but that since the Court of Appeal decision in *Formby v Barker* [1903] 2 Ch 539 it was, and that *Formby v Barker* (and two other decisions of the Court of Appeal) were the authorities for that view.
80 (1869) 4 Ch App 654.
81 (1859) 4 De G & J 276, at 282.
82 (1878) 9 Ch D 125.
83 (1879) 11 Ch D 866.
84 (1881) 8 Q B D 403.
85 *Ibid*, at 408.
86 *Ibid*, at 411.
87 (1882) 20 Ch D 562.
88 (1881) 8 Q B D 403.
89 'The covenant to repair can only be enforced by making the owner put his hand into his pocket, and there is nothing which would justify us in going to that length', per Cotton, LJ.
90 (1882) 20 Ch D 562, at 583.
91 J.C.V. Behan, *The Use of Land affected by Covenants,* Sweet and Maxwell, 1924.
92 For a full account of Behan's argument, see *ibid*, pp. 43-51. Whilst not invalidating his general conclusions he may have overstated his case by referring to 'the six categories of accepted easements', bearing in mind the words of Lord St. Leonards in

Dyce v Hay (1852) 1 Macq 305: 'The category of...easements must alter and expand with the changes that take place in the circumstances of mankind'.
93   (1885) 29 Ch D 750.
94   *Ibid,* at 773.
95   (1879) 13 Ch D 324.
96   (1881) 52 LJ Ch 34.
97   (1884) 28 Ch D 103.
98   (1882) 47 LT 243.
99   (889) 43 Ch D 265.
100   (1875) 1 Ch D 673.
101   [1893] 1 Ch 195.
102   The plan was prepared primarily for submission to the sanitary authority.
103   [1893] 1 Ch 195, at 205.
104   (1887) 57 L J Ch 6.
105   [1896] 1 Ch 653, [1896] 2 Ch 294.
106   (1888) 14 App Cas 12.
107   *Ibid,* at 25.
108   Gray, *Elements of Land Law,* 2nd edition, 1993, p.1161.
109   Law Commission, Report No.11, *Transfer of Land: Report on Restrictive Covenants,* 1967, p.8, para 14.
110   Evidence of their 'popularity' may be gauged from the number of applications for the discharge or modification of restrictive covenants (under section 84(1) of the Law of Property Act, 1925) which related to covenants imposed during this period (late 19th early 20th century).
111   It was during this period also that legislation relating to town planning first appeared on the Statute Book in the Housing, Town Planning, etc. Acts of 1909 and 1919 and the Town Planning Act of 1925.
112   [1903] 2 Ch 539.
113   *Ibid,* at 552.
114   He cited with approval the judgment of Collins, LJ in *Rogers v Hosegood* [1900] 2 Ch 388 CA where, at 407, it is noted that 'the purchaser's conscience is not affected by notice of covenants which [are] part of the original bargain on the first sale, but [are] merely personal and collateral, while it is affected by notice of those which touch and concern the land. The covenant must be one that is capable of running with the land before the question of the purchaser's conscience and the equity affecting it can come into discussion'.
115   [1914] 3 KB 642 CA.
116   *Ibid* at 660.
117   (1583) 5 Co Rep 16a.
118   *London County Council v Allen* [1914] 3 KB 642, at 660.
119   *Ibid,* at 672.
120   *Ibid,* at 673.
121   J.C.V. Behan, *The Use of Land as affected by Covenants,* 1924, p. 38.
122   [1914] 3 KB 642 CA.
123   For example, Local Authorities (under the Housing Acts) and the National Trust.
124   The atmosphere of constraint affected not only the running of the burden but also the running of the benefit. *Rogers v Hosegood* [1900] 2 Ch 388 CA shows that (at that time) if the benefit was to run on the basis that it was 'annexed' to the land of the covenantee, it was vital that the intention of the parties be expressed with utmost clarity.
125   By reason of his having acquired the legal estate and his conscience being clear.
126   Eventually, the doctrine of notice would, to an extent, be replaced by registration.

127   [1906] 1 Ch 386 CA.
128   [1911] 2 KB 473 CA.
129   *Ibid*, at 483.
130   *Ibid*, at 488.
131   [1908] 2 Ch 374, [1908] 2 Ch 665 CA. Parker, J's statement of the requisites for enforcing restrictive covenants as between different purchasers was approved by the Court of Appeal, affirming his decision.
132   [1908] 2 Ch 374, at 384.
133   *Ibid*, at 385.
134   Megarry & Wade, *The Law of Real Property*, 5th edition, p. 790.
135   [1900] 1 Ch 412
136   (1900) 16 TLR 431.
137   (1900) 17 TLR 43.
138   [1903] 2 Ch 446.
139   [1922] 2 Ch 309.
140   [1909] 2 Ch 305.
141   *Ibid*, at 319.
142   [1913] 2 Ch 513.
143   *Ibid*, at 529.
144   (1923) 92 LJKB 750.
145   *Ibid*, at 752.
146   *Ibid*, at 753.

2 The Restrictive Covenant after 1925

The Period from 1926 to the End of the 1960's

This period is defined by reference to the property legislation of 1925 at its commencement and the Law of Property Act, 1969 at its conclusion and has, as a major milestone along the way, the Town & Country Planning Act, 1947.

As every student of land law is made early aware, the reforming legislation of 1925 is without parallel for its historical and continuing significance. It has played, and continues to play, a leading rôle in the modernisation of an essentially feudal system so that it might accommodate the very different needs of an industrial society.[1] It affects restrictive covenants in a number of ways including their impact on third parties coming to the burdened land and their discharge or modification. But before referring to these issues it should first be noted that at the termination of this period the Law of Property Act, 1969 also had important implications for the discharge or modification of restrictive covenants, while at the halfway stage the Town & Country Planning Act, 1947, by subjecting all land to planning control, had unprecedented consequences for land use and development.

The effects of the 1925 legislative reforms on restrictive covenants, respecting the 'running of the burden', as likewise for their discharge or modification, were fundamental. Regarding the former, the Law Commission in its 1967 Report on Restrictive Covenants explains the matter in the following terms:[2]

[Restrictive Covenants] were included in the category of land charges registrable under Section 10 of the Land Charges Act, 1925 [now Section 2 of the Land Charges Act, 1972] in the case of unregistered land, and were made subject to protection by notice in the register of title in the case of registered land ... Registration under the Land Charges Act, or, in the case of registered

45

land, noting in the register of title, operates as statutory notice to all persons dealing with the burdened land and failure by the person entitled to the benefit to register them or have them noted... makes them void against a purchaser.

The result of this far-reaching change was that 'as regards covenants made after 1925 the equitable doctrine of notice no longer applies'.[3] Regarding the latter, i.e. discharge or modification, the Law of Property Act, 1925 develops certain equitable principles under which a person can be deprived of the right to enforce a restrictive covenant by making it possible for persons to seek, in a range of situations, an order discharging or modifying a covenant.[4]

In consequence, the restrictive covenant no longer lay purely in the domain of Equity, for the control régime acquired a statutory appendage. Even so the restrictive covenant as it developed remained very much 'Equity's child'. Following the pattern already established we deal first with the general principles, then with the building scheme and finally, occasioned by section 84 of the Law of Property Act, 1925, we append a brief commentary of certain aspects of the case law relating to discharge or modification.

General Principles

Our starting point is the Court of Appeal's decision in *Re Union of London & Smith's Bank Limited's Conveyance, Miles v Easter*,[5] one of a number of cases in the 1930's which contributed substantially to that aspect of the doctrine concerning the acquisition of the benefit of a covenant - in this instance the running of the benefit by *assignment*.

While the case is noteworthy for the way in which Romer, LJ brings together the criteria for a valid assignment, its critical value is for the establishment of the rule that the 'assignment of the covenant and the conveyance of the land to which it relates must be contemporaneous'.[6] With the protection of the covenantee's land being the only reason for the permitting of the benefit of a covenant to run, the assignment of the benefit is effective only if it takes place at the same time as the assignment of the relevant land. As Cheshire and Burn put it, 'the covenant has spent its force if the covenantee has not required its aid in disposing of the dominant land',[7] and, as the learned Lord Justice himself observed, if the covenantee 'has been able to sell any particular part of his property without assigning to the purchaser the benefit of the covenant, there seems no reason why he should at a later date and as an independent transaction be at liberty to confer upon the purchaser such benefit'.[8]

Just as the judges of the time were concerned with the passing of the benefit of a restrictive covenant by assignment, so too were they involved in the intricacies of the passing of the benefit by *annexation*. In *Re Ballard's Conveyance*,[9] the question arose as to the enforcement of restrictive covenants in respect of a very large estate (some 1700 acres), where there was no building scheme, and assignees of the whole of the dominant land sought the advantage of the covenants on the basis of annexation. In this they failed, it being held that the property for the benefit of which the restrictions were imposed was the *whole* of the estate and that the restrictions, being the usual building restrictions, could not possibly benefit the whole of so large an area and were therefore unenforceable. Moreover, even if there were some part of the land which the covenant actually did 'touch or concern' the court was not prepared to sever it and regard it as in fact annexed to that particular part. Interestingly, as the Court of Appeal decision in *Marquess of Zetland v Driver*[10] was to show soon after, the way forward in the case of express annexation to a large dominant tenement was to make sure that the benefit of the covenant was annexed to 'each and every part of the tenement'.[11]

In addition to the attention given in this period to the aspect of the passing of a benefit from person to person, light was also being thrown on the way in which, by reason of section 56 of the Law of Property Act, 1925, the benefit of a restrictive covenant could be bestowed, at the time the covenant was taken, on a person other than the covenantee. Such a possibility was the concern of the leading case of *Re Ecclesiastical Commissioners for England's Conveyance*.[12] In this case, a conveyance provided that restrictions expressed therein should 'run with and bind the said land' and by a separate covenant contained therein, that such restrictive covenants should enure for the benefit of 'lands adjoining or adjacent to the said land'. Several plots of freehold land had been conveyed by the original vendors to various purchasers before the date of the conveyance. It was held that on the true construction of the covenant, the land referred to as 'adjacent' included certain plots of land 'near to but not adjoining it' and that the original purchasers of the land so held to be adjoining or adjacent, and the present owners of such land, were entitled to enforce the covenant, although the original covenantees were not parties to the conveyance.

Before the end of the 1930's a section 56 issue arose again, this time in *White v Bijou Mansions Limited*.[13] This case emphasises the fact that the operation of the section is restricted and can only be used by a person who is ascertainable at the time the deed is made purporting to make a covenant available to him. It cannot bestow the advantage of a covenant on a future owner of specified land.[14]

Returning to the matter of the passing of the benefit from person to person it is worth while to reflect upon the care which was being taken to contain the restrictive covenant. Boundaries were being defined for the curtailment of its potential. When it came to the later years of this period, however, the attitude appears to have changed in that a more relaxed approach is on occasion taken. Two well known cases serve to illustrate the point.

The first is *Newton Abbot Co-operative Society Limited v Williamson & Treadgold Limited*.[15] Here, the owner of a shop, 'Devonia', carried on an ironmongery business at the premises. She sold a shop opposite to a purchaser who traded as a grocer, the purchaser covenanting not to trade there as an ironmonger. Eventually a successor in title of the vendor brought an action to enforce the covenant against a successor in title of the purchaser and the question arose as to whether the benefit of the covenant had passed, either by annexation or, alternatively, by assignment.

Upjohn, J (as he then was) came to the view that, because in the conveyance in which the covenant was created there was nothing clearly to identify the land for the benefit of which the covenant was taken, the benefit could not have passed by *annexation*.[16] However, he concluded that the benefit was capable of, and did, pass by *assignment*. First, the covenant was taken not merely to protect business goodwill but to enhance the value of 'Devonia' upon a re-sale.[17] Secondly, the land which was intended to benefit was defined with sufficient clarity. It did not matter, in the view of the learned judge, that the conveyance in question did not clearly identify the land to be benefited, but only described the vendor as 'of Devonia', for the court was able to have regard to the surrounding circumstances to see whether the land was shown in some other way with reasonable certainty. From the circumstances, particularly the closeness of the respective shops, Upjohn, J believed the only reasonable inference was that the covenant had been taken to protect the property. It is his willingness so to approach the matter that is important and significant in the consideration of the evolution of the restrictive covenant.

The second case, *Marten & Another v Flight Refuelling & Another*[18] raised the question whether it was possible for the benefit of a restrictive covenant to be *annexed by implication* from circumstances. Part of an agricultural estate had been sold, and the case involved a covenant not to use the land for non-agricultural purposes. It was argued that the conveyance did not annex the benefit of the covenant so that it would pass automatically, that it did not indicate that it was made for the benefit of any land and that, even if it was so made, it did not identify the land. Wilberforce, J was prepared however to take a favourable stance and to hold that annexation could be implied. He was willing to have regard to the circumstances surrounding the conveyance and to take 'a broad and reasonable view of the proof of the identity of the estate'. Adopting a generous view of the matter, the learned judge was ready, even though there was no express annexation, to infer it, if to do otherwise would be an affront to justice and common sense.[19]

As with the situation in the earlier years of this period social conditions continued swiftly to change. This state of affairs was reflected in changing patterns of land use and in turn occasioned a cluster of cases in the 1930's on the subject of equitable defences.

To the fore is *Chatsworth Estates Company v Fewell*,[20] in which an action was brought to enforce a restrictive covenant designed to keep an estate residential in character. The defendant relied upon two equitable defences namely (i) the general change in the character of the neighbourhood and (ii) an allegation that this change was brought about by the acts or omissions of the plaintiffs or their predecessors. It was held that in order to succeed on the first ground the defendant must show so total a change in the character of a neighbourhood as to render the covenants valueless to the plaintiffs and in order to succeed on the second ground the defendant must show that the plaintiffs' acts or omissions were such as to justify a reasonable person taking the view that the covenants were no longer enforceable.[21]

To keep the estate purely residential covenants had been imposed preventing any house being used 'otherwise than as a private dwelling house', and although the plaintiffs (or their predecessors) had licensed a number of schools, some blocks of flats, a hotel and three boarding houses, it was held that this did not prevent the plaintiffs from restraining the defendant from using his house as a guest house, and further that the area was not so changed as to render the covenants valueless to the plaintiffs. Accordingly, an injunction was granted.

On the first defence Farwell, J adopted a remarkably rigorous stance. In his view, a person who has taken covenants for the protection of his property cannot be deprived of his rights under them unless such a state of affairs has been brought about as to deprive those covenants of all their worth, 'so that an action to enforce them would be unmeritorious [and] not *bona fide* at all'.[22]

On the second defence, in an interesting comment on the plaintiffs' conduct and approach, he went on to note that the plaintiffs had not unduly insisted on their covenants saying:[23]

> I cannot think that plaintiffs lose their rights merely because they treat their neighbours with consideration. They are doing what they think sufficient to preserve the character of the neighbourhood. Whether they do enough is another matter, but I am quite satisfied that they are not intending by their acts or omissions to commit this area to be turned into anything other than a mainly residential area.

Always a matter of degree he concluded that it could not be thought that the plaintiffs had here, by their conduct, represented to the defendants that the covenants were no longer enforceable.[24]

In the second of the cases, *White v Bijou Mansions Ltd.*,[25] Simonds, J gave as the final matter for his consideration the question whether, should the plaintiff be in a position to enforce a certain covenant, there might be available to the defendant 'any equitable defence based on a change in the character of the neighbourhood, or the conduct of the plaintiff himself'.[26] Having concluded that the plaintiff was unable to enforce the covenant, it became unnecessary to deal in depth with any defences, but the learned judge nevertheless went on to observe that 'although there [might] have been some changes in the neighbourhood [they were not] changes for which the plaintiff himself was substantially responsible'.[27]

Of significance here was the use of the word 'substantial'. Although the point was, in the circumstances, academic it seems that there was no ready anxiety to denude a party of the benefit of a covenant. Together, *Chatsworth Estates* and *Bijou Mansions* clearly show that the degree of the change in circumstances or the extent of the plaintiffs' conduct must be considerable for the protection of a covenant to be lost.

A similar message was signalled by *Westripp v Baldock*[28] not long afterwards. In this case, in response to a claim of breach of a covenant against the carrying on of trade, the defence was again brought of a change in the character of the neighbourhood. The Court of Appeal concluded that the neighbourhood in question, being yet largely of a residential nature, had not sustained such a change as to render the covenant unenforceable. For Slesser, LJ the whole character of the neighbourhood had to have been altered to the extent that 'the object for which the covenant was originally entered into must be considered at an end'.[29] It had been argued that the test in *Chatsworth Estates* was too stringent and that a neighbourhood must develop and not be sterilised, but to no avail. As is intimated in the editorial note, 'the judgment ...again emphasises the heavy burden that is placed upon a party who seeks to show that a restrictive covenant has become unenforceable by reason of a change in the character of the neighbourhood'.[30]

These 1930's cases, dealing with 'change of character', not only reflect the rôle of the restrictive covenant as a forceful shield against the undermining of value and amenity, they indicate also the continuing great respect of the judiciary for property rights.

Albeit obliquely, the strength of the restrictive covenant as a land management tool is further underscored by a decision in the House of Lords at the very end of the 1960's. *Esso Petroleum Co. Ltd. v Harpers Garage (Stourport) Ltd.*[31] raised the 'restraint of trade doctrine', a common law doctrine which has long struck down certain agreements which unreasonably restrain trade.[32] The House of Lords was called upon to consider certain agreements restraining the respondents from buying or selling at their garages motor fuels other than those of the appellants. In the circumstances, it was concluded that such agreements were within the restraint of trade doctrine but what is relevant here is the approach to the question of whether or not ordinary restrictive covenants were embraced by the doctrine. That they were not is succinctly explained thus in the headnote :[33]

[O]rdinary negative covenants preventing the use of a particular site for trading are not within the doctrine of restraint of trade, because a person buying or leasing a particular piece of land has no previous right to trade there and, when he took possession subject to a negative covenant, he gave up no freedom which he had previously possessed.

The importance of their exclusion from the grasp of the restraint of trade doctrine plainly speaks for itself.

By way of conclusion to the 'general principles' aspect of this stage in its history, it is submitted that the strength of the restrictive covenant was now founded on two matters first, the fact that Equity had set boundaries to an otherwise potentially volatile concept and secondly, the advent of a statutory mechanism for their discharge or modification. In the context of the former, the case of *Tophams Ltd. v Earl of Sefton*[34] may serve as an appropriate finale. This, another case which reached the House of Lords, involved a covenant, taken on the sale by the Earl of Sefton of freehold land used as a racecourse, that the purchasers (Tophams Ltd.) would not *inter alia* cause or permit the land to be used other than for horse racing and for agricultural purposes. In due course, Tophams Ltd. agreed to sell the land to Capital and Counties Property Co. Ltd. (a development company) who, to the former's knowledge, intended to develop it for housing. The Earl then sought an injunction to restrain Tophams from causing or permitting the land to be used for other than the permitted uses and to restrain Tophams and the development company from carrying their agreement into effect.

The cynosure of the case was the question whether Tophams, by selling the land to the development company knowing that the latter were intending to build on it, were 'permitting' development in breach of the covenant, the matter on which the majority of the House of Lords decided in the negative. For the purpose of an historical account, however, what is perhaps of equal interest lies rather in the fact that no land was kept by the covenantee which could benefit from the covenant and it was therefore agreed that it was enforceable only against Tophams, in other words its burden could not run. As Lord Guest observed:[35]

> It was ... accepted that if the conveyance [were] completed the covenant would not run against Capital & Counties Property Co. Ltd. as the respondent (the Earl of Sefton) has no adjacent land to benefit by the covenant.

In chapter 1 we accorded considerable emphasis to the way in which, in *London County Council v Allen*,[36] the Court of Appeal had insisted upon the need for the retention of benefited land if the burden of a restrictive covenant was to run. With this insistence, the doctrine of the restrictive covenant had become firmly linked to the objective of the protection of land and so (as this case illustrates) the position was to remain. With this principle lodged at the heart of the doctrine, the placing of 'unwarranted and useless burdens upon subsequent purchasers from the covenantor'[37] would always be avoided and hence the essentially practical nature of the doctrine maintained.

The Building Scheme

Cases in the period reveal on the one hand a perception of the intrinsic value of the 'building scheme' and on the other an awareness also of its potency and hence of the need for clarity in the setting of its confines. Such a tension was apparent in *Torbay Hotel Limited v Jenkins & Lawley*.[38] Here, while certain estate owners had not followed the classic building scheme order of parcelling out vacant land in plots for sale, they had adopted a systematic policy of granting the fee simple when sales of the freehold became practicable and in so doing imposed a regular system of covenants to benefit *inter se* all those who from time to time became owners of portions of the estate. Notwithstanding that these circumstances differed from those of an ordinary building scheme, Clauson, J was of the view that 'the principle of the common intention of the parties on which the building scheme cases proceed would apply to [such a] case'.[39] However, he then went on to explain that the common intention would be carried into effect by enforcing the restrictions on any owner for the time being 'only if, the court can ascertain with reasonably clear definitiveness the geographical area within which those mutual obligations are intended to operate',[40] and in this instance the plea in question failed for want of evidence sufficient to define the area.[41]

Tension between intrinsic value and potency arose in a different manner just a few years later in *Pearce v Maryon-Wilson*[42] which involved the issue of entitlement to relax a restrictive covenant in a building scheme. Briefly, the facts were that the defendant, successor of the original lessor, owned an estate (assumed to be embraced by a scheme) comprising houses let subject to identical covenants including one against occupancy other than as a private dwelling house 'without the consent in writing of ... the lessor'. The plaintiff sought an injunction to restrain the relaxation of the covenant, arguing that there must be, in equity, an implied condition in the scheme to the effect that the defendant could not relax the covenant over parts of the estate so as to depreciate the value of other parts of the estate.

The argument failed, it being held that the words 'without the consent' bestowed the widest possible power of giving or withholding consent and conferred an entitlement to authorise any use of property desired. It might perhaps be thought that this decision challenges the very raison d'être of the building scheme concept which is based on principles of 'mutuality' and 'reciprocity' of benefit and burden for its rôle in controlling use and development to the advantage of all embraced by a particular scheme. It is possible that the court took the view that, as it was dealing with a leasehold situation, the defendant would not sanction any use or development which might 'injure' the value of his reversion and that therefore what he had permitted could not be of such a grievous nature as to harm the plaintiff.

In his *Elements of Land Law*, Gray adverts to the fact that Parker, J had laid down in *Elliston v Reacher*,[43] the most stringent requirements for the existence of an enforceable building scheme, conditions indeed 'so ferocious' that between 1908 and 1965 in hardly any cases was such a scheme upheld.[44] One case where a scheme was held to exist was *Newman v Real Estate Debenture Corporation*[45] decided at the outbreak of the 1939-45 war.

The case involved a block of leased flats in which the leases in question contained covenants restricting the use of the flats to residential purposes only. The plaintiff, having suffered serious nuisance when the building was altered so as to facilitate business use, successfully contended *inter alia* that the building was the subject of a scheme and that, accordingly, there was an implied obligation on the lessor not to let flats other than for residential use.[46]

It is suggested that this is a case that repays attention not only for the successful contention of the existence of a scheme, but also for the fact that its existence was established in respect of 'a small number of flats in a single building'. The principle of the building scheme is commonly applied to a substantial area and no lower limit to the size of the 'building estate' had previously been suggested. If, as it appears from this decision, it was logical that the principle should be applied even to a small number of flats in a single building, since the user of any one part of the premises must materially affect the comfort of the remainder, could it be concluded that the minimum 'size' for a building scheme would be a pair of semi-detached houses?

An examination of building scheme cases has illustrated, with some force, the way in which equity came, in due course, to require the fulfilment of strict conditions for a building scheme to exist - conditions as set out by Parker, J in *Elliston v Reacher*.[47] One of these was that a common vendor should, prior to making sales, have laid out a defined area of land in lots. In the mid 1960's however, with the advent of the decision in *Baxter and Others v Four Oaks Properties Limited*,[48] this was no longer to be so. In Baxter's case a vendor sold, over a period of ten years, the whole of an estate, taking restrictive covenants from the various purchasers. Certain flats, having been built in breach of covenant, the question arose as to whether or not a building scheme existed, and Cross, J was of the opinion that the fact there had been no laying out of the land in lots prior to any selling off did not preclude the establishment of a scheme's existence.

In the view of the learned judge, the absence of prior division would be an argument against 'there having been intention on [the vendor's] part and on the part of the various purchasers that there should be a building scheme'[49] but, even so, it was not, he thought, the intention of Parker, J to lay down any rule that any such absence must 'as a matter of law, preclude the court from giving effect to a clearly proved intention that the purchasers were to have rights *inter se* to enforce the provisions of the common law'.[50]

This less stringent approach to the pre-requisites of a building scheme would, as will emerge later, be continued in the 1970's and, in so doing, reflect a desire to hark back to the much earlier stance on schemes when the basis of the equity was perceived to rest on a simple communality of intention. However, the decision in *Baxter's case* did not escape criticism. In the 1967 Report of the Royal Commission on Restrictive Covenants it was considered that the position there adopted meant that certainty had been lost. To the extent that there was no longer any requirement for a prior parcelling out in lots 'the objective character of the test [had] been replaced by the understanding of the parties'.[51]

An appropriate conclusion to this review of building scheme cases may be drawn from the decision in *In re Pinewood Estate, Farnborough*.[52] This case brought out a question whether, in addition to the three well established ways of transmitting the benefit of a restrictive covenant there might be a fourth method. Under consideration was the suggestion that a benefit might flow to successors of the covenantee not only via annexation, assignment or a scheme, but also on the ground merely that if there is a deed showing a group of parties intend mutually to be bound by certain restrictive stipulations, that very mutuality suffices to carry to a transferee the benefit of those stipulations. In the event, the view was taken that no such fourth 'vehicle' of transmission was known to equity.

Cases Concerning Section 84 of the Law of Property Act, 1925

In our introduction to this period, reference was made to the enactment of section 84 of the Law of Property Act, 1925, and its facilitation of the discharge or modification of restrictive covenants. In its original form sub-section (1) of section 84[53] provided for applications to be made to the Official Arbitrator (later the Lands Tribunal[54]) to have restrictive covenants discharged or modified on a number of grounds, such as that the restriction was obsolete (as a result of changes in the character of the property or the neighbourhood), or that its continued existence would impede the reasonable use of the land, or that the proposed discharge or modification would not injure persons entitled to the benefit of the restriction. Appeals could be made from the Official Arbitrator to the Chancery Division by way of a re-hearing, and later from the Lands Tribunal to the Court of Appeal by way of case stated.

Inasmuch as it warrants study in its own right the operation of this statutory régime is considered later, and at length, in chapters 3, 4 and 5. However, certain appellate decisions occasioned by the régime merit attention here in that the respect displayed in them by the courts for property rights echoes that shown in the cases relating to equitable defences.

First, is the decision of Farwell, J in *In re Henderson's Conveyance*[55] in 1940. A purchaser of property, which was the subject of a restrictive covenant, desirous of building thereon had successfully applied for the covenant's discharge or modification. The order was made subject to the payment of compensation to the person benefiting from the restriction and he, having opposed the application, appealed to the court.

The learned judge set the order aside. He held that there was no change in the character of the property or neighbourhood, there had been a failure to show impediment to reasonable development, and the covenant continued to be of value. In so holding, Farwell, J observed that he did not 'view [section 84] of the Act as designed to expropriate the private rights of another purely for his own profit'.[56] There might be cases where a covenant should be discharged or modified against the will of the benefiting person but, as he saw it, the section was not 'designed with a view to benefiting one private individual at the expense of another private individual'.[57] Here again was demonstrated the high regard for a right of property which the same judge had revealed some years earlier in the *Chatsworth case*.[58]

For a continuation of that same level of esteem two cases of the mid-1950's may be cited as illustrations, namely *In re Truman*[59] and *Driscoll v Church Commissioners for England*.[60] In the former the Court of Appeal heard an appeal from the dismissal by the Lands Tribunal of an application by brewers to have a restrictive covenant intended to maintain the residential quality of an area so modified as to enable them to erect a public house.

The Lands Tribunal had dismissed the application on the grounds first, that the degree of change in the area which had occurred was not sufficient to justify the conclusion that the covenant had in consequence become 'obsolete' and second, that the proposed development would seriously injure the objectors who were entitled to the benefit of the restriction. Affirming the decision, the Court of Appeal considered that with change of character a point might eventually arrive when a covenant's purpose could no longer be fulfilled and hence it would be 'obsolete'. However, the finding by the Tribunal of serious injury to those entitled to its benefit were the covenant to be discharged, and hence its affording to them of real protection, meant it could not be said here that it had become 'obsolete'.

Driscoll's case[61] likewise involved an appeal from an application for discharge or modification of a covenant designed to preserve residential character, but this time so as to facilitate the use of large houses as clubs and hotels. The application, based on obsolescence and impediment of reasonable user failed, the Lands Tribunal finding *inter alia* that despite changes in the area it was yet residential and those entitled to benefit from the restriction remained entitled to the protection it afforded.

An appeal was made to the Court of Appeal but without success, the approach being taken that the covenants in question still afforded real protection, did not impede reasonable user, and were not obsolete. On the matter of obsolescence, Morris, LJ noted findings of the Tribunal that, whereas few people could now afford large private residences the area was still essentially residential and he agreed with the Tribunal that this was sufficient to warrant the conclusion that the restriction was not obsolete.[62] Further, in the view of Denning, LJ (as he then was) if a covenant is deployed reasonably for a useful purpose it is not obsolete 'even though that purpose goes beyond what was contemplated 90 years ago', however if it 'is shown no longer to serve any useful purpose, then, of course, it is obsolete'.[63]

It is worthy of mention that *Driscoll's case* raised before the Court of Appeal not only the important issue of the sufficiency of the establishment of grounds for discharge but also the equally significant matter of the nature of the Tribunal's power under section 84. It was argued that the words 'the authority shall have the power by order wholly or partially to discharge or modify any restriction' imposed a duty on the Lands Tribunal to modify the restriction in some way or other, though it had discretion as to the precise way to be adopted. The idea contained in this submission, namely that the discretion extended only to the manner of modification, did not find favour. In the view of the majority of the judges there was no such implicit duty. Denning, LJ observed that to him it seemed the section gave a discretion to the Tribunal 'whether to modify the restriction *at all*'.[64]

It should perhaps be added that whereas there was thus no desire to curtail the sphere of discretion in the fashion suggested, there is nevertheless an inherent limitation in the sense of the range of considerations which may be taken into account upon its exercise.This was made clear by the Court of Appeal in a case towards the end of the period, namely *Gee v The National Trust for Places of Historic Interest or Natural Beauty*.[65] This case involved an application for discharge or modification of a restrictive covenant from which the National Trust (as custodian of places of natural beauty) benefited,[66] in order that a house might be built on land in the area of the Helford River in Cornwall. The application was made on the ground that discharge or modification could not injure those entitled to the benefit of the restriction and the Lands Tribunal concluded that the proposed dwelling would not adversely impinge upon the beauty of the area. Nevertheless, the Tribunal refused the application on the basis of fears that to do otherwise might hinder the obtaining of such covenants and appeals by the Trust for funds in the future. From this decision the applicant made an appeal and with success. It was held that the Lands Tribunal having accepted that the proposed house was not injurious had no basis for the grounds on which it declined to exercise its discretion to modify the covenant. In the eyes of the Court of Appeal the matters to which the Tribunal had given consideration were plainly extraneous, even if laudable.

Section 84(2) of the Act, like sub-section (1), contains provisions of practical value to estate managers. Briefly, it gives the court power to declare whether any freehold land is affected by restriction, or to declare what is the nature and extent of a restriction, and whether the same is enforceable.[67] It is to be noted that it is the court, not the Lands Tribunal, which is the recipient of the power, a point to which Upjohn, LJ (as he then was) adverted in *In re Purkiss' Application*[68] when he observed that the [Lands Tribunal] has no jurisdiction to determine any question falling properly within the ambit of sub-section (2)'.[69]

A case which illustrates the operation of sub section (2) is *Re Freeman-Thomas Indenture*.[70] Here, a local authority applied for a declaration that the land on which it desired to build a school was no longer affected by restrictive covenants to maintain the land 'as a public park or common' and 'not to erect any building on any part of the land' without the consent of the owner or the trustees of the 'large settled estate'. It was held that as the estate had been 'broken up into small plots', as there was no owner of the 'large settled estate', as the covenants were obsolete, and as there was no-one legally able to enforce them, the court in the exercise of its discretion would issue a declaration that the land was no longer affected by the restrictive covenant.

The period from 1926 to the end of the 1960's had comprised, in development terms, several distinct phases. First, was the growth of council housing estate construction in the late 1920's and 1930's. Secondly, as a result of the 1939-45 war and consequential financial and administrative (e.g. licensing control) constraints, there followed a virtually moribund period (certainly in respect of house building) for the whole of the 1940's. Thirdly, there followed in the 1950's and 1960's a time of post-war reconstruction and re-development which, though embracing commercial and industrial as well as residential development, was particularly characterised by 'feverish' house building activity (including high-rise flats) confined initially to local authority housing in the main but to be followed later by extensive private housing estate development.

This house building activity, in volume previously only exceeded in the last quarter of the 19th century, met the demand created by physical (wartime) destruction, population growth and inward migration and involved both public and private development. It was a revival which took place in the very different climate of public regulation brought about by the enactment of the Town & Country Planning Act, 1947.[71] The new large 'estates', both council and private, were the subject of town and country planning control and, insofar as much private estate development was concerned, supplemented by restrictive covenant control.

It was a period of great change and movement embodying increasing social aspirations for enhanced living conditions. As people sought higher standards of amenity by, for instance, the protection of the character of the area in which they were to live, the provision of open space, the retention of access to light and air and the imposition of tolerable levels of density, so they ensured for the doctrine of the restrictive covenant a position of undiminished significance.

To the judges there fell the rôle of nurturing the régime, involving them in a series of implicit 'balancing acts'. When dealing with general principles they had need to achieve a structure which was both secure and flexible, when considering building schemes to measure 'worth' against 'potency', and when interpreting section 84 to weigh respect for 'property' against the scarcity of a natural resource, for example the degree of availability of land for house building. That they fulfilled that task is demonstrated by the fact that the doctrine of the restrictive covenant prospered. It was, indeed, destined to prove its continuing worth in the years which lay ahead.

The Period from 1970 to the Present Day

The last period was defined by reference to two significant statutory interventions, namely the Law of Property Act, 1925 and the Law of Property Act, 1969, it being observed that the latter considerably amended the régime for the discharge or modification of restrictive covenants.

The 1969 Act not only provided *per se* a suitable break point in the history of the restrictive covenant, it also marked the appearance of a shifting perception of what may be called 'property-related values'. As society moved from the 1960's to the 1970's there was exhibited a culture change from a time in which 'quantity' and comprehensive development were the main criteria, to one in which 'quality' of development and conservation and environmental issues were to become of increasing importance and value.[72] Although, as has been earlier observed, there is artificiality in the division of a continuum, it may be appropriate to enter this final period of the history of the restrictive covenant at the stage where there were beginning to emerge those desiderata which enjoy so high a profile in our present day.

Again, for ease of exposition, the material is taken under three headings, dealing first with cases highlighting matters of general principle, followed by decisions involving building schemes, and finally by cases relating to certain issues raised by 'Section 84'.

General Principles

Early in this period the case of *Wrotham Park Estate Company v Parkside Homes Ltd. and Others*[73] brought forward matters of distinct practical significance for the lawyer and estate manger alike, namely whether the benefit of the particular covenant was still a 'real benefit', and the principles concerning the exercise of the mandatory injunction, damages in lieu and the quantum of damages. The substance of the case was whether the particular 'layout stipulation' (compliance with which was the subject of the restrictive covenant) was enforceable as between the present parties,[74] whether the development carried out was in breach, and what the remedy should be.

In the process of holding that the layout stipulation was enforceable as between the plaintiffs and the defendants on the principle of annexation, particular attention was paid to the question whether the dominant land had been and was still capable of benefiting, and the conclusion reached that 'the validity of the restriction should be upheld so long as an estate owner might reasonably take the view that the restriction remained of value to his estate and that the restriction should not be discarded merely because others might reasonably argue that the restriction [was] spent'.[75]

It having been found also that the development carried out by the defendants was a clear and material breach of the layout stipulation, it was concluded that the plaintiffs were not entitled to relief by way of a mandatory injunction because 'it would be an unpardonable waste of much needed houses to direct that they now be pulled down',[76] and furthermore, 'it [was] totally unnecessary to demolish the houses in order to preserve the integrity of the restrictive covenants imposed on the rest of the area'.[77]

Inasmuch as the court had jurisdiction to grant a mandatory injunction against the defendants for building in breach of the covenant, the court had power in consequence to award damages in lieu of an injunction and accordingly the next matter was to consider the proper amount. The approach taken proceeded from the basis that while the breach of the covenant had not diminished the value of the Wrotham Park Estate, the plaintiffs should not merely be given nominal damages, for this would result in the defendants being 'left in undisturbed possession of the fruits of their wrongdoing'. Justice would be served, it was thought, by the award of such a sum as might reasonably have been demanded for the relaxation of the covenant.

This is a case which raises a number of important points. First, on the matter of the assessment of damages, Newsom, in a note on the decision,[78] commented that basing it on the so-called 'wayleave principle' was a useful alternative to nominal damages in situations where a mandatory injunction would be unjustifiable.[79] Secondly, on the question of the value of a restrictive covenant in estate management and environmental terms, the litigation highlighted the polarity of the approaches taken to the issue by the party benefiting and the party burdened. The former emphasised the value of control over character and amenity, the latter the reduction in worth 'as the tide of development advances'. Thirdly, on the decision to refuse a mandatory injunction it may be asked whether this decision, albeit difficult, may not only reflect a remarkably sympathetic view of the defendants' breach but also sit somewhat uncomfortably with the learned judge's observation that 'the fact that these houses will remain does not spell out a charter entitling others to despoil adjacent areas of land in breach of valid restrictions imposed by the conveyances'.[80]

It will be observed that on the fundamental question as to whether or not the dominant land could be regarded as capable of benefiting from the restriction a favourable approach was adopted. The view was taken that it is for the defendant to show there is no such capability.[81] A generous approach to the issue of basic enforceability had also appeared only a year previously in *Earl of Leicester v Wells-next-the-sea Urban District Council.*[82] Here, a very small part of an extremely large estate had been sold and a covenant taken against use for purposes other than smallholdings and allotments. The purchasers later proposing to sell the land for a purpose involving a breach of the covenant, a restraining injunction was successfully sought. It was held, *inter alia*, that although the area in issue was only tiny in proportion to the estate in its entirety that did not mean the covenant could not benefit the estate *as a whole*.

Although not on the same point, the regard for enforceability shown in this case was to be seen far more vividly in the next decade with the leading decision of the Court of Appeal in *Federated Homes Ltd. v Mill Lodge Properties Ltd.*[83]

This case focussed on the long-standing question of whether or not the benefit of a restrictive covenant might run not by express or implied annexation, but by statutory annexation. Section 78(1) of the Law of Property Act, 1925 provides that 'a covenant relating to any land of the covenantee shall be deemed to be made with the covenantee and his successors in title and the person deriving title under him or them'. As Gray intimates, this provision appears to have provided an efficacious formula of annexation but strangely it had not been regarded 'as supplying a general statutory implication of the necessary words of annexation'.[84] Clear words evidencing the necessary intention were required, as for instance in *Rogers v Hosegood*[85] where a covenant ran which was couched in terms that its benefit might enure for the vendors, their heirs and assigns and others claiming under them to all or any of their lands adjoining or near to the said premises.

Adopting Gray's vivid imagery, the spell cast over this long dormant statutory provision was 'finally broken'[86] in *Federated Homes*. To the forefront of the many issues raised by this case was the question whether a covenant not to build houses above a certain density was enforceable by a successor of the covenantee. So far as a part of the land was concerned, there was no problem, as the benefit passed by assignment. The difficulty appeared in connection with the other part, in respect of which reliance had to be placed upon annexation. While the deed made it clear that the land to be benefited was adjoining land retained by the covenantee there were no express words sufficiently annexing the benefit of the covenant to that land.

In a decision which aroused widespread interest, the Court of Appeal took the line that in spite of this lack, the benefit of the covenant had passed and the covenant was enforceable by the successor of the covenantee. In the view of the court, so long as the covenant in question actually touched and concerned the land of the covenantee, its benefit was able, by virtue of section 78, to pass to a successor of the covenantee and there was no 'need to use appropriate language from which an intention to annex might be inferred'.[87] Here, the phraseology of the deed sufficiently intimated that the covenant related to the land of the covenantee and hence its benefit might run.

In taking this stance, Brightman, LJ rejected a long-standing narrow interpretation of the section, to the effect namely that it provided no more than 'word-saving shorthand'. For the future, this robust holding[88] would make it so much easier to ensure the passing of the benefit by annexation that it could be said that this particular part of the equitable régime was transformed.[89]

Successful resort to the notion of statutory annexation via section 78 was had not long ago with the decision in *Robins v Berkeley Homes (Kent) Ltd.*[90] where it was held that the section would achieve annexation unless, which was not there the case, the covenant was purporting to achieve a different purpose. However, the reach of the section was not to prove so extensive as it might at first sight have seemed. Before the end of the 1980's two cases indicated certain significant limitations.

The first was that of *Roake and Others v Chadha and Another,*[91] in which the benefit of a covenant was expressly stated *not* to enure for a successor unless it was specifically assigned. The plaintiffs argued that annexation had come about through section 78, because its provisions could not be excluded by the expression of a contrary intention, but without success. Judge Paul Baker, QC, whilst having no difficulty in accepting that the covenant was one that came within section 78, was 'far from satisfied that section 78 [had] the mandatory operation ...claimed for it'.[92] In his view, one still had 'to construe the covenant as a whole to see whether the benefit of the covenant [was] annexed'.[93] Intention was thus, still, a fundamental consideration.

The second case, *J Sainsbury plc and Another v Enfield London Borough Council,*[94] concerned a successful application for a declaration that certain land was not the subject of certain restrictive covenants. It was held that the restrictive covenants, having been entered into prior to 1926, were not subject to section 78. They were governed by the more narrowly worded provision contained in section 58 of the Conveyancing Act, 1881, which was not apt to bring about an effect of automatic annexation. In so doing the court was drawing attention to the fact that old restrictive covenants are not amenable to the 'generous' *Federated Homes* approach and, given the number of old covenants, this plainly serves to diminish the *Federated Homes* impact.

Apart from the necessary constraint exhibited in these two last cases, and the perhaps understandable disinclination to order demolition in *Wrotham Park,*[95] it will be seen that the general climate for the enforceability of restrictive covenants (both in terms of capacity to run and the mechanics of running) was favourable. This, it is suggested, testifies to a continuing regard for the mechanism as being one of distinct practical worth, a perception only recently further reflected in *Robins,*[96] whence it emerges that there is still a *heavy* burden to discharge upon any who seek to argue the obsolescence of a covenant on account of neighbourhood change.

Of this seeming desire to 'foster' the restrictive covenant the decision in *Federated Homes*[97] may be considered the plainest illustration. Indeed, this case could be regarded as the most important of the current period. However, it should share that distinction with a case of equal, if more indirect, significance, namely the case of *Rhone and Another v Stephens.*[98]

In this case, which came ultimately before the House of Lords, the owner of a property called 'Walford House' sold and conveyed parts of it known as 'Walford Cottage' as a separate dwelling. Part of the roof of Walford House covering Walford Cottage, the vendor covenanted for himself and his successors to maintain that part of the roof in wind and water-tight condition. Both dwellings having subsequently come into other hands, and the overhanging roof leaking badly, the owner of Walford Cottage sought to enforce the covenant. Affirming the rule in *Austerberry v Oldham Corporation*[99] that the burden of a positive covenant between freeholders could not run, the House of Lords held that the action had to fail.

In the course of his speech, Lord Templeman noted the common law rule as enshrined in *Austerberry* that the burden of a positive covenant does not run, and then proceeded to point out that it was a situation in which equity could not assist. Observing that equity supplemented but did not contradict the common law his Lordship explained that, when equity protected the interest conferred by a restrictive covenant, it was not contradicting the common law by enforcing a covenant against a successor, but in fact preventing 'the successor exercising a right which he [had] never acquired'.[100]

His Lordship then went on to make it clear that 'a negative covenant deprives the owner of a right over property' and its enforcement 'lies in property', whereas 'a positive covenant compels the owner to exercise his rights', and its enforcement 'lies in contract'.[101] If equity were to compel compliance with a positive covenant entered into by a predecessor it would flatly contradict 'the common law rule that a person cannot be made liable upon a contract unless he were a party to it'.[102] By contrast however equity could prevent the breaking of a negative covenant, the simple essence of which is to 'deprive an owner of a right which he could otherwise exercise'.[103]

Refusing the invitation which was extended to overrule the decision in *Austerberry*, Lord Templeman made it plain that he had no wish to undermine the established orthodoxy. He summed up his understanding in these words:[104]

> For over 100 years it has been clear and accepted law that equity would enforce negative covenants against freehold land but has no power to enforce positive covenants against successors in title of the land. To enforce a positive covenant would be to enforce a personal obligation against a person who has not covenanted. To enforce negative covenants is only to treat the land as subject to a restriction.

This decision of the House of Lords is important for two reasons. First, in paying attention to the boundary between the common law's regulation of positive covenants and equity's governance of restrictive covenants it necessarily throws light upon the nature of the latter. Secondly, in a consideration of the mechanisms for the control of land use, by characterising the effect of the restrictive covenant as being 'only to treat land as subject to a restriction', it highlights the parallel that may be drawn between the 'private' device of the restrictive covenant and the 'public' régime of town and country planning.

The Building Scheme

The consideration given to cases concerning building schemes in the last period revealed how, for many years, the rigorous pre-conditions for the existence of a scheme which had been laid down in *Elliston v Reacher*[105] early in the century had persisted and only very occasionally were schemes upheld. Later, a more relaxed view was taken with emphasis being placed (as it had been in much earlier times) upon the general concept of 'community of interest', as for example in *Baxter v Four Oaks Properties Ltd.*[106] where a scheme was found to exist despite there having been being no advance division of the land into lots.

Cases dating from the early 1970's show that the more relaxed attitude to the establishment of a scheme was to become the trend. Two well known cases which followed the broad approach taken in *Baxter* are *In re Dolphins Conveyance*[107] and *Brunner and Another v Greenslade.*[108] First, however, it is worth while to reflect upon another case decided at the same time, namely *Eagling and Another v Gardner.*[109] In this case the plaintiff succeeded in an action to restrain the building of a house in a garden in breach of a covenant, a building scheme having been found to exist on the pre-conditions as laid down by Parker, J rather than on any less stringent basis. In a footnote in Maudsley and Burn it is observed that it is curious that this case was 'founded entirely upon *Elliston v Reacher*, with neither *Baxter's case* nor *Dolphin's case*, which had been decided only six weeks previously, seemingly having been cited'.[110]

The question which arose in *Dolphin's case* was as to whether or not certain land was affected by restrictive covenants designed to ensure the building only of *detached* houses with at least a quarter of an acre attached to each dwelling. Applying *Baxter's case* the court held that a scheme was established in that covenants had been imposed for common benefit and with the intention that each purchaser should be able to enforce them against the other purchasers. That the purchasers did not all buy their respective pieces of land from a common vendor did not matter, inasmuch as the sales made by the successive vendors (who were members of the same family) were subjected to identical covenants. Proceeding from the basis of a wide equity founded on community of interest and intention, Stamp, J concluded that there had been laid down for the estate a 'local law' which was 'for the common benefit of all the several purchasers of it'.[111]

The second case, *Brunner v Greenslade*,[112] is not only an illustration of a wide approach to building schemes[113] but also a witness to the practical value of such an approach where the point at issue is whether or not a scheme is operative as between sub-purchasers of one lot. Here, the sub-purchasers had not entered into any covenant other than by way of indemnity but the restrictions of the scheme were nevertheless mutually enforceable as between them. The scheme raised an equity which was independent of contract but rather one based on community of interest and reciprocity of obligation. The desirability of being able to reach such a conclusion was considerable in that, were the conclusion to have been otherwise, the consequence would have been the defeat of a 'local law' inasmuch as an inability of sub-purchasers to enforce covenants *inter se* would create 'islands of immunity'.

Gray[114] ventures the view that with the return to its 'broad origins in obligations of reciprocity and conscience, the courts have been able to refashion the 'scheme of development' so that it once more becomes a useful and workable device'. He continues:[115]

> Accordingly, it is now generally accepted that a 'scheme of development' arises where there is an intention that a well-defined area should be sold off in... plots and that, for the benefit of the common purchasers *inter se*, restrictive obligations should be placed on the user of each portion sold.

To that author it appears that at the heart of the situation were two essentials, namely the existence of an identifiable 'scheme' and a mutually perceived common intention.[116] Indeed, other decisions in the period testify to the fact that whereas the approach had become more generous it would not degenerate into laxity. For example, in *Lund v Taylor*[117] the contention that a scheme existed failed in the absence of the establishment of a defined area, while in *Harlow v Hartog*[118] the contention of the presence of a scheme foundered on account of there being no evidence that there was an estate plan. Again, in *Jamaica Mutual Life Assurance Society v Hillsborough Ltd. and Others*,[119] where the question arose as to whether or not certain land was affected by restrictive covenants the Judicial Committee of the Privy Council were at pains to point out that for the existence of a building scheme it was crucial to establish reciprocity of obligations between the purchasers and, in the absence of evidence thereof, no scheme could be taken to exist.

The undiminished care taken by the judges over the requisites for the existence of schemes clearly reflects a continuing regard for their potency. Appropriately, this regard is highlighted in three cases.

First, in *Re Hunt's Application*,[120] a very recent case in which, in respect of a dwelling already erected in breach, an application was made for the discharge of a covenant in a scheme. Refusing the application the Lands Tribunal drew attention to the legitimacy of having regard to the scheme of covenants as a whole and the importance of maintaining the integrity of the scheme. It was noted that here was a scheme which was carefully and successfully maintained and that were the application to be granted the consequences might be the creation of increasing density and the loss of character.

The second case, *Texaco Antilles Ltd. v Kernochan and Another*,[121] coming from the early 1970's, underscores with some particularity the significance of the concept of schemes inasmuch as it sanctions, in their context, a departure from the usual rules relating to restrictive covenants. As is illustrated by *In re Tiltwood, Sussex*,[122] the position with restrictive covenants generally is that where the fee simple of land benefited and land burdened by the covenants become vested in the same person the covenants are extinguished unless the common owner should recreate them. The situation with building schemes however is different. In *Texaco Antilles* it was held by the Privy Council that:[123]

> [I]f there is a scheme of development, unity of seisin does not automatically discharge a covenant ... and ... on severance it revives, unless there is evidence from the circumstances surrounding the severance that the parties intended that it should not do so.

Finally, there is the decision in *Re Lee's Application*,[124] which is a further recent case involving an application for the discharge of a covenant under a scheme. It exhibits a particularly interesting illustration of the special aura attached to schemes, inasmuch as it holds not only that the scheme establishes a system of local law but also that the impact of a scheme is to create 'a greater presumption that restrictions imposed under it will be upheld'. This raises the question as to whether a distinction is being drawn - in terms of relative 'strength' - between covenants which are within or without a scheme?

Cases Concerning Section 84 of the Law of Property Act, 1925

As observed elsewhere, if the idea of enforceable restraints on land use is to remain acceptable an effective discharge or modification régime is crucial and moreover such régime should be flexible and capable of broad application. The former attribute is provided by the system's 'discretionary' base and the latter by the court's continuing to so interpret the provisions as to ensure freedom from unnecessary constraints.

A case signalling the unwillingness of the court to fetter the discretion of the Lands Tribunal is *Jones and Another v Rhys-Jones*.[125] A covenant restrictive of building having been entered into some years previously, planning permission was obtained by the covenantor for a bungalow and an application made for modification of the covenant. The Lands Tribunal, despite finding that no injury would be occasioned to those benefiting from the covenant, even so dismissed the application on the ground that 'it would be contrary to public policy and an abuse of the Tribunal's powers to grant an application within four years of the date on which the covenant was imposed'. The matter eventually coming before the Court of Appeal, it was emphasised by the Court that modification was a matter of discretion for the Tribunal and that there was no general principle that the elapsing of only a short period of time between entry into the covenant and application for its modification would forbid the granting of the application. Indeed, only a few years earlier, in *Creswell and Another v Proctor and Others*,[126] the Court of Appeal had intimated that the Tribunal had jurisdiction to modify a covenant the day after it had been made where it thought fit so to do.

Bearing on an aspect of a covenant even more fundamental than its age, was the decision in *Shepherd Homes Ltd. v Sandham (No. 2)*,[127] in which similarly the court was not disposed to reach a conclusion leading to the exclusion of the Tribunal's jurisdiction. Here, in the course of litigation flowing from the erection of a fence in breach of covenant and a consequential desire for the discharge or modification of that covenant, the question arose as to whether or not in the particular circumstances the Lands Tribunal had jurisdiction. It arose for reasons including, *inter alia*, whether, on the true construction of section 84(1) the Tribunal had jurisdiction not only over covenants which ran with the land but also over those of a merely personal nature. That part of the sub-section which Megarry, J was called upon to interpret states that:

> The Lands Tribunal shall ...have power ... on the application of any person interested in any freehold land affected by any restriction arising under covenant or otherwise as to the user thereof or the building thereon ... to discharge or modify any such restrictions.

In the view of the learned judge, covenants which were merely personal, as much as covenants whose burden ran, might 'affect land' for the purpose of the sub-section, and it embraced them both. Significant was his observation that the jurisdiction of the Lands Tribunal was of 'a general nature, and [was] not to be whittled down by fine distinctions or limited exceptions'.[128]

In a different connotation the point arose again a decade or so later in litigation, the appreciation of which requires a preliminary explanation of certain of the provisions of section 84. By virtue of a combination of the provisions contained in section 84 (1)(aa) and (1A), the Lands Tribunal can, in certain cases, discharge or modify a covenant if its continued existence would impede some reasonable user of the land. Those cases include the situation in which the Tribunal is satisfied that, *inter alia,* the covenant does not secure to persons entitled to its benefit any practical benefits of substantial value. The case in question, *Gilbert v Spoor and Others,*[129] arose from the purchase by the applicant to the Tribunal of land governed by a building scheme and thereby subject to a covenant against building other than one dwelling. Having obtained planning permission for two further houses the applicant sought the discharge or modification of the covenant and objections were made thereto by successors of other properties embraced by the scheme. The Tribunal found that from the immediate vicinity of the objectors' property, though not from those properties *themselves*, there was a view of outstanding landscape quality.[130] Further, it was found that the erection of the proposed houses would interfere with this view but that any such interference was prevented by the covenant. In these circumstances the Tribunal concluded that the covenant secured to those entitled to its benefit practical benefits of substantial value, and dismissed the application. Appeal was made to the Court of Appeal, the applicant contending, *inter alia,* that the statutory provision is concerned with covenants the burden of which runs with the land and that such covenants have to benefit the land of the covenantee. This being so, when section 84(1A) speaks of 'practical benefit' it must mean only benefit directly benefiting the covenantee's land and, as the view was not actually enjoyed from the objectors' pieces of land themselves, it could not constitute a 'practical benefit' within the section. The argument failed and the appeal was dismissed. If it was to constitute a 'practical benefit' within the meaning of the section, the view did not have to be enjoyable from the objectors' properties themselves because section 84 was not confined to covenants whose burden ran with the land and hence there was no need to benefit the very land of the covenantee.[131]

The concern of the Court of Appeal to give as broad a scope as possible to the relevant portion of section 84(1A) was paralleled also by a desire, expressed in *obiter dicta*, to fend off the imposition of any unnecessary fetter upon the Tribunal's discretion. An argument that the acquisition of detailed planning permission should have precluded the taking into account of the view in the exercise of discretion was rejected. The wording of section 84(1B), which requires the Tribunal to take planning matters into account in its deliberations, in no sense made 'planning decisions decisive'.[132]

Over the past three decades the way of the restrictive covenant has not been without its landmarks despite the fact that the doctrine had already been so finely honed. In addition to the pivotal affirmation of the fundamental distinctions between positive and restrictive covenants, the cases here reported have revealed such significant features as the desire to soften the rigours of the pre-requisites for annexation and for building schemes and to ensure the continuance of an efficacious discharge or modification system.

Regarding these concerns some observations are called for. First, there is surely to be discerned a link. As Gray observes:[133]

It is indeed likely that the modern relaxation of many of the threshold requirements affecting the recognition of enforceable covenants owes much to the increasingly wide scope of the statutory power to deal with inappropriate land obligations.

Secondly, while simplification has in its train obvious benefits, there can be drawbacks. Adverting to the legal changes made to both annexation and building schemes, the Law Commission, in its 1984 Report on Positive Covenants, observed that:[134]

[These] shifts in the law as interpreted by the courts may be wholly beneficial so far as future covenants are concerned, but they must of course apply equally to existing covenants, and here their effects are much more mixed. If a landowner sought advice periodically about the enforceability of a particular covenant, he would have to be told different things at different times; and his lot would not be a happy one if he had acted in good faith on advice given in one year only to find it invalidated the next.

The Commission was concerned about the uncertainties (as also the complexities) of the law of restrictive covenants and expressed it vividly - 'a traveller in this area of the law. old though it is, walks on ground which is still shifting'.[135] It is a criticism which could justifiably still be made today but, on the other hand, the doctrine is an evolving one and here, as in other areas of the law, the defect of uncertainty is accompanied by the merit of adaptability. The law cannot stand still. Eventually there may be statutory reform but when that would occur seems equally uncertain.

The matters briefly addressed in this 'endnote' are broad in their thrust. However, it is proposed to conclude by revisiting *Gilbert v Spoor and Others*.[136] It will be recalled that in that case the Court of Appeal rejected, *inter alia,* an argument involving the notion that section 84 of the Law of Property Act, 1925 was concerned only with covenants the burden of which 'ran' and upheld the Lands Tribunal's dismissal of an application for the discharge or modification of a restrictive covenant regulating building. In so doing, the Court of Appeal continued to secure for the objectors to the application the enjoyment of a resplendent landscape view. The effective deployment of the restrictive covenant in such a cause is all the more striking when set against the centuries old stance of the common law which perceives a 'view' as too indefinite for any claimed right thereto to exist as an easement.[137] In these days of heightened environmental awareness it is perhaps appropriate that this outline of the history of the restrictive covenant should have, as the final case, one in which the restrictive covenant played such a special rôle.

Notes

1 Cheshire & Burn's *Modern Law of Real Property*, 15th edition, opens with the specific observation that: 'Modern English land law is based on the reforms enacted in a series of statutes which were passed in 1925'.
2 Report No. 11, *Transfer of Land: Report on Restrictive Covenants*, para. 15.
3 *Ibid.*

4   Section 84(2) of the Act also made it possible for a person to seek a High Court declaration as to whether land is affected by a restrictive covenant and whether it is enforceable and if so by whom.
5   [1933] 1 Ch 611.
6   See Cheshire & Burn's *Modern Law of Real Property*, 15th edition, p. 628 for a crystallisation of the equitable rules as achieved by Romer, LJ, including also that the covenant be taken for the benefit of the land of the covenantee and that the land be capable of benefiting from the covenant.
7   *Ibid,* p. 629.
8   [1933] 1 Ch 611, at 632.
9   [1937] 1 Ch 473.
10 [1939] 1 Ch 1.
11 As Gray points out in *Elements of Land Law*, 2nd edition, p 1151, footnote 20, 'the Marquess of Zetland succeeded in depriving the citizens of Redcar in Yorkshire of the facility of an eating-house for the consumption of fried fish'.
12 [1936] 1 Ch 430.
13 [1937] 1 Ch 610, [1938] 1 Ch 351 CA, affirming Simonds, J.
14 It is worthy of note that, some years later, in *Smith and Snipes Hall Farm Ltd. v River Douglas Catchment Board* [1949] 2 KB 500 (a case involving the passing of the benefit of a positive covenant), Lord Denning strove to introduce and extend the limited interpretation that Simonds, J had placed upon section 56, stating (at 517) that 'there is no reason why the section should not be given its full scope [to the unequivocal extent that] a person may enforce an agreement respecting property made for his benefit, although he was not a party to it'.
15 [1952] 1 Ch 286.
16 The conveyance did not define any dominant land for the benefit of which the covenant was taken but simply described the vendor as 'of Devonia'.
17 That is with the benefit of the covenant.
18 [1962] 1 Ch 115.
19 In Gray, *Elements of Land Law,* 2nd edition, p 1153, however, it is observed that even today it is 'still somewhat uncertain to what extent annexation of a covenanted benefit may arise by implication from circumstances'.
20 [1931] 1 Ch 224.
21 In other words, the defendant must establish a 'sort of estoppel'.
22 [1931] 1 Ch 224, at 230.
23 *Ibid.*
24 *Ibid.* at 232.
25 [1937] 1 Ch 610.
26 *Ibid,* at 619.
27 *Ibid,* at 626.
28 [1939] 1 All ER 279 CA.
29 *Ibid,* at 281.
30 *Ibid,* at 280. It is of note that the street whose character was in issue (it was explained) had for the most part been 'town-planned' as a residential street - part of a scheme which had been submitted to the Minister for his approval.
31 [1968] AC 269.
32 Unreasonably, that is, viewed from the interests of the parties and the interests of the public.

33 [1968] AC 269, at 271.
34 [1967] AC 50.
35 *Ibid*, at 69.
36 [1914] 3 KB 642.
37 See Cheshire & Burn's *Modern Law of Real Property,* 15th edition, p. 618.
38 [1927] 2 Ch 225.
39 *Ibid*, at 241.
40 *Ibid.*
41 The plea was for an injunction to restrain breach of a covenant designed to protect property from a lessening in value or interference with its material enjoyment.
42 [1935] 1 Ch 188.
43 [1908] 2 Ch 374.
44 Gray, *Elements of Land Law,* 2nd. edition, p. 1161.
45 [1939] 1 All ER 131.
46 Atkinson, J having set out the principles of *Elliston v Reacher,* observed that 'if one applies what is there said to a block of flats, a scheme certainly is established' (*ibid*, at 140). He was of the view that 'the reservation [in the leases] was clearly intended to be... for the benefit of the flats and their tenants', and the learned judge had 'no doubt that each lessee either knew or took it for granted that the restrictions imposed on him were also imposed on the other lessees, and were so imposed for their mutual benfit *inter se*' (*ibid*, at 137-8).
47 [1908] 2 Ch 374.
48 [1965] 1 Ch 816.
49 *Ibid*, at 828.
50 *Ibid.*
51 Report No.11, *Transfer of Land: Report on Restrictive Covenants*, para 23.
52 [1958] 1 Ch 280.
53 Substantial changes were made to section 84 by the Law of Property Act, 1969.
54 Following the introduction of the Lands Tribunal Act, 1949.
55 [1940] 1 Ch 835.
56 *Ibid*, at 846.
57 *Ibid.* Here indeed was an adverse commentary on the then growing practice of 'buying out restrictive covenants' which was being pursued by the Official Arbitrator in respect of the Orders which he was making.
58 *Chatsworth Estates Co. v Fewell* [1931] 1 Ch 224.
59 *In re Truman, Hanbury, Buxton & Co. Ltd's Application* [1956] 1 QB 261 CA.
60 [1957] 1 QB 330; and see further the observations of Lord Evershed, MR in *In re Ghey and Galton's Application* [1957] 2 QB 650 CA, at 659-60.
61 *Driscoll v Church Commissioners for England* [1957] 1 QB 330.
62 *Ibid*, at 349.
63 *Ibid*, at 341. Denning, LJ (as he then was) thought that while, when the premises in issue were first let, the contemplation would be for use only as single private dwellings, and that altered social conditions had compelled their being turned into flats or guest houses, even so the covenant enabled the landlords to keep the area residential rather than commercial. (It may be noted that section 84(12) makes provision for the application of the section to long leases).
64 *Ibid*, at 342 (emphasis added).
65 [1966] 1 WLR 170.

66 Section 8 of the National Trust Act, 1937 entitles the Trust to enforce restrictive covenants as if they were entitled to adjacent land.

67 Section 84(2) was slightly amended by section 28(4) of the Law of Property Act, 1969.

68 [1962] 1 WLR 902.

69 *Ibid*, at 911-12.

70 [1957] 1 All ER 532.

71 The Town & Country Planning Act, 1947, which came into operation on 1 July 1948, made all 'development' (with minor exceptions) the subject of 'public control'.

72 This change in attitude is most clearly demonstrated in the decisions of the Lands Tribunal in respect of applications under section 84(1) of the Law of Property Act, 1925 (as amended by the 1969 Act).

73 [1974] 2 All ER 321.

74 Both the burdened and the benfited land had passed to successors.

75 [1974] 2 All ER 321, at 335, per Brightman, J.

76 *Ibid*, at 337.

77 *Ibid.*

78 G.H. Newsom, *Restrictive Covenants -2*, [1974] JPL 130.

79 In cases where a defendant profitably trespasses by making use of a plaintiff's underground ways and does not diminish the value of the latter's property, justice can be done by awarding damages based on a reasonable wayleave rent. (On the matter of an appropriate remedy, attention may also be drawn to the more recent case of *Brown v Heathlands Mental Health NHS Trust* [1996] 1 All ER 133.)

80 [1974] 2 All ER 321, at 337-8. He continued - 'a developer who tries that course may be in for a rude awakening'. But, one wonders, just how rude an awakening?

81 See Cheshire & Burn's *Modern Law of Real Property,* 15th edition. pp. 618 and 626.

82 [1973] 1 Ch 110.

83 [1980] 1 WLR 594.

84 *Elements of Land Law,* 2nd. edition, p. 1154.

85 [1900] 2 Ch 388.

86 *Elements of Land Law,* 2nd. edition, p. 1154.

87 Cheshire & Burn's *Modern Law of Real Property*, 15th edition,. p. 624.

88 An excellent account of *Federated Homes* and its implications is given (with references also to its various critics) in Gray's *Elements of Land Law,* 2nd. edition, at pp. 1154-56. Amongst its far-reaching consequences is the possibility that 'it has removed much of the scope left for the law of assignment of covenanted benefits'.

89 It may be added that it appears the case may have impinged also upon a further facet of annexation. In a situation where the benefit of a covenant had been annexed to the entirety of an area of land, if a successor of the covenantee purchased part of the land and sought to enforce the covenant he would have had to show the benefit was annexed to that particular part or to each and every part. Since *Federated Homes,* however, it seems that where the benefit of a covenant is annexed to the *whole* of an estate, it is also implicitly intended to benefit each and every part, without any need in the conveyance *expressly* so to state. (It is also of note, as MacKenzie & Phillips in *A Practical Approach to Land Law,* 7th edition, at p. 362 observe, that a 'strange' feature of the case is that the defendant was the original covenantor. Therefore there was no need to show that the burden had run with the land in equity, and accordingly, the court need only have been concerned with whether the benefit ran at common law).

90   [1996] EGCS 75 (ChD).
91   [1984] 1 WLR 40.
92   *Ibid*, at 46.
93   *Ibid.*
94   [1989] 2 All ER 817.
95   *Wrotham Park Estate Co. v Parkside Homes Ltd. & Others* [1974] 2 All ER 321.
96   *Robins v Berkeley Homes (Kent) Ltd.* [1996] EGCS 75 (Ch D). A similar generosity of approach had been experienced at the end of the 1980's in *R v Westminster City Council and the London Electricity Board, ex parte Leicester Square Coventry Street Association Ltd.* (1989) 59 P & CR 51. Being satisfied that the burden of the covenant ran with the land and that the benefit was annexed to the covenantee's land, the court held that it did not matter that nothing was known about the dominant land and who presently enjoyed the benefit. Westminster City Council, the present owners of Leicester Square were bound by the covenant: 'I conclude that this covenant remains binding on Westminster, its benefit a 'hidden treasure' in the hands of the present owner (whoever he may be) of Tulk's retained land' (per Simon Brown, J).
97   *Federated Homes Ltd. v Mill Lodge Properties Ltd.* [1980] 1 WLR 594.
98   [1994] 2 All ER 65 HL.
99   (1885) 29 Ch D 750.
100 [1994] 2 All ER 65 HL, at 68.
101 *Ibid*, at 69.
102 *Ibid*, at 68-9.
103 *Ibid*, at 68.
104 *Ibid*, at 77.
105 [1908] 2 Ch 374, per Parker, J.
106 [1965] Ch 816.
107 [1970] 1 Ch 654.
108 [1971] 1 Ch 993.
109 [1970] 2 All ER 838.
110 *Land Law Cases and Materials*, 6th edition, p. 882, footnote 12.
111 [1970] 1 Ch 654, at 662.
112 [1971] 1 Ch 993.
113 A viewpoint of particular interest emerged in the course of Megarry, J's judgment. He said: 'It may be, indeed, that this is one of those branches of equity which work best when explained least'.
114 *Elements of Land Law,* 2nd edition, p. 1162.
115 *Ibid.*
116 *Ibid*, at 1163.
117 (1975) 31 P & CR 167.
118 (1977) 245 EG 140.
119 [1989] 1 WLR 1101.
120 (1997) 73 P & CR 126.
121 [1973] AC 609.
122 [1978] 1 Ch 269.
123 Cheshire & Burn's *Modern Law of Real Property,* 15th edition, p. 640.
124 (1996) 72 P & CR 439.
125 (1974) 30 P & CR 451.
126 [1968] 1 WLR 906.

127 [1971] 1 WLR 1062.
128 *Ibid*, at 1069.
129 [1983] 1 Ch 27 CA.
130 The view was described by Waller, LJ as 'priceless'.
131 It may be added that the Court thought, however, that in any event the loss of the view might have an adverse effect on the objectors' land itself in that it could prove detrimental to the estate as a whole.
132 [1983] 1 Ch 27, at 34.
133 *Elements of Land Law*, 2nd edition, p. 1165.
134 Report No. 127, *Transfer of Land: The Law of Positive and Restrictive Covenants*, p.30.
135 *Ibid.*
136 [1983] 1 Ch 27 CA.
137 *William Aldred's Case* (1610) 9 Co Rep 57b, at 58b.

PART II

THE DISCHARGE OR
MODIFICATION OF
RESTRICTIVE COVENANTS

3 Discharge or Modification and the Official Arbitrator

Introduction

The need for a statutory mechanism to facilitate the development of land and property the subject of obsolescent, irrelevant or inappropriate restrictive covenants was most clearly expressed by G.H. Newsom:[1]

> Before 1926 an owner of land who wished to develop it but who had on his title restrictive covenants, however old or obscure, incompatible with such development, was compelled to take the risk that he would be sued upon them if he put his plans into effect.

The danger of legal proceedings may have been illusory in many cases but the fear was nonetheless real, risking an injunction or, since Lord Cairns's Act, 1858, damages by way of compensation in lieu.[2] It was to address this dilemma that section 84 of the Law of Property Act, 1925 was introduced. Under section 84(2) a landowner is enabled to test through the courts the validity and effect of restrictive covenants. The Chancery Division, upon the application of any person interested, has the power to declare in any particular case whether any freehold land is affected by a restriction and, if so, the nature and extent of the restriction, whether it is enforceable and by whom.

Further, under section 84(1) an application may be made for either the discharge or modification of a restrictive covenant. Originally it was provided that applications should be to 'the Authority', i.e. an Official Arbitrator appointed for the purposes of the Acquisition of Land (Assessment of Compensation) Act, 1919 and selected by the Reference Committee under that Act. Such a person was normally one concerned with compensation for the compulsory acquisition of land and the arrangement did not perhaps allow sufficiently for the difficult questions of law to which section 84(1) gives rise and furthermore tended to suggest that the problem was not so much whether the restriction should be discharged or modified as to how much should be paid by way of compensation for the discharge or modification sought. The Lands Tribunal Act, 1949 substituted for 'the Authority', the Lands Tribunal (a mixed body of lawyers and surveyors) and applications for discharge or modification are now heard by that body.

Decisions of the Authority (before 1950) and of the Lands Tribunal (since 1949) are subject to appeal. Appeal from the Authority was to the Chancery Division by way of a re-hearing, a comparatively expensive method which left the whole matter open to the court's consideration, and was available only where the Authority had modified or discharged a restriction. Appeal from decisions of the Lands Tribunal lies to the Court of Appeal, by way of case stated, and consequently the powers of the Court of Appeal are more limited than were those of the Chancery Division under the former procedure, although appeals can now be heard in cases where the application had been dismissed as well as in those where it had been granted by way of discharge or modification.

Before 1950, decisions of the Authority (the Official Arbitrator) were seldom the subject of official reporting, although many featured in 'unofficial' reports in the Estates Gazette. Unfortunately the Official Arbitrator gave no reasons for his decisions - apparently he was not required so to do - although towards the end of his period of tenure he adopted the practice of indicating his reasons, albeit briefly. Nevertheless an analysis of his decisions as reported in the Estates Gazette is instructive and illustrates the way in which section 84(1) was being used in practice and the influence that external factors, in particular town planning issues, were having on the decisions of the Official Arbitrator.

Since 1949 the Lands Tribunal decisions, together with reasons for those decisions, have been reported, and in the Property, Planning and Compensation Reports alone (over a period of more than 40 years) hundreds of cases have now been documented. An analysis of these decisions, the earliest of which start from a time when town and country planning legislation in the form of the Town & Country Planning Act, 1947 was starting to have a significant effect on the control of land use and development, charts the way in which the private control of land through the restrictive covenant was seen by the Lands Tribunal and the Courts as either supplementing, complementing or inhibiting the 'public' control of the use and development of land.

Analysis of the decisions, with particular reference to the way in which the Official Arbitrator and later the Lands Tribunal has interpreted and ruled upon section 84(1) in the light of planning and environmental issues and the changing economic and social clime is considered in three parts. The first covers the years from 1926 to 1949 - the Era of the Official Arbitrator - and examines and interprets the Orders of the Arbitrator during that period. The second considers the Jurisdiction of the Lands Tribunal and its Decisions from its inception up to the end of 1969. The third covers the Jurisdiction and Decisions of the Lands Tribunal, following the important amendments to section 84 made by the Law of Property Act, 1969, up to the present day.

The interpretation of section 84(1) is, or at least should be, central to the deliberations of both the Official Arbitrator and the Lands Tribunal. Constant reference to that section (sometimes by omission rather than commission) occurs in the cases analysed and the full text of section 84(1), as first enacted, is accordingly set out in Appendix 1.[3]

The Era of the Official Arbitrator

As already observed, from 1 January 1926 applications for the discharge or modification of restrictive covenants under section 84 of the Law of Property Act, 1925 were, until the introduction of the Lands Tribunal Act, 1949, dealt with by the Official Arbitrator and although his decisions (orders) rarely contained reasons for his conclusions many were reported in the Estates Gazette and occasionally in the Journals of the Chartered Surveyors' Institution (as it then was). The reports in the Estates Gazette became over the years more detailed and the evidence of both the applicants and the objectors came increasingly to be reported at length as similarly did the Official Arbitrator's Order. The absence of the Official Arbitrator's 'stated reasons' means that any conclusions concerning the basis of his decisions must to a degree be speculative but analysis of the evidence as reported and the decision of the arbitrator, taken together, permits of some general assumptions as to the criteria on which he based his order. Such assumptions and conclusions become more certain as a pattern emerges from a consideration of a number of cases over a period of time. By contrast, the decisions of the Lands Tribunal (post 1949), to be considered later, do not suffer from the same disability in that they have been reported fully in the Planning and Compensation Reports (later the Property, Planning and Compensation Reports) together with the Tribunal's reasons and supporting conclusions.

It is important to attempt to discern the way in which the Official Arbitrator came to his decisions during the period of his authority (1926-1949) which coincided with the development of town planning law from the first statute dealing solely with town planning (the Town Planning Act, 1925) to the introduction of the Town & Country Planning Act, 1947, which still forms the basis of town and country planning law as we know it today. Reference to planning schemes and planning decisions appear, as will be seen later, to assume ever greater importance and indeed influence on the arbitrator's order. Such influence needs to be interpreted alongside the development of planning law between 1925 and 1947, through three Acts in particular, namely the Town & Country Planning Act, 1932, which was the first Act to deal with country planning as well as town planning and which imposed on local authorities the power to make planning schemes; secondly, the Restriction of Ribbon Development Act, 1935, which contained powers restricting development along highways, and lastly the Town & Country Planning (Interim Development) Act, 1943, which imposed planning control over all land in England and Wales and dealt with control during the period before a scheme finally became operative.

The decisions of the Official Arbitrator are dealt with in two main periods. The first period (1926-1935) covers the formative years during which the Official Arbitrator was developing a framework (and even a code of practice) for dealing with applications, as evidenced by his issue of rulings and increasing tendency to question witnesses (and even comment on their replies) and impose conditions in his order (conditions which would not disgrace an over-zealous planning authority of today). Some 60 cases are considered in this particular period. Far fewer cases are reported and considered in the second period (1936-1949), which is understandable in view of the almost complete moratorium on domestic building during the period of the 1939-45 war and its immediate aftermath.

The Orders of the Official Arbitrator, 1926-1935

The 60 cases consulted from the period 1926-1935 are identified by the name of the applicant and the Estates Gazette reference, followed by a brief description of the modification (discharge) sought. These form the basis for the overall analysis, with cases cited specifically in the text being identified by an asterisk. A full list is included at this point, however, because it not only helps to 'set the scene' but also demonstrates the variety of subject matter with which the Official Arbitrator was dealing.

Cases Consulted

*   Michaels (1926) 108 EG 741 & 846 ....Houses to lock-up garages
   Davies (1926) 108 EG 840 ....Discharge restriction prohibiting opening
*   Christmas & Wythe's Trustees (1926) 108 EG 812 & (1927) 109 EG 117.......Increase housing density
   Cowan (1927) 109 EG 157 & 450 .... Garden to school tennis courts
   Hobbs, Lewis & Lambert (1927) 109 EG 625 & 110 EG 160 ....Houses to business purposes
*   Gas Light & Coke Co. (1927) 109 EG 842 & 110 EG 160 ....House to showroom & stores
   Bacon (1927) 110 EG 93 & 180 ....Increase housing density
   Sir Berkeley Sheffield (1927) 110 EG 93 & 221........ ....House to professional or business purposes
   Spiller (1927) 110 EG 372..House to hotel, hostel or school
   Searle & Others (1927) 110 EG 793 ....Houses to shops
*   Death (1927) 110 EG 829 & (1928) 111 EG 89 ....Houses to shops
*   Hayward (1928) 111 EG 194 & 466......................................Increase housing density
*   Hayes Ltd. (1928) 111 EG 390 & 784............................Reduce 'prime cost' of houses
   Allen (1928) 111 EG 685...Increase housing density
*   Evershed & Vignoles Ltd. (1928) 111 EG 784 & 112 EG24 ....Discharge restriction prohibiting trade or manufacture
*   Higgs, Murrell & Wooding (1928) 112 EG 24 & 666..............Increase housing density
*   Crampton (1928) 112 EG 24 & 235 .....Discharge restriction save for noise or nuisance
   Proctor (1928) 112 EG 50 & 261....................................Houses to shops & showrooms
   Sharp (1928) 112 EG 630 & 691 ....Increase housing density
*   Bremner (1928) 112 EG 630 & 771 ....Houses to club premises
   Kirton (1929) 113 EG 181 & 219 ....House to club
*   Parkes (1929) 113 EG 219...Increase housing density
   Lambert (1929) 114 EG 52 & 197...............................Houses to factory or warehouse
*   Wilson & Chitty (1929) 114 EG 600 & 777..................House to institutional purposes nursinghome or flats
   Spooner (1929) 114 EG 636 & (1930) 115 EG 114 ....Increase housing density
   Wright (1930) 115 EG 221 & 768..Increase housing density
*   Marshall (1930) 115 EG 268..Houses to shops
   Bexhill Pavilion Ltd. (1930) 115 EG 331 & 903..........Discharge restriction protecting views to permit houses, shops, swimming baths, etc.
*   Tunbridge Wells Gas Co. (1930) 116 EG 23 & 172....Discharge restriction prohibiting development to permit gasometer
   Stone (1930) 116 EG 139...House plot to use as road acces
*   Trustees of William Earp (1930) EG 492 & 582 & (1931) 117 EG 12............House to hotel, school or other educational purpose
   Yewens (1930) 116 EG 546 & (1931) 117 EG 12 ....Houses to builders yard, shops, offices & storage

Brandt (1931) 117 EG 416 & 918 ....House & mews to flats and garages
* Chamberlain (1931) EG 140 & 331 ....Increase housing density
Basser (1931) 118 EG 862 .... House & grounds to flats and dwellings
* Newcombe Estates Co. (1932) 119 EG 673 & 120 EG 601 ....Increase housing
density & permit shops & business premises
Lambert (1932) 120 EG 953 ....House to hotel or boarding house
* Gas Light & Coke Co. (1933) 121 EG 57 ....Increase height of flats
Revill (1933) 121 EG 219..Increase housing density
Foster (1933) 121 EG 611 ....Reduce 'prime cost' of houses
How (1933) 121 EG 929...Houses to self-contained flats
Nash (1933) 122 EG 287................................Houses, nursing home or hotel to offices
Pard Estate Ltd. (1933) 122 EG 780 ....Reduce 'prime cost' of houses and
permit use as public sports ground
* Mortimer (1933) 122 EG 973 ....Increase housing density
Tull & the Public Trustee (1933) 122 EG 1011........................Houses to blocks of flats
* Frost & Brand Estates Ltd. (1934) 123 EG 306 ....Increase housing density &
reduce 'prime cost'
* Fulford (1934) 123 EG 436 ....Reduce 'prime cost' of houses
Chamberlain (1934) 123 EG 1011........Increase housing density & reduce 'prime cost'
Slaughter (1934) 123 EG 1012 ....Shops to bakery
Bell Property Trust Ltd. (1934) 123 EG 1012............................Houses to block of flats
* Smith & Cooke (1934) 123 EG 1054.................Discharge restriction prohibiting hotel,
public house, trade or manufacture
* London County Council (1934) 124 EG 243 ....Coroner's court & weights
& measures office to 'Drainage' depot, stores & workshop
Streather (1935) 125 EG 245..Houses to flats
Methodist Chapel Trustees (1935) 125 EG 245...........Discharge restriction prohibiting
trade or manufacture
Adams (1935) 125 EG 246...Houses to shops
Sharvatt (1935) 125 EG 741 ....Increase housing density or permit block of flats
Ground (1935) 125 EG 949 ....Houses to flats
* Haywards (Brighton) Ltd. (1935) 126 EG 325 ....Residential to garage, showrooms,
shops, etc.
Tricker (1935) 126 EG 326 ....Houses to shops
Cox-Johnson (1935) 126 EG 966.....................Houses to lock-up shops with flats over

(1) The Arbitrator's Order - in Terms of its Effect

Of the 60 cases reported in the Estates Gazette (1926-1935) on only five
occasions did the arbitrator dismiss the application. Apart from a few cases
where he made no decision (e.g. where the matter was adjourned for a
particular legal issue to be determined by the High Court) in all other
instances the arbitrator's order modified (but rarely discharged entirely) the
restrictive covenant. In many of these instances the modification was in the
form of a compromise between that sought by the applicant and the
substance of the objector's opposition, such orders frequently being subject

to the payment of compensation and increasingly subject to detailed conditions. Any conclusions from an analysis of these decisions have to be treated, it is believed, with some caution (because of the nature of reporting and the possibly arbitrary nature of selection) but the small number of cases dismissed and the compromise modifications made (often accompanied by compensation) lead the authors to the conclusion that the arbitrator was more concerned with the 'commercial value' of the restrictive covenant rather than the 'environment and amenities' which it protected. This is, perhaps, to be expected as the restrictive covenants entered into in the last decades of the 19th century and the early 20th century were primarily to 'protect property values' and only incidentally to 'protect amenity', although the latter may well in certain circumstances have been the basis for the former.

(2) The Location of Land subject to the Restrictive Covenant

Some two-thirds of the applications reported related to land and property in the Greater London area. With one notable exception (in the north east) the remainder were located in the south east, the 'prosperous' south coast resorts and the home counties. There may be a number of reasons for this distribution. First, these were the areas least affected by the great depression of the 1920's and 1930's and were the subject of such limited growth as occurred during that period; secondly, they were areas where freehold estates had been broken up and developed in the latter part of the 19th century and the early 20th century (as compared with the midlands and north west where much development had been 'working class' and the 'wealthier' estate development had taken place under leasehold control, e.g. the Calthorpe Estate in Birmingham), and lastly, as the heart of the property market lay in the city and the west end of London where the major property agents and legal advisers to the large estates were located, their influence and initiative to use the new section 84 on behalf of their clients must not be discounted.

(3) The Date of Origin of the Restrictive Covenant

The date of imposition of the restrictive covenant is not always recorded but where so recorded the majority fell within the period 1875-1914, although the age of the restrictive covenant does not appear to have been a factor in the Official Arbitrator's decision. In three cases[4] he modified restrictive covenants that had been in operation for only three, two and six years respectively. The modifications were comparatively minor and in the last case were only made after hearing evidence as to the local authority's planning scheme. In *Re Hayes Ltd's Application*[5] he would appear to have been influenced by the fact that after part of an estate had been sold subject to restrictive covenants the remainder had been sold without such covenants, thus seemingly discounting the objector's submission that no changes in the character of the neighbourhood had occurred since the restrictive covenants were imposed.

(4) Community Aspects - The Number of Objectors, their Status and the Issue of 'Public Need'

In the earlier cases the Official Arbitrator shows signs of having been 'influenced' by the sheer body of objection. Later, however, he draws a clear distinction between those objectors who can substantiate a claim to the benefit of the restrictive covenant and those he is prepared to hear as interested members of the general public.

The first recorded and reported case was that of *Re Michaels' Application*[6] heard on 23 November 1926. Although only reported in brief it is interesting, apart from being the first case to be heard under section 84 of the Law of Property Act, 1925, in that the stated grounds for the application included, apart from what was to become the almost universal reason of 'change in character of the neighbourhood or property', the additional ground of 'demonstrated need'. The application was to modify a restrictive covenant which prohibited any use other than as a private dwelling house in order to permit the erection of 40 lock-up garages in the grounds of a house (over 1 acre) for the storage of motor cars only 'to meet the needs of 1270 houses in the locality with no garage accommodation'. Having heard from the objectors that there had been no change in character such as to render the restrictive covenant obsolete and that 'garages would spoil amenities and depreciate value of properties (RV) and constitute a nuisance in this valuable residential district' - the 'demonstrated need' apparently not being challenged - the Official Arbitrator dismissed the application, it being reported that some 268 objectors were believed to be concerned and represented. Later, as will emerge, evidence of 'public need' was to be more favourably received by the Official Arbitrator.

The Act, in referring to restrictions impeding the reasonable use of land, equates both 'public and private purposes', apparently not distinguishing between them so as to give greater weight to public than private purposes. In *Re Marshall's Application*[7] the Arbitrator accepted a 'public need' for local shops to serve a rapidly expanding housing estate development and modified a restrictive covenant so as to permit shops where otherwise only housing was allowed - a true expression of a 'public purpose' to satisfy a local 'public interest' or need.

The Arbitrator, however, accepted submissions of 'public purpose' as not only covering 'public interest' but, seemingly without distinction, covering the needs of a public body or authority to discharge its public duty. In *Re Tunbridge Wells Gas Co's Application*[8] he discharged a restrictive covenant in order to permit the erection of a Gasometer and in *Re London County Council's Application*[9] he modified a restrictive covenant so as to permit a Council 'Main Drainage' Depot in place of a Coroner's Court and Council Office. But, it is thought, the need of a public authority to discharge its public duty or responsibility cannot *prima facie* be a sufficient reason to override the 'public interest' of those persons living in the vicinity of the activity to be protected from, for example, noise and toxic fumes.

The Official Arbitrator (and, as will be seen later, the Lands Tribunal) has not always drawn a clear distinction in such cases and has tended to let 'public purpose', as in the *'Gasometer'* case, nullify the proviso in section 84(1)(a) that to discharge or modify a restrictive covenant for reasons of public (or indeed private) purposes the restriction must be one that no longer secures 'practical benefits to other persons'.

(5) The Main Relaxation or Modification Sought

Generally, it appears that the restrictive covenant for which discharge or modification was sought in this period applied to housing development in one form or another and the type of relaxation or modification sought fell into one of three categories, namely:
(a) To retain the residential use but to modify the type of development (e.g. in place of detached private dwellings, to permit semi-detached dwellings, flats or tenements); to increase housing density, or to reduce the 'prime cost' of housing.
(b) To change the use from residential to, for example, shops and showrooms, or workshops, stores and manufactory, or offices, commercial and business uses.
(c) To change the use from housing to private schools and institutional

uses, or to hotels and licensed premises.

Further, there was a fourth category in which, in a limited number of cases, the applicant applied for the discharge of the restrictive covenant without putting forward specific proposals for either the use of the land or the type of development.

(6) The Main Grounds of the Application

It is convenient to consider the grounds on which applications were made under the headings of the three categories mentioned above.

(a) Apart from 'changes in the character of the neighbourhood (and of the property)' the main grounds for modifying restrictions relating to the type of housing that could be developed were that the continuance of the restrictive covenant impeded reasonable user, that no person entitled to the benefit would be injured and later, although not a statutory ground, the difficulty of sale or other disposition of the land or property with the restrictive covenant in force.[10] It had been the practice in many restrictive covenants to lay down maximum densities and minimum 'prime costs' of building. The social change that had taken place since the restrictive covenant was entered into had often resulted in 'desirable residential estates' being 'swamped and surrounded by higher density and lower cost housing' making it difficult to find developers prepared to conform with the restrictive covenants to meet a demand which no longer existed by reason of the change in character and the extent of surrounding development. This situation was exacerbated in respect of the more recently imposed restrictive covenants laying down minimum 'prime costs' in that the period saw a reduction in house-building costs, making the achievement of the 'prime cost' requirement both uneconomic and unrealistic.[11]

(b) The modification of restrictive covenants to permit the development of land (previously restricted to some form of residential development) for either shops and showrooms, workshops, stores and manufactory or offices, commercial and business uses, was often based on grounds (apart from changes in the character of the neighbourhood) that continuance of the restrictive covenant impeded reasonable user, that no property would be harmed by the modification and that no person entitled to the benefit of the restrictive covenant would be injured. But it is within this category that

the 'change in the character of the neighbourhood' dominates and that issues of nuisance, including noise and traffic, start to feature in the evidence and in the conditions imposed by the Arbitrator. The majority of applications concerned isolated pockets of land and property which had become or were becoming surrounded by non-residential development. Typical examples were where, since the restrictive covenant was imposed, a community had expanded and shopping and other commercial uses had been introduced either by way of conversions of dwelling houses or by, for example, the construction of shopping parades, workshops and 'service industry'. In all the reported cases the Arbitrator's Orders effected some modification (often less than that sought) and were more often than not accompanied by conditions excluding noisome, noxious or other objectionable uses and frequently the payment of compensation.

(c) The third main category concerned applications to modify covenants (restricting development to some form of private housing) to permit the use, conversion or development of land and buildings for uses such as private schools, other institutional uses (private hospitals and hostels) and hotels (including licensed premises). The grounds for such applications were, variously, changes in the character of the neighbourhood, demand for the proposed use coupled with no demand for the restricted use and the assertion that 'no persons or other land' would be harmed. Most of these applications occurred in what were described as 'high-class residential areas' and involved either the conversion of existing large dwellings (sometimes with significant extensions) or new buildings in the grounds. It is in this category in particular that environmental and amenity issues (loss of light, air, views and privacy) and concerns relating to nuisance (noise, traffic and danger) were raised in evidence and featured in the Arbitrator's Order by way of explicit conditions.[12]

(7) The Objector's Main Grounds and Concerns

Apart from refuting the 'universal' grounds for modification by submitting that there had been no change in the character of the neighbourhood sufficient to make the restrictive covenant obsolete or that reasonable user was possible within the restriction, the most frequent grounds, in order of importance attached to them by the objectors, were:
(a) Modification of the restrictive covenants as required by the applicant would result in development which would 'lower the tone' of the

neighbourhood and depreciate property values.

(b) The development proposed would result in nuisance by way of noise, traffic and danger.

(c) The development proposed would spoil existing amenities through loss of light, air, views and privacy.

A fear that the 'tone of the neighbourhood would be lowered' (or less euphemistically that property values would be depreciated) featured most prominently in those applications for a relaxation permitting multiple occupation, higher density or lower building costs and were often accompanied by claims for compensation for depreciation in property values. Objections relating to the loss of amenities (light, air, views and privacy), particularly where they occurred in applications for private schools, other institutional uses and hotels in 'high-class residential areas' were generally pursued more rigorously on environmental and amenity grounds or accompanied by such statements as 'money cannot compensate for their loss'. In the world of 'private' property it would seem, certainly from the cases reported, that the poor man's 'environment' is more easily to be bought out while the more affluent are in a better position to resist and thus safeguard their amenity.[13]

In a few cases objectors raised the issue of 'injustice' if the restrictive covenant were to be modified or discharged. Thus, in *Re Chamberlain's Application*[14] the objectors maintained that it would be an 'injustice to all other owners on the estate if the restrictive covenant were modified', they having complied with (or been bound by) the covenant, and similarly in *Re Newcombe Estate Company's Application*[15] the objectors claimed that as they had complied with the restrictive covenant it would be an injustice if it were now to be modified in favour of the applicant. In both these cases, however, the Arbitrator proceeded to modify the restrictive covenants.

(8) The Influence of Town Planning Schemes and Planning Authority Decisions

During the course of the first ten years of the operation of section 84 of the Law of Property Act, 1925 town planning schemes and decisions featured ever increasingly in the evidence of both applicants and objectors and influenced in no small degree the Official Arbitrator in the formulation of his Order. As early as 1926 it was reported in *Re Christmas and Wythe's Trustees' Application*[16] that the 'LCC as town planning authority' had no objection to the application to modify the restrictive covenant and in 1927 in *Re Death's Application*,[17] following evidence by the UDC Engineer & Surveyor that Middlesex CC and the District Council had 'selected the area as an established centre for shops' and zoned it accordingly, the Arbitrator modified the restrictive covenant so as to permit shops.

In 1932 in *Re Newcombe Estate Company's Application*,[18] evidence having been given that the town planning scheme for Great Stanmore allowed 6 houses per acre on the land, the Arbitrator proceeded to modify a restrictive covenant limiting development to a maximum density of 4 houses per acre so as to permit 6 houses per acre in line with the town planning scheme. A year later, in 1933, in *Re Foster's Application*[19] the Town Clerk of Twickenham gives evidence to the effect that whereas the corporation is not directly concerned in estate covenants it welcomes them 'where they enured to supplement the schemes of the corporation for the effective town planning of the district'. And in the following year, in *Re Frost's Application (freeholder) and Brand Estates Limited's Application (purchaser)*,[20] Brand Estates, having applied to modify a restrictive covenant to enable development of part of the land at 6 houses per acre and the remainder at 12 houses per acre, was permitted during the course of the hearing to submit a revised plan based on zoning at 4.5 houses per acre rising by stages to 10 houses per acre. After evidence by an official of Epsom UDC that this layout was preferred by its Town Planning Committee which was prepared to recommend it to the Council, the applicant went on to submit that 'zoning under the town planning scheme indicated that the restrictions ought to be deemed obsolete'. The Arbritrator modified the restrictive covenant.

The intervention of a local authority was further demonstrated in *Re Fulford's Application*[21] where the Coulsdon & Purley UDC opposed an application under two heads, namely town planning and rating.[22] Although land within the area was originally zoned in the town planning scheme at 6 houses per acre, following objection the town planning scheme had been modified to zone part at 2 houses per acre. The Arbitrator's Order provided for a modification of the restrictive covenant but he appears not to have been convinced by the 'rating argument' nor, in this case, by the 'planning argument', in that his modification provided for part of the land to be developed at 4 houses per acre and the remainder at 6 houses per acre.

One last case from this period underlines the increasing importance that the process and the Official Arbitrator were attaching to planning proposals. In *Re Smith and Cook's Application*[23] the objectors, a brewery company, objected to the modification of a restrictive covenant so as to remove the prohibition of the use of the property as a 'hotel, tavern, public house or bar shop', as did the Twickenham Town Council.[24] The Town Council, while agreeing that the present restrictions were obsolete, having regard to developments in the area, opposed the use as a public house, off-licence or factory and 'felt it was desirable that any restrictive covenant should as far as possible synchronise with town planning proposals'. The Official Arbitrator seems to have been of a similar mind for, after an adjournment, the parties (applicants and Town Council) announced they would 'endeavour to agree town planning arrangements and enter into an agreement under section 34 of the Town & Country Planning Act, 1932', whereupon the Arbitrator by his Order discharged the restrictions subject to an agreement between the applicants and the Corporation of Twickenham.

These decisions, in the way they almost mirror the proposals in town planning schemes and local authority planning decisions, are, as will be seen later, in marked contrast to the attitude the Lands Tribunal adopted during the early years of its jurisdiction.

(9) Conditions Imposed by the Official Arbitrator's Order

In those cases where the relaxation or modification of the restrictive covenant concerned housing but without any change to a non-residential use, the standard conditions imposed by the Arbitrator related to housing density (including height of buildings, aspect and building lines), housing cost (expressed in terms of prime cost) and housing type (for example restrictions against flats and tenements). Often the Order would provide for housing at lower densities and higher prime costs on important road frontages and attach detailed conditions as to house type, particularly where flats or conversions to flats were permitted. Where the modification provided for a change of use from housing to, for example, shopping or commercial such modification more often than not was subject to a standard condition against nuisance, noise, noxious uses, etc.

Increasingly the Arbitrator's Order hedged the modification with more and more detailed conditions and in the 1930's (particularly after the Town & Country Planning Act, 1932) 'environmental' conditions came to be included. As early as 1929 in *Re Wilson and Chitty's Application*,[25] an application to permit the use of premises for 'prevention and rescue work either for institutional purposes, nursing home or conversion into flats', resulted in the Arbitrator's Order modifying the restrictive covenant as requested but subject to conditions relating to (i) retention of the private appearance of the premises, (ii) fencing, (iii) the height of the existing premises not to be increased, (iv) garden and grounds to be reasonably maintained, (v) no building within 100 feet of property in an abutting road, (vi) no flats (other than the conversion of the premises), and (vii) no trees to be felled or lopped except for safety grounds or for the erection of such dwellings as were permitted (by the deed of mutual covenants dated January 1853), which conditions will run with the land and be binding on any sale.

In *Re Frost's Application (freeholder) and Brand Estates Limited's Application (purchaser)*,[26] a joint application already referred to, the Arbitrator's Order included *inter alia* conditions that 'trees and timber-like trees on [two plots of land indicated on the plan] are not to be felled unless...dangerous...the intention of the applicants being to convey these two plots...to the Epsom UDC to be preserved as a screen...'; houses are to be restricted to use as private dwellings only; garages for private motor cars only are to be restricted to the use of the occupiers of the house erected on the same or adjoining plot; no outbuilding is to exceed nine feet in height; fences in front of the building line are not to exceed 3ft. 6ins.; no timber or timber-like trees except as necessary for the development (or dangerous) are to be felled, and 'the large copper beech at the junction of Grafton Road and Cromwell Road is to be preserved'.[27]

Subsequent cases contain further examples of detailed 'planning conditions' imposed by the Official Arbitrator in his Order but these two examples suffice to indicate how the Arbitrator was emulating the role of the local planning authority and the comprehensive range of detailed conditions of a 'planning' nature he was attaching to his decisions.[28] Apart from the fact that some of these conditions were of a 'positive' nature, as for example the requirement for fencing and the condition regarding maintenance of the garden and grounds, it is questionable as to whether strictly under the provisions of the Act he was entitled to add conditions at all.

(10) Some Observations on Powers, Procedure and Interpretation

The interpretation of section 84(1) and its intended effect were the subject of rulings by the Official Arbitrator and submissions or observations by both applicants and objectors. In no small measure, due to the innovative nature of the modification (discharge) procedure, they represent a disparate miscellany of issues (difficult to co-relate) but nevertheless illustrating the diversity of problems arising within the Official Arbitrator's realm. Before attempting to draw interim conclusions as to the way in which section 84(1) was being interpreted it is instructive to examine these briefly, dealing first with the rulings of the Official Arbitrator.

Rulings of the Official Arbitrator   In *Re Higgs, Murrell & Wooding's Application*[29] the Arbitrator (apparently for the first time) ruled that 'unless an objector was entitled to the benefit of the covenant he could not seek compensation' but that 'one might object as a matter of public policy'. From this case onwards the Arbitrator draws a clear distinction between those objectors who are entitled to the benefit and those objecting 'as a matter of public policy' to the harm that modification of the restrictive covenant will do to their properties.[30]

The issue of compensation, together with that of costs, was the subject of a memorandum of procedure produced by the Official Arbitrators for the special benefit of members of the Chartered Surveyors' Institution (as it then was) and published in the Institution's Journal.[31] First, the Official Arbitrators confirmed that they act on the assumption that an objector is not entitled to compensation unless he is legally entitled to the benefit of the restriction, thus acknowledging the 'rule' that they had adopted at least since '*Higgs*' case in 1928, and that when compensation is 'awarded' the Order only becomes Operative after an endorsement by the Official Arbitrator certifying that all compensation has been paid. Secondly, the Official Arbitrators considered that they had no power to deal with costs as 'Under Section 84 the Official Arbitrator makes an 'Order', which cannot be regarded as an Award; consequently they are of the opinion that the Arbitration Act, which empowers an Arbitrator to deal with costs, does not apply'. This omission was soon thereafter to be remedied by the Administration of Justice Act, 1932, section 6 which gave the 'Authority' (the Official Arbitrators) wide powers, exercisable in its discretion, to deal with costs, including the ability to 'direct by whom and to whom and in what manner the costs...are to be paid'.

In 1928, in *Re Crampton's Application*[32] the Arbitrator discharged a restrictive covenant except for a condition relating to 'noise, etc.', specifically stipulating (almost certainly in excess of his jurisdiction) that such condition should 'run with the land and be binding on the aforesaid land and premises into whosoever's possession the same may come'. And in the same year, in *Re Bremner's Application,*[33] where the London County

Council objected to a relaxation of a restrictive covenant 'unless sufficient land was given up for widening the road [Bacon Lane] to a width of 40 feet', the Arbitrator modified the restrictive covenant to permit the use applied for subject to 'reserving (and permitting) land for widening of Bacon Lane'. By what authority the Official Arbitrator used a hearing under section 84(1) to reserve land for a highway authority is not clear, other than a general proposition that he felt he should not modify a restrictive covenant in such a way as to impede the use of land for a 'public purpose'.

Interpretation and Procedure In a number of cases (the most significant of which are here considered) submissions or observations of applicants or objectors led to fresh light, or at the least a gloss, on interpretation and procedure. In *Re Gaslight & Coke Company's Application*[34] the objector submitted that 'The Act never meant that [development by a busy and active corporation] could be done at the expense of a small man who had observed the stipulations himself'. Nevertheless, the Arbitrator proceeded to modify the restrictive covenant to permit showrooms and stores on land subject to a restrictive covenant limiting use to that of a private dwelling house only.[35]

In *Re Evershed & Vignoles Limited's Application,*[36] in refuting the objection that discharge of the covenant would tend to force down rents and depreciate property by 'diminishing light and air', counsel for the applicant suggested that these rights could be upheld by the common law, as most of the houses had been erected more than 20 years and 'even if the Arbitrator released the restriction they would still have their common law rights to light and air'. This submission was not an issue in the Arbitrator's Order as there were sufficient grounds, based on change in character and impediment to reasonable user apart from the fact that 'persons entitled to benefit had agreed by implication by their acts and omissions to the restrictive covenant being discharged', to justify modification.[37]

In *Re Parkes' Application*[38] the Arbitrator, having reminded the hearing that he had laid down the rule that an objector could not receive compensation unless entitled to the benefit, heard submissions to the effect that the Law of Property Act, 1925, section 84 (1) provided for compensation to 'any person suffering loss in consequence of the Order'. The case was adjourned pending consideration whether the point of law should be raised in the High Court but apparently it never was and, following his ruling in 1928,[39] the Official Arbitrator never 'awarded' compensation to persons other than those legally entitled to the benefit.

In *Re Fulford's Application*[40] the objector submitted that the Arbitrator could not modify a restrictive covenant unless he was satisfied that it 'did not secure practical benefit to other persons...even if the covenant sterilised the land...' and that as the restrictive covenant was of practical benefit to owners in the immediate neighbourhood he could not modify it. The Arbitrator's Order provided for a modest compromise modification, with apparently no response to the submission that he had no power to modify in the particular circumstances of the case.

The Chatsworth and Wytham Estates In *Re Trustees of William Earp's Application*[41] some interesting light is thrown on how one of the large estates viewed the importance of the restrictive covenant. Land at Eastbourne (part of the Chatsworth Estate) had been in the posonesion of the Dukes of Devonshire since the 18th century who had 'done their best to avoid haphazard and speculative development. They felt strongly their moral obligation to the freeholders to whom they sold and they were seeking to enforce covenants which were for the benefit of those freeholders'. The substance of the application was not simply a removal of a restriction but 'the removal of the consent of the Chatsworth Estate'. Removal would affect the Duke's successors in 'the control and development of the whole of the estate...it would injure persons who were entitled to benefit from the amenities and good management...'. Having heard from the Eastbourne Corporation that they had no objection except to buildings on the gardens 'likely to spoil the present fine view' the Arbitrator by order made a modest modification subject to stringent conditions and the submission of plans to the Chatsworth Estate for approval.[42]

In *Re Mortimer's Application*[43] the modification of a restrictive covenant so as to permit housing development at a higher density was objected to by the Wytham Estate on the grounds that the development would be prominent 'from the southern slope of Wytham Woods' and the loss of 'views' would adversely affect property values. Complementing the line taken in the *'Chatsworth Estate case'* the owner of Wytham Estate emphasised the important environmental rôle of the restrictive covenant by asserting that 'there are important questions of principle entailed, not only questions that affect the people who are next door, or even those in sight of it, the question goes a good deal beyond that. What we should regard are not only the interests of private individuals, but the interests of the public'. This statement and that in the *'Chatsworth Estate case'* give credence to the view that the large estate owners saw the restrictive covenant (amongst other management tools) as a means of achieving that to which in due course public planning control would aspire.

The Purpose and Legal Intention of Section 84 In *Re Hayward's (Brighton) Limited's Application*[44] the impact of the local planning authority's proposals on the Arbitrator's decision were such as to question whether the original intent of section 84(1) had not been lost and that it was being used to further local planning authority ambitions. The application was to discharge or modify a restrictive covenant in order to permit the erection of a motor garage and showrooms, shops with flats or offices over and a block of flats or offices with shops on the ground floor. The objectors claimed that there was no need for more shops (Worthing had reached 'saturation point') and a garage would be 'noisy' and a nuisance from vehicles. The application was supported by the Worthing Corporation (there being little evidence from the applicant himself) on the ground of need (the police were of the view that 'there was a need for a central garage in the centre of Worthing to accommodate not fewer than 5000 [sic] cars') and the Council were of the opinion that the proposed scheme would be an improvement from the 'point of view of appearance, traffic conditions and general amenities of the district'. Counsel for the applicant submitted that as the objectors had produced no evidence to say the scheme was not wanted and that all they had claimed was compensation, in consequence the application must be considered as uncontested. The Arbitrator's Order modified the restrictions to permit the uses and development as specified in the application in accordance with plans approved by the Housing & Town Planning Committee of Worthing Corporation, subject to conditions. Thus, ten years after its introduction, section 84(1) of the Law of Property Act, 1925 is quite blatantly being used to achieve local planning objectives and doing so expressly, or at least effectively, on planning grounds.

Following this analysis of some 60 cases heard by the Official Arbitrator over the first ten years some interim conclusions may be drawn. Such conclusions, however, must be set within the context of the criteria that were required to be satisfied by section 84(1), which in summary were: (i) by reason of changes in the character of the property or the neighbourhood the restriction ought to be deemed obsolete, or (ii) continued existence of the restriction would impede the reasonable user of the land without securing practical benefits to other persons, or (iii) the proposed discharge or modification would not injure the persons entitled to the benefit of the restriction.

On a strict interpretation, if changes in character of the property or neighbourhood are such as to render the restriction obsolete then it has no value and no compensation should follow. However, in many cases the Official Arbitrator, seeking a compromise, appears to decide in favour of a modification subject to the payment of compensation, on the grounds presumably of partial obsolescence. This attitude encouraged objectors to claim compensation rather than retention of the benefit of the right, but the object of the Act was to modify or discharge obsolete restrictive covenants, not to facilitate the buying-out of property interests.

Similarly, the criteria in respect of impeding 'reasonable user' came to be interpreted as impeding 'a more profitable user' and restrictions were modified, with or without compensation, to permit the more profitable even though the less profitable might still have been achieved in time.

The criteria relating to the concept that 'the proposed discharge or modification will not injure the persons entitled to the benefit of the restriction', if construed in a strict sense, would have at least called in question a number of the Arbitrator's decisions. Section 84(1)(c) appears not to have been much used. This must be a matter of comment as, where a person is so entitled and can substantiate benefit, that must be a surer defence than contesting matters of opinion relating to changes in character or impediment to reasonable user. Applicants, as noted, tended to proceed under section 84(1)(a) and, having made their case under one or the other 'limb' of that section, objectors seemingly were either unable to raise (or discouraged from raising) a defence based on section 84(1)(c).

Finally, it must be concluded at this stage in its operation that section 84(1) was being used to bolster planning schemes and decisions on the one hand and to buy out property rights on the other, both being objectives outside its purpose and intention. An examination of cases over the remaining years until the powers of the Official Arbitrator were transferred to the Lands Tribunal will show whether these approaches would be sustained or reversed.

The Orders of the Official Arbitrator, 1936-1949

A further 33 cases covering the period 1936-1949, as reported in the Estates Gazette, have been analysed in a similar manner to that adopted for the 60 cases in the first period. Using the convention previously adopted they are identified by the name of the applicant and the Estates Gazette reference, followed by a brief description of the discharge or modification sought. Cases cited in the text are identified by an asterisk. As before, the inclusion of a full list of cases at this point helps to 'set the scene' and demonstrate the variety of subject matter with which the Official Arbitrator was concerned.

Cases Consulted

Blake & Leake (1936) 127 EG 726 ....Houses with no development on backland,to Blocks of flats and houses over the whole area

Bennett, Worskett & Bennett (1936) 127 EG 818.........Discharge restriction prohibiting use of strip of land as a 'pathway' access

Collins (1936) 127 EG 884..............Houses to School, hotel, club, nursing home or flats

* Jarman & Jarman (1936) 128 EG 918......................................Increase housing density

* Wavertree Green (1936) 128 EG 1044.........................Discharge restriction prohibiting all structures to permit Cinema & flats

Reuben & Touchan (1938) 131 EG 31 ....House to Block of flats

Price (1938) 131 EG 31.................Discharge restriction limiting development to houses

* Croydon & South London Building Co. Ltd. (1938) 131 EG 593..........Increase housing density

Ramuz (1938) 131 EG 778 ....House to Block of flats

* Hinsley, O'Grady & Others (1938) 131 EG 958 ......House to Residential hostel for boys

* Stanford (1938) 132 EG 854..Modify Building line

* Countess de Cardi & Others (1939) 133 EG 31.......................Houses to Flats & garages

* British & Dominions Film Corporation Ltd (1939) 133 EG 571 ...Film studio to Houses, shops, business premises and factories

* Samuel, Abraham & Mackover (1939) 133EG 1076 ....House to Hostel for mothers and babies

* Robertson (1939) 134 EG 1076.........................House to School, flats, club, hospital etc.

Knight & Co. Ltd. (1939) 133 EG 1125.................House to Club, school, offices or flats

* Salt (1939) 134 EG 325 ....Open space to Theatre, hall, car park & bowling green

* Gates (1939) 134 EG 628..Increase housing density

* Porn (1939) 134 EG 866 ....House to self-contained flats

Victoria Hall Trustees (1940) 135 EG 258.......................Residential to Hall & Institute

Corner & the Earl Spencer (1940) 135 EG 530.........Houses & 'smallholdings' to Shops & Public Buildings

* Tilley & Trenor & Ashton & Jones (1940) 136 EG 224 ....Houses to Shops with flats over

* Corden (1941) 138 EG 545....................Residential to Monumental Mason's showroom

*	Wilson (1943) 141 EG 498 ....Residential to Film Studios	
*	Simonds Ltd. & Bennett & Kersley (1944) 144EG 65 ....House to Public House	
*	Thornbank Ltd. & Liverpool Victoria Friendly Society (1945) 144 EG 182......School to Convalescent Home for women	
*	West Ham Corporation (1946) 147 EG 538.........House to Holiday Home for old people	
*	Lang (1946) 148 EG 555 ....Modify restriction prohibiting factory to permit light engineering workshop	
	Bell (1947) 149 EG 404 ....Houses to flats	
*	Curton Ltd. (1948) 152 EG 75 & 111 & 130 ..Houses to Flats, Nursing Home & School	
*	Baker & Co. Ltd. (1948) 152 EG 494.....................Houses to Offices & 'approach road'	
*	Ramsden & Son Ltd. (1949) 153 EG 443 ....Discharge restriction prohibiting any 'noisy or noxious' trade, business or process	
*	Coles (1950) 155 EG 149 ....Houses to furnished or unfurnished flats	

The Influence of Planning Legislation

Although consideration of the cases from the later period exhibits a similar general pattern to that already discerned, the 'section 84 régime' was changing in both concept and practical effect. The two main influences were first the developing law of town and country planning and second the burgeoning social and environmental aspirations (social welfare, full employment, good housing and a pleasant healthy environment) formulated in the late 1930's, published in the early 1940's in various Official Reports (Beveridge[45], Barlow[46], Scott[47] and Uthwatt[48]) and epitomised in the programme for post-war reconstruction. The second of these influences started to affect the nature and content of the evidence presented to the Official Arbitrator and his subsequent Orders towards the very end of the period now under review. Naturally it features more prominently in the cases considered by the Lands Tribunal, post 1949.

The influence of the developing town and country planning legislation is, however, to be seen throughout the whole of the period during which cases under section 84 were dealt with by the Official Arbitrator. It has already been remarked that by 1935 reference to the 'planning position' appeared regularly in evidence at the Hearings and became an element which 'influenced' the Arbitrator in his decisions. This influence assumes increasing importance during the period 1936-1949 and a brief reference to the statutory provisions in force and those brought into operation during that period is necessary for a full understanding of the background against which section 84 applications were being determined.

The Town Planning Act, 1925 (operative from 1 July 1925) pre-dated by six months the coming into operation of section 84 of the Law of

Property Act, 1925. Although enacted in the same year as the six Statutes collectively referred to as 'the Property Statutes of 1925' the Town Planning Act of that year, which laid the foundations for the comprehensive town planning legislation of today, passed almost unnoticed. Had it been foreseen in 1925 how this modest piece of legislation (a Planning Act containing only 21 sections) would lead to a town and country planning régime with far-reaching implications for the property lawyer it might well have been included as one of 'the Property Statutes' of that year.

Under the Town Planning Act, 1925 a Town Planning Scheme could be made for 'any land in course of development or which appears likely to be used for building purposes' with the object of securing 'proper sanitary conditions, amenity and convenience' (section 1). It was the duty of every Borough or Urban District with a population exceeding 20,000 (at 1921 census) to prepare a Scheme and submit it to the Minister of Health by 1 January 1929 (section 3). The Act also provided for the compulsory purchase of land comprised in Schemes (section 8) and compensation for property injuriously affected (section 10). A Schedule to the Act listed the matters which could be dealt with in the Town Planning Scheme.

These provisions were extended by the Town & Country Planning Act, 1932 which provided for the making of a Scheme for 'any land (built on or not)' with the object of 'controlling development, securing proper sanitary conditions, amenity and convenience and preserving buildings of architectural, historic or artistic interest and places of natural interest or beauty and generally protecting amenities' (section 1). The duty of preparing Schemes was placed in the hands of County Councils and County Borough Councils who were empowered to form Joint Committees of two or more authoriries to prepare Schemes (section 2). A Schedule to the Act listed the matters to be dealt with, supplementing to a modest degree the matters listed in the comparable Schedule to the 1925 Act.

Apart from placing the duty on County Councils and County Borough Councils, the main changes made by the 1932 Act were to make the control of development universal throughout the whole of the area covered by a Scheme and to extend the remit of that control to cover the built and natural heritage.

The 1932 Act formed the main body of the law relating to town and country planning until the Town & Country Planning Act, 1947. There were, however, other Acts concerning 'town planning' related issues during this period. The Restriction of Ribbon Development Act, 1935 contained powers restricting development along the frontages of highways and powers restricting access to highways and these powers were exercisable by the Government Department responsible for Transport. The Housing Act, 1936, dealing with the development of land subject to Clearance Orders and to land in Redevelopment Areas, whilst providing that regard be had to any Planning Scheme relating to that land, placed the control of the development of that land in the hands of the Government Department responsible for Housing.

The powers of the Government Department responsible for Planning were those contained in the 1932 Act as supplemented by the Town & Country Planning (Interim Development) Act, 1943, which brought all land in England and Wales under planning control and dealt with control during the period before a Scheme became operative, and the Town & Country Planning Act, 1944, the main purpose of which being to empower Local Authorities to purchase land so as to enable it to be properly planned under the Town & Country Planning Act, 1932.[49]

It is against the background of the 'Town Planning' law operating during this period that the arbitration cases (1936-1949) are analysed. Having dealt with the generality of the decisions that the Official Arbitrator made during the early years, commentary on his decisions in the later years (1936-1949) concentrates on three main issues, namely:

(1) The Influence of Town Planning Schemes and Planning Authority Decisions, including planning policies ('Town Planning Issues').

(2) The Conditions Imposed by the Arbitrator's Order, including in particular matters relating to the environment and amenity ('Environmental and Amenity Issues').

(3) Some Observations on Powers, Procedure & Interpretation, including legal submissions and points of legal interest and the introduction of new matter and new interpretation ('Legal and Administrative Issues').

Town Planning Issues

The decisions of the Official Arbitrator during this later period start to exhibit the attitude which was later to be adopted by the Lands Tribunal, namely that whilst Town Planning Schemes and Planning Authority Decisions and Policies may be relevant to the Hearing, there is no obligation on the Arbitrator to follow them in his decision.[50] The inconsistency of the Arbitrator in this area is well illustrated in four cases determined in this period.

In *Re Jarman & Jarman's Application*[51] an application to modify a restrictive covenant (dating from 1865) limiting development to one detached or one pair of semi-detached houses on a plot of about half an acre, so as to permit the erection of not less than three private dwellings was dismissed by the Arbitrator's Order. The objectors submitted that no property on the estate (which had altered little in the last 30 years) had such small gardens (38 feet) as proposed and no property so small a site area as one-sixth of an acre. Evidence that the Town Planning Scheme (in course of preparation) zoned the land at 8 houses per acre apparently had no influence on the Arbitrator who by his dismissal of the application confirmed development at a maximum density of four houses per acre.

Contra, in *Re Countess de Cardi and Other's Application*[52] an application to modify a restrictive covenant (entered into as recently as 1920) limiting use to private residences only, so as to permit the erection of flats and garages, on the grounds that it would be uneconomic to modernise or to rebuild houses, was allowed, despite objection that there had been no physical change in the character of the area, that it would be possible to develop the site with a cul-de-sac and say 20 houses, and that flats would depreciate property values. The town planning assistant to Ealing Borough having given evidence that plans for a three storey block of flats with garages had been approved under 'Town Planning and the Restriction of Ribbon Development Act', the Arbitrator issued an Order modifying the restrictive covenant to permit flats (maximum three storeys), subject to conditions relating to siting, screening, elevational treatment and tree preservation and awarding compensation to three adjoining owners provided they were legally entitled to the benefit of the restrictive covenant. That the restrictive covenant was still of value was acknowledged by the Arbitrator in his award of compensation but the Planning Authority's approval of plans and the applicant's submission that houses would be uneconomic appear on the face of it to have carried more weight than the absence of either change in the character of the area or evidence that the continuance of a restrictive covenant (entered into as recently as 1920) was impeding reasonable user.

In *Re Porn's Application*[53] the Official Arbitrator appears not to have been impressed by evidence of the Hampstead Borough Council. The case involved an application to modify a restrictive covenant (in a lease of 96 years from 1884, with 55 years expired and 41 years to run), so as to permit the conversion of a dwelling house on land at Strathray Gardens,

Hampstead (part of Eton College Estate) to four self-contained flats. The applicant's grounds included, *inter alia*, changes in the character of the neighbourhood; no demand for (large) houses for private occupation, and that the amenities of the area would not be affected by granting the application as 'people who lived in flats were not necessarily of a different class from those who occupied houses - the question was one of the class of accommodation provided'. The objectors feared that the conversion would 'create a precedent' and Hampstead Borough Council considered that in planning policy terms 'Strathray Gardens was not the type of road in which a house should be permitted to be converted into four flats'. Nevertheless the Arbitrator's Order modified the restrictive covenant to permit the conversion into four self-contained flats (subject to 15 conditions and the approval of plans by the lessors).

A post 1939-45 war case illustrates even more dramatically the Arbitrator's independence of planning considerations. In *Re West Ham Corporation's Application*[54], upon an application to modify a restrictive covenant (1893) on a private dwelling house to permit its use as a holiday home for old people from West Ham Social Services Institution, the Arbitrator by his Order modified the restrictive covenant to permit the use of the dwelling house as a holiday home for a maximum of 15 elderly people from West Ham Social Services, despite the evidence of an unsuccessful appeal (in 1945) against the refusal by Southend Corporation (within whose planning jurisdiction the property lay) to allow the dwelling house to be so used.

Three cases from the year 1939 illustrate the degree of reliance being placed by applicants, objectors and the Arbitrator on town planning criteria and proposals. *Re Samuel, Abraham & Mackover's Application*[55] concerned an application to discharge or modify a restrictive covenant (dating from 1844) limiting development and use to that of a private residence, in order to permit use as a hostel for mothers and babies requiring medical treatment (or for some other use, including flats, hotel or guest house). The premises were required as an adjunct to the Royal Free Hospital, the London County Council as Town Planning Authority having approved plans and the proposed use. Changes in the neighbourhood had been confined to multiple occupation and the objectors, whilst agreeing to conversion to flats objected strongly to a hostel in a quiet residential area. The Arbitrator's Order modified the restrictive covenant to permit conversion of the existing building into self-contained flats or the erection of a number of private residences not exceeding the number permitted by the Town Planning Authority. Thus, whilst rejecting the Town Planning Authority's approval regarding use he nevertheless made his Order subject to a condition requiring the approval of the Town Planning Authority.

In *Re Robertson's Application*[56] the proposal was to modify a restrictive covenant (dating from 1855, as modified in 1925) permitting 'taking in paying guests' in a private dwelling house, to allow (by further modification) use as 'school, flats, flatlets, residential or bridge club, boarding house, guest house (transient), nursing home, hospital, learned or artistic professional use, offices or business premises, but not a home or hospital for contagious diseases or persons of unsound mind, nor shops, nor trade or business of a noisy or offensive nature'. The objector would agree to flats, residential or bridge club, boarding house or learned or artistic professional use but objected to all the other uses; on the other hand the Planning Authority (Hampstead Borough Council) objected only to the flatlets, bridge club, offices and business premises. By his Order the Arbitrator modified the restrictive covenant to permit the conversion or adaptation to self-contained flats, residential club (supervised), boarding house (supervised), artistic or learned professional use or private school (up to 14 years of age), subject to preserving the present elevational treatment. In this case the criteria in section 84(1) appear (at least as reported) not to have been raised either in the application or in the case for the objector. The only ground stated for the applicant was the impossibility of selling the property as a private house. Of the comprehensive list of uses featuring in the application, the Arbitrator appears to have accepted the range endorsed by the Hampstead Borough Council as Planning Authority in preference to the rather more limited range agreeable to the objector.

In *Re Gates' Application*[57] the applicant sought to modify a restrictive covenant (dating from 1929) limiting development to one dwelling per plot to allow development (of apparently smaller plots and therefore more dwellings) such as would be permitted or required by the local Town Planning Scheme and the Town Planning and other Local Authorities. In other words the form of this application is clearly to equate the restrictive covenant as modified with the town planning requirement. A considerable opposition (some 70 objectors) contended that the restrictions were of benefit to adjoining owners and that 'the purchasers of adjoining lots had to rely as much, if not more, on the restrictions as to value as on town planning. Even in areas zoned 6 houses to the acre, development of an unfortunate nature could occur'. The Arbitrator's Order, whilst permitting some reduction in the 'prime costs' of houses, the relaxation of building lines and the distance of building from plot boundaries, nevertheless refused any modification which would have increased density, regardless as to whether or not it be permitted or required by the local planning and other authorities.

One final example illustrates an almost reverential attitude to the omnipotence of planning in the immediate post-war period. *Re Long's Application*[58] concerned an application to modify a restrictive covenant (dating from 1844) 'that the land should not be used as a cemetery, burial ground or tarpit, nor should there be erected and built on the land...any Union house, workhouse, nunnery, factory, steam engine house or gasometer, nor should there...be carried on any noisy, noisome or offensive trade or business', so as to permit a light engineering workshop. The application had the support of the Ministry of Works for a licence to erect a factory and the support of the Urban District Council that in its Town Planning Scheme (operative from 1937) the land was in an area zoned for industrial or general business purposes. The objector's main concern was that the 13 feet high factory wall at the bottom of his garden would interfere with light, air, sun and view. The Arbitrator modified the restrictive covenant by excluding the word 'factory' (thus enabling the erection of a light engineering workshop) and substituting for 'noisy, noisome or offensive trade or business' words securing the exclusion of 'processes, industries, businesses or trades' in Clauses (i), (ii) and (iii) of the Third Schedule to the Friern Barnet Planning Scheme No. 1 and subject to no building exceeding 14 feet in height. Apart from ignoring the objector's concern about the height of the building, the Arbitrator inextricably linked the modification of the restrictive covenant to the specific wording of a Town Planning Scheme.[59]

Environmental and Amenity Issues

The protection of the environment appears, from the facts as reported in the Estates Gazette, to have been the overriding issue in the mind of the Official Arbitrator in the *'Wavertree Green' Application*.[60] Land at Wavertree Green, Liverpool had 'since the reign of George III' been subject to restrictions prohibiting 'the erection of buildings or walls, fences or other structures more than 4ft. 6ins. high'. The modification sought was to permit the erection of a cinema and 8 blocks of flats on 6 acres of the Green at present used for sports purposes. It was submitted on behalf of the applicant that the Act of George III (under which the restrictions were imposed) was a Private Act passed to control the rights between the Lord of the Manor of Wavertree and the Copyholders of the Manor and 'the Act lays down specifically that it is to be enforced by the Copyholders [who] ceased to exist in 1925'. This being so (it was argued) none of the 61 objectors was entitled to enforce the restrictions. After hearing evidence from the applicant that the changed character of the neighbourhood had rendered the restrictions obsolete and that their continuance would impede reasonable user of the land (and that the plans for the cinema had been passed by the local authority), the Arbitrator (without apparently hearing any evidence on behalf of the objectors) adjourned the proceedings pending submission of full details of the buildings proposed (and the rentals of the flats), commenting that in applications of this kind 'great care had to be taken with regard to the protection of the neighbourhood'. Whilst the final outcome of this case is not reported, the observations of the Official Arbitrator are significant in that this case dating from 1936 appears to be the first instance in which the 'environmental issue' is significant.

In *Re Croydon & South London Building Co. Ltd's Application*[61] the Official Arbitrator dismissed an application to modify a restrictive covenant (dating from 1874) for a modest increase from a permitted development of 50 houses to permit a further three on land not yet built on, in spite of evidence to the fact that the resulting density of 10 houses per acre on the applicant's part of the site had the approval of the local Town Planning Committee. Submissions were made on behalf of the objectors that removal of the restrictions would 'lead to further undesirable development of a speculative nature'[62] and that retention of the unbuilt on land 'as an open space would contribute substantially to the health of the people in the immediate district'.[63]

The preservation of a 'class' structure and standards had throughout been a prominent feature in restrictive covenants, especially those restricting development to private houses where restrictions laid down maximum density (often as low as one or two houses per acre) and minimum prime building costs. Reference is repeatedly made to 'high-class residential areas' and *Re Hinsley, O'Grady and Others Application*[64] illustrates the problem of siting 'socially impaired' groups in residential areas. In an application to modify a restrictive covenant limiting development to private houses in order to permit premises to be used as a residential hostel for men and boys it was submitted that 40 boys (aged 15 to 18) would live on the premises under the supervision of four priests.

They were 'perfectly respectable boys, of elementary school type' employed in the district and 'no less respectable citizens than the people residing in [neighbouring houses in the same road] though they would perhaps be from a slightly lower class in the social estate'. In spite of changes in the neighbourhood (multiple occupation and a number of nursing homes and schools) the objectors (a large number) contended that the area remained 'high class residential' and that its character was retained because of the covenants. The applicants 'had the whole of the suburbs to choose from and it seemed very unfortunate that they should have selected a site in the heart of a good residential estate'. In an Order recognising 'social need' covertly and 'residential respectability' overtly, the Arbitrator modified the restrictive covenant to permit the use of the dwelling house as a hostel for working men and boys subject to conditions, *inter alia*, that no person charged with a criminal offence (other than under the Road Trafffic Act) be admitted and that nothing be done to destroy the character of the premises as a private dwelling.

During this period an increasing number of the Arbitrator's decisions contained conditions relating to noise, materials, elevational treatment and rights of light, air and privacy. Brief reference to a few of the cases illustrates not only the range of issues but the increasing importance being given to them by the Official Arbitrator. In *Re British & Dominions Film Corporation Limited's Application*[65] the Arbitrator modified a restrictive covenant limiting land to the use of the Elstree Studios in connection with their business of producing cinematographic films, so as to permit the erection of 'light industry' factories subject to, *inter alia,* 'a 200 ft cordon sanitaire in which development shall not emit noise exceeding 65 phons'.[66]

In *Re Robertson's Application*[67] the Arbitrator's Order, in permitting conversion of a dwelling house to flats, residential club, boarding house or private school made such modification subject to 'preserving the present elevational treatment'. In *Re Corden's Application*[68] his Order was made subject, *inter alia,* to the use of 'appropriate brickwork' and maintenance of the verge alongside the public footway and again, in *Re Thornbank Ltd & Liverpool Victoria Friendly Society's Application,*[69] his Order to permit a building (at present used for scholastic purposes) to be used as a convalescent home for women, was made subject to 'no material alteration to the layout of the front and any further building to conform with elevation and appearance of existing buildings'.

In those cases where the modification of a restrictive covenant resulted in a conflict between meeting 'public need' on the one hand and preserving 'amenity' on the other, environmental considerations appear to have carried less weight in influencing decisions of the Official Arbitrator than in those cases where the applicant and the 'beneficiary' were both private individuals.

Re Salt's Application[70] was for the modification of restrictive covenants (dating from 1824, 1831 and 1870) banning all building operations, i.e. to keep the land described as The Dell, Warwick Terrace, Leamington Spa and comprising some 4860 sq. yds. as an open space properly fenced - shades of *Tulk v Moxhay* - so as to permit the erection of a theatre, assembly hall, underground car park and a four-rink indoor bowling green (or otherwise as the Arbitrator deemed just). Considerable changes in the character of the area had taken place in the last 100 years and an area once entirely residential now included flats, a factory, shops and (proposed) a police and fire station. There was a need for the theatre and assembly hall and the 'underground garage might also have a useful ARP function'. Whilst agreeing that changes had taken place in the past 100 years the objectors contended that the area was still a quiet, pleasant residential district, using such expressions as 'we came because there was an open space', 'we can look out on trees and see the sunset' and the development would involve 'the wanton destruction of an open space of a type which was growing all too rare in our towns'.

Following a submission on behalf of the applicant that 'the restrictions were so old that the objectors were no longer entitled to the benefit of them', the Arbitrator by his Order modified the restrictive covenant to permit development as applied for, substantially in accordance with plans already submitted to the local authority for approval. Apparently it was not submitted that the objectors were not legally entitled to the benefit of the restrictive covenants but that *by reason of the age of those covenants* they 'were no longer entitled to the benefit of them' - a wholly untenable proposition. On the evidence of the objectors it is clear that the restrictive covenants were of benefit to the enjoyment of their properties, but nevertheless the Arbitrator quite inconsistently and, it is suggested, without legal foundation set aside the provisions of section 84(1) and substituted therefor the 'public good' as enshrined in the anticipated planning approval of the local authority, even though that approval had not yet been granted. It would not be until after the war that the hearings would revert to a stricter application of the wording of the Statute, as demonstrated in the later cases coming before the Official Arbitrator and more particularly those under the aegis of the Lands Tribunal.

Legal and Administrative Issues

At least two attempts to use section 84 to achieve objectives outwith its
remit were dismissed by the Official Arbitrator. In *Re Stanford's
Application*[71] an application was made to modify a building line from 50
feet to 20 feet in order to 'enable the owner and the District Valuer to settle
a dispute regarding the purchase price' of the land subject to the restrictive
covenant. The Beckenham Borough Council in pursuance of their powers
in Clause 35 of their Planning Scheme (in operation since 1930) had made
in 1937 an Order fixing a building line at 20 feet and, a Compulsory
Purchase Order for the land having been confirmed, the only issue
concerned the building line and its effect on the market value of the land.
The parties chose to proceed under section 84(1) of the Law of Property
Act, 1925 rather than by arbitration under the Acquisition of Land
(Assessment of Compensation) Act, 1919. The restrictions did not prevent
the land being used for public purposes, the ultimate user of the land was
not in dispute and the objectors could not enforce the restrictive covenant
against the authority. The Official Arbitrator ruled that the proceedings
were 'misconceived and not *bona fide*' and dismissed the application as
having no merit at all.[72]

In *Re Cole's Application*[73] (the last report of a decision by the Official
Arbitrator as recorded in the Estates Gazette), an application to modify a
restrictive covenant (dating from 1881) limiting the use to a private
dwelling house so as to permit its letting out as serviced or non-serviced
furnished or unfurnished flats, was dismissed by the Official Arbitrator.
Permission to use the premises as five non-self-contained flats had been
given in an Interim Development Order in 1946 and it was contended that
the existence of this planning permission (in principle the same as a
permission under the 1947 Act) was proof of change in the character of the
neighbourhood. The objector (Cadogan Estate) submitted that 'the real
purpose of the appplication was to secure to [the applicant] the benefit of
the Rent Restriction Acts', his lease expiring in June 1952; that there was
no evidence that the covenant was not of great value to the lessor and other
tenants holding under similar terms, and that whilst the dwelling houses
could be used as self-contained flats without detriment their letting as
unfurnished apartments or non-self-contained flats would injure the estate.

Four cases show how, with varying degrees of success, section 84(1)
was being used, as it were, to 'remedy' breaches of restrictive covenants
and provide a clear title free from covenants the breach of which had been

acquiesced in. In *Re Tilley and Trenor's Application and Ashton and Jones' Application*[74] joint applications were made to modify restrictive covenants so as to permit the erection of shops with flats over. Development by way of conversion to shops had been partly carried out but not in accord with the Arbitrator's Order of 1938 which had provided for modification of the restrictive covenants. The reason for the application was to 'have a clear title' but following a submission by the objectors that the application could not properly be made under section 84(1) - the breach had already been committed and it was merely an attempt to put right the title - the Arbitrator dismissed both applications. However, in *Re Wilson's Application*[75] an application to permit properties to be used as film studios, they having been used as such for the last ten years in breach of a restrictive covenant, in spite of objection and evidence that the land was zoned as residential in the Town Planning Scheme, the Arbitrator proceeded to modify the restrictive covenant to permit the use of the premises as film studios in the terms of the application.

Again, in *Re Simonds Ltd's Application and Bennett & Kersley's Application*,[76] a joint application to discharge restrictive covenants (dating from 1882) that no building on the land should be used for the sale of intoxicationg liquors, on the grounds that the covenant had been breached since 1924 and no action taken and none likely after 20 years, the Arbitrator discharged the restrictive covenants in full.[77] Similarly, in *Re Ramsden & Son Ltd's Application*,[78] an application to discharge a restrictive covenant (dating from 1853) against the carrying on of 'any trade business process or deposit which shall be noisy noxious dangerous or offensive' in order to permit the continuation of the use of the property as a factory and provide a clear title, resulted in the Arbitrator, by his Order, discharging the restrictive covenant in its entirety. The main concern of the objectors was that of noise. The development of the area was quite different from that which had been intended when the restrictive covenants had been imposed, there being much industrial development and the noise complained of emanated from factories other than that of the applicants who in respect of complaints regarding noise had carried out extensive remedial measures. It was further submitted on behalf of the applicants that the breach had been acquiesced in for many years and that having regard to what had happened in the area 'the appropriate protection was that provided by common law and not by the covenants'. There being no enforceable right (presumably as a result of long acquiescence) there was no loss and therefore no liability to compensation.

Two cases decided in 1948 (at the very end of the period of the Official Arbitrator's jurisdiction) are important in that they presage the changes that would take place when the applications for discharge or modification of restrictive covenants under section 84(1) would come under the Lands Tribunal. They exhibit a return to an appropriate consideration of the requirements of section 84(1) - even if at one stage a rather bizarre interpretation - and the introduction by the Official Arbitrator of the practice of giving reasons for his decisions.

Re Curton Ltd's Application[79] concerned an application to modify a restrictive covenant (dating from 1922) not to erect other than private houses, so as to permit, in addition, blocks of flats, a nursing home and/or a private school. The stated grounds in the application to modify were changes in the character of the neighbourhood and 'other circumstances'. As the 'other circumstances' were not specified in the application, counsel for the objectors submitted that he would 'object to evidence directed to anything but change in the character of the property or neighbourhood': this submission was overruled by the Arbitrator who was 'anxious to get any evidence' he could. Regarding 'changes in the character of the neighbourhood', counsel submitted that as the whole of section 84(1) is governed by the conception of 'change in the character' the applicants could not plead 'impediment to reasonable user' unless they showed change in the character first and the Arbitrator's jurisdiction arose only if there had been changes: the Arbitrator after commenting on the presence of the word 'or' separating the two limbs of section 84(1)(a) ruled that 'the hearing must proceed [and] if my Order is wrong in law you have your right of appeal'. A further submission, that the only reason for modifying the restrictive covenant was because of the war and the desire to meet 'temporary circumstances', drew the response from the Official Arbitrator that he was entitled to take into account all the circumstances at the time of the application (including present building difficulties). In dismissing the application (apart from a modification to allow a private school and flats on part of the land) the Arbitrator gave as reasons for his decision that the restrictive covenants (unmodified) did not impede reasonable user; that the modification as sought would injure persons entitled to the benefit, and that compensation was not in this case appropriate.

Finally, the case of *Re Barker & Co. Ltd's Application*[80] had all the hallmarks of a planning appeal under the Town & Country Planning Acts and may well have influenced the terms of reference for, and the 'stricter control' of, proceedings by the Lands Tribunal. The application was to modify a restrictive covenant (1924) on land at Kensington Square to permit its use in connection with the business of 'general drapers and storekeepers' and to provide an approach road to gain access to the rear of the premises and to a proposed loading dock. The applicant called Police evidence as to the traffic congestion and the need to provide space off the highway and evidence of a planning consultant that the proposals would not be detrimental as the general character of the square would be maintained. The objector's case was supported by evidence of an architect member of the Town & Country Planning Advisory Committee on Buildings of Architectural and Historic Interest as to the architectural value of this 'very important and attractive group of representative houses of the whole of the 18th and the beginning of the 19th century' and evidence of a London County Council employed architect that construction of the access would be detrimental to the residential amenities of the square.

Following evidence as to change in the character, need, impediment to reasonable user, absence of injury to persons entitled and the breaches of the covenant by others in the Square, the hearing then proceeded to consider the 'environmental' impact of three alternative schemes illustrating ways in which the applicant's objectives could be achieved. By his Order the Arbitrator modified the restrictive covenants so as to permit the uses as applied for, subject to the approach road being accessed from the rear and exiting through an archway on to Kensington Square and to such modifications as the Town Planning (or any other) Authority sought fit to impose, seemingly regardless of the fact that in evidence they had opposed the scheme and presumably would carry that opposition to a consideration of any planning application. Giving reasons for his Order he found that changes had taken place which 'changed the character' and that enforcement of the restrictions conferred 'no practical benefit' on persons entitled, following which he (quite illogically) awarded compensation to a number of adjoining property owners. This case demonstrates, probably more clearly than any other, the abuse of section 84 of the Law of Property Act, 1925 and the need for a body such as the Lands Tribunal to restore the credibility of section 84(1) applications for the discharge or modification of restrictive covenants.

Before considering the Lands Tribunal cases (post 1949) it is useful to draw a few general conclusions from the analysis of the 93 cases decided by the Official Arbitrator as a background to the 'climate' in which the

Lands Tribunal took over.

The main criticisms of the hearings and of the Official Arbitrator may be summarised as follows:

(1) The proceedings and the Arbitrator's Order showed increasingly over the years a departure from (and even an abuse of) the statutory provisions of section 84(1) as legislated, generally to achieve planning ends or to facilitate the development of land. This, in spite of the judgment of Farwell, J in *Re Henderson's Conveyance*[81] that the Official Arbitrator had been wrong to discharge a restrictive covenant, which had neither become obsolete nor prevented the reasonable user of land, on the payment of compensation: the 'purpose of section 84(1) is not a matter of the development of land but of the personal benefit of one owner as against another'.

(2) There was an increasing tendency to allow 'public' need to override 'private' property rights and as such to take section 84(1) outside its legitimate function as a provision designed to reconcile and update the rights and obligations as between 'private' property interests.

(3) The proceedings provided a forum for members of the general public to be heard as objectors even when it had been accepted by all parties that they were not persons entitled to the benefit of the restrictive covenant, leading to confusion in the determination of 'inter-party' property rights and obligations.

(4) An apparent inconsistency of decisions, probably due to the desire of the Arbitrator (in the very nature of his calling) to arrive at a compromise through the device of awarding compensation as part of the modification Order. There is a fine line between cases where the benefit is still of such value as to dictate that no modification should be made and those cases where compensation can recompense for the element of benefit remaining.

These criticisms were to an extent tempered, certainly towards the end of the period, allowing the favourable conclusions to be summarised as follows:

(1) The proceedings and the Official Arbitrator himself came to acknowledge the 'planning issues' as considerations which the Arbitrator could take into account but which were clearly not overriding considerations that he had necessarily to follow.

(2) An acknowledgement that the restrictive covenant may protect property values in more than just financial terms. The value of a restrictive covenant in safeguarding environmental issues such as amenity, traffic and industrial pollution, noise levels, views, etc. was reflected in a reduction in the

number of cases where compensation was awarded in order to facilitate (or even justify) modification or where section 84(1) was used as an instrument to enable the 'buying out' of property rights (as between individuals).

(3) At the close of the Official Arbitrator's period of jurisdiction following the end of the 1939-45 war he started to accompany his Order with findings, conclusions and reasons for his decision.

(4) The later cases reveal a return to a consideration of the intention of section 84(1) and an application to the legal interpretation and legal effect of the section.

Two elements in particular, namely the issue of compensation and the influence of town planning, made a more balanced form of hearing, i.e. the Lands Tribunal, virtually inevitable if section 84(1) applications were to be dealt with as prescribed under the Act. The new body needed to be able:

(a) to deal with the legal aspects and questions that arise;

(b) to counter the 'valuation approach' by recognising 'amenity (environmental)' value as well as 'financial' value, and

(c) to distinguish the town planning (public interest) wider dimension from the narrower section 84(1) consideration of private property rights and obligations.

How far the Lands Tribunal achieved these objectives is the subject of the next chapter.

Notes

1   G.H. Newsom, *Planning and Compensation Reports,* Vol.7, 1957, at xvii.

2   The Chancery Amendment Act, 1858, section 2, now replaced by the Supreme Court Act, 1981, section 50.

3   The full text of section 84 (1), as amended by the Law of Property Act, 1969, is reproduced in Appendix 2.

4   *Re Hayes Ltd's Application* (1928) 111 EG 390 & 784; *Re Gaslight & Coke Co's Application* (1933) 121 EG 57; *Re Foster's Application* (1933) 121 EG 611.

5   (1928) 111 EG 390 & 784.

6   (1926) 108 EG 741 & 846.

7   (1930) 115 EG 268.

8   (1930) 116 EG 23 & 172.

9   (1934) 124 EG 243.

10 Whilst in itself the problem of disposition is not a statutory ground it could arguably be brought within the ambit of 'impeding reasonable user' and within the general proposition that the law views with distaste fetters on the free alienation of land.

11 The question of relaxation of 'prime cost' is dealt with more fully in *(9) Conditions*

Imposed by the Official Arbitrator's Order.

12   See *(7) The Objector's Main Grounds and Concerns* and *(9) Conditions Imposed by the Official Arbitrator's Order.*

13   For examples of cases dealing with amenities and nuisance see: *Re Haywood's Application* (1928) 111 EG 194 & 466; *Re Wilson & Chitty's Application* (1929) 114 EG 600 & 777; *Re Trustees of William Earp's Application* (1930) 116 EG 492 &528 and (1931) 117 EG 12.

14   (1931) 118 EG 140 & 331.

15   (1932) 119 EG 673 & 120 EG 601.

16   (1926) 108 EG 812 & (1927) 109 EG 117.

17   (1927) 110 EG 829 & (1928) 111 EG 89.

18   (1932) 119 EG 673 & 120 EG 601.

19   (1933) 121 EG 611.

20   (1934) 123 EG 306.

21   (1934) 123 EG 436.

22   The objection on rating grounds was to the loss of rateable value of existing houses and the 'uneconomic' return from low rated properties - 'the local authority had a line below which properties of a certain rateable value were receiving more services than they produced in rates, and therefore it was of the greatest benefit to the Council that they should retain as far as possible the premises which had a large rateable value'.

23   (1934) 123 EG 1054.

24   Although it was submitted on behalf of the applicant that the 'Town Council had adequate powers under the Town & Country Planning Act, 1932 to control development within their area', thus questioning their status at the arbitration hearing, their evidence and intervention appears to have been crucial to the Official Arbitrator's conduct of the case and his subsequent decision.

25   (1929) 114 EG 600 & 777.

26   (1934) 123 EG 306.

27   Probably the first example of a 'Tree Preservation Order'.

28   Hart's, *Introduction to the Law of Local Government Administration,* 9th edition, at p.549 points out that town planning legislation 'confers on local authorities powers which are derived from the practice of landowners' - a clear reference to the practice of control over land use exercised through estate management by way of covenants in leases and, more particularly, restrictive covenants. At this stage in the operation of section 84(1) of the Law of Property Act, 1925 it would not perhaps be unfair to suggest that 'the Official Arbitrator is attempting to impose on landowners decisions which are derived from the practice of local planning authorities'.

29   (1928) 112 EG 24 & 666.

30   Where there is doubt as to the legal entitlement of an objector to the benefit of the restrictive covenant the Official Arbitrator will, where his Order is made subject to the payment of compensation, make such compensation subject to the objector being legally entitled to the benefit of the restrictive covenant, thus avoiding an adjournment of the hearing whilst the point is being decided by the High Court.

31   *Journal of the Chartered Surveyors' Institution,* Vol. X1 (1931-32), p.71: Memorandum by J. Willmott & H.C. Webster, Official Arbitrators.

32   (1928) 112 EG 24 & 235.

33   (1928) 112 EG 630 & 771.

34   (1927) 109 EG 842 & 110 EG 160.

35 Apparently section 84(1)(c) was not considered; neither apparently was the maxim that 'Equality is Equity'.

36 (1928) 111 EG 784 & 112 EG 24.

37 This case does, however, raise the question as to whether a restrictive covenant which does no more than confer rights which are already, or have through the passage of time become, available at common law, is thereby to be deemed obsolete on the sole ground that the restriction is superfluous?

38 (1929) 113 EG 219.

39 In *Re Higgs, Murrell & Wooding's Application*(1928) 112 EG 24 & 666.

40 (1934) 123 EG 436.

41 (1930) 116 EG 492 & 582; (1931) 117 EG 12.

42 Contrast this with subsequent cases where the Arbitrator consistently discharged any obligation to obtain the vendor's approval to plans.

43 (1933) 122 EG 973.

44 (1935) 126 EG 325.

45 Report on *Social Insurance & Allied Services*, Cmd. 6404, 1942.

46 Report of the Royal Commission on *The Distribution of the Industrial Population*, Cmd. 6153, 1940.

47 Report of the Committee on *Land Utilisation in Rural Areas*, Cmd. 6378, 1942.

48 Final Report of the Expert Committee on *Compensation & Betterment*, Cmd. 6386, 1942.

49 Town planning issues at this time came under three separate Government Departments and three separate Ministers. Despite criticism in the Scott Report of the confusion and conflict caused by a division of responsibility, it would last until the creation of the Department of the Environment, Transport and the Regions in 1997.

50 They were considerations but not in modern parlance in the nature of 'material considerations' in that they could be ignored with impunity and departed from without reason.

51 (1936) 128 EG 918.

52 (1939) 133 EG 31.

53 (1939) 134 EG 866.

54 (1946) 147 EG 538.

55 (1939) 133 EG 1076.

56 (1939) 133 EG 1076.

57 (1939) 134 EG 628.

58 (1946) 148 EG 555.

59 Apparently no thought was given to what might be the effect on the modified restrictive covenant when the Town Planning Scheme was later to be superseded by a Development Plan under the Town & Country Planning Act, 1947. It seems, however, from the reported cases that no other instance occurs where the link between the modified restrictive covenant and a Town Planning Scheme was so firmly interwoven.

60 (1936) 128 EG 1044.

61 (1938) 131 EG 593.

62 The 'thin end of the wedge' argument later to be, in general, rejected by the Lands Tribunal.

63 This is in line with, and may have been influenced by, a growing acceptance of the planning requirement, following the 1932 Town & Country Planning Act, for the provision in Town Planning Schemes of amenity open spaces in new housing

development.
64 (1938) 131 EG 958.
65 (1939) 133 EG 571.
66 A restriction prohibiting the acquisition of any rights of light or air was discharged by the Arbitrator's Order, subject to the right to take steps to prevent the acquisition of such rights.
67 (1939) 133 EG 1076.
68 (1941) 138 EG 545.
69 (1945) 145 EG 182.
70 (1939) 134 EG 325.
71 (1938) 132 EG 854.
72 Presumably the parties saw the section 84(1) procedure as a means of settling independently the question of the relevant building line, be it 50', 20' or something in between. An Order of the Official Arbitrator would have provided an agreed basis for the compulsory purchase valuation.
73 (1950) 155 EG 149.
74 (1940) 136 EG 224.
75 (1943) 141 EG 498.
76 (1944) 144 EG 65.
77 This case is important in another respect, namely the revival of specific reference to section 84(1) which, according to the report of the case, was quoted in full as the grounds for discharging the restrictive covenant.
78 (1949) 153 EG 443.
79 (1948) 152 EG 75, 111 & 130.
80 (1948) 152 EG 494.
81 [1940] Ch 835.

4 Discharge or Modification and the Lands Tribunal before 1970

Introduction

On 1 January 1950 the Lands Tribunal Act, 1949 came into operation and thenceforth applications for the discharge or modification of restrictive covenants under section 84 of the Law of Property Act, 1925 were dealt with by the Lands Tribunal. The deficiencies in the operation of section 84 in arbitration proceedings presided over by the Official Arbitrator were noted in chapter 3. The Official Arbitrator, selected by the Reference Committee under the Acquisition of Land (Assessment of Compensation) Act, 1919, was normally someone concerned with compensation for the compulsory acquisition of land and rarely sufficiently versed in the law to deal with the legal questions to which section 84(1) from time to time gives rise. Furthermore, the appointment of a valuation surveyor as Official Arbitrator tended to suggest that the problem was not so much whether a restriction should be discharged or modified as to how much should be paid by way of compensation for the discharge or modification sought. The transfer of authority to the Lands Tribunal, comprising both lawyers and surveyors and whose President is always an eminent silk, did much to remedy these problems.

The difficulties experienced in an analysis of the decisions of the Official Arbitrator, namely the considerable variations in both the detail and quality of reporting, and the absence of conclusions and reasons for the Official Arbitrator's decision, do not apply to the decisions of the Lands Tribunal. From 1950 onwards the Lands Tribunal decisions, together with reasons, have been reported fully, and in the Property, Planning & Compensation Reports alone, hundreds of cases have been documented.

Following the analysis of some 93 cases reported in the Estates Gazette the three main issues that the Lands Tribunal needed to address have been identified. The analysis which follows seeks to deal with those issues, namely: (i) the relationship between town planning and the restrictive

121

covenant; (ii) the environment versus compensation issue, and (iii) the evolving legal and administrative issues. However. it does not replicate the traditional approach adopted in standard works, as for example Preston & Newsom, of considering seriatim jurisdiction under sub-sections (a), (b) & (c) of section 84(1) and, following amendment by the Law of Property Act, 1969, sub-section (aa), but adopts a division related to subject matter rather than juridical grounds. This aims to achieve a more informative and practical approach to the rôle of the restrictive covenant in the control of land use and development and, in particular, the land management perspective of restrictive covenant control.

A further subdivision of the analysis is necessary by reason of the substantial amendments made to section 84(1) by the Law of Property Act, 1969, which provided, *inter alia*, a 'formula' for dealing with town planning matters in the decision-making process of the Lands Tribunal and a 're-statement' of the circumstances governing the award of compensation which the Lands Tribunal in its formative years strove so strenuously to resist. These changes had such a fundamental effect on the decisions of the Lands Tribunal that a consideration of cases in two parts is called for, namely those cases decided before the coming into operation of the Law of Property Act, 1969 and those after, which form the subject matter of chapter 5. The Lands Tribunal cases taken from the period leading up to the Law of Property Act, 1969 relate primarily to those issues where overlap or conflict was most likely to occur as between public and private control of the use and development of land and are deliberately selective in order to permit examination in some degree of detail and depth of the town planning, environmental and legal issues involved.

Town Planning Issues

The Lands Tribunal cases decided in this period exhibit an ambivalent attitude towards town planning. At times the Tribunal embraces the views and decisions of the Local Planning Authority and at other times takes great pains to distance itself from such views and decisions, often in terms which leave little doubt as to the low regard in which it held public control in general and town planning control in particular. To an extent the attitude of the Lands Tribunal reflects the changing popular attitudes and public perceptions and it is important, therefore, to consider the cases in chronological order to confirm or refute the proposition that the Tribunal might in some way have been influenced by the changing fortunes and credibility of town planning.

The first reported case, viz. *Re Davis' Application*[1] addressed the issue head on. An application to modify a restrictive covenant limiting development to private dwelling houses only, on the grounds that such development was contrary to good town planning as evidenced by the granting of a planning consent for flats, was refused, it being held that 'a private covenant which still offers valuable protection will not be set aside on planning grounds'. In *Re Hickman & Sons Ltd's Application*,[2] a restrictive covenant limiting use firstly to allotments and later to 'one private dwelling house per plot' was discharged, following evidence that the Local Authority had approved a development plan for mainly light industrial purposes, on the grounds that 'the Local Authority's Development Plan was a reasonable one and provided sufficient safeguards' and that the restrictions were cumbersome, obsolete, within the category of 'other circumstances' in section 84(1)(a), and ineffective. On the other hand it held in *Re M. Howard (Mitchum) Ltd's Application*[3] that, where the Local Authority had approved a higher density development than that permissible under the restrictive covenant, 'though the applicants' proposed development had received planning permission and was reasonable, it was not the only reasonable form of user of the plot' and furthermore the restriction did not impede reasonable user, was not obsolete and was still of benefit to the persons entitled. Accordingly the application was dismissed.

A further case decided in 1956 illustrates a situation where a planning authority 'used' the Lands Tribunal to achieve its objective. In *Re Hedges' Application*,[4] following a modification made by the Lands Tribunal in March 1955 to permit a block of 6 maisonettes, a further modification was sought for a block of 10 maisonettes for which planning permission had been granted in September 1955. The planning authority appeared at the Tribunal as an objector intimating that it regretted having granted planning permission and that the right number was 6 (or possibly 8) but had not revoked the permission for fear of a claim for compensation. The Lands Tribunal, dismissing the application on the grounds that it failed under both section 84(1)(a) & (c), commented that 'the planning history of this case shows how little assistance the Tribunal, in exercising its jurisdiction under section 84(1) of the Act, can receive from the decision of a planning authority'.

Possibly the nadir was reached in the same year. Although not a Lands

Tribunal case, *Bell v Norman C. Ashton Ltd*[5] in the Chancery Division concerned an action to enforce a restrictive covenant imposed under a building scheme limiting development to not more than two houses on any one plot. Planning permission had been granted for a higher density. The defendant's surveyor in evidence is reported as having said that:

> town planning approval had been obtained for houses on this scale of density; modern conditions demand that suburban planning should be on that kind of scale; that is the right density at which suburban people ought to live, and if they do not they are obsolete and they ought to be disregarded as being anti-social persons wanting more room than in a crowded country it is right that they should occupy.

Commenting thereon, Harman, J confessed that he 'was much incensed by this evidence. There does remain in a world full of restrictions just a little freedom of contract'. He went on to state unequivocally that the fact that planning permission had been granted was immaterial.

These cases in the mid 1950's reflect what was then an almost universal disenchantment with town planning. The Town & Country Planning Act, 1947 had been heralded as the instrument, along with other legislation such as the New Towns Act, 1946, to achieve the 'post-war reconstruction' which had been promised in the early 1940's in such reports as *Barlow*,[6] *Scott*[7] and *Uthwatt*[8] and in White Papers such as *'The Control of Land Use'*.[9] The post-war planning legislation however, had not and could not of itself achieve these objectives for two main reasons. The legislation was primarily restrictive in nature and that part which was positive, for example comprehensive development, was largely unimplemented due to lack of finance and the generally depressed economic situation of the country. The development which took place in the decade following the 1939-45 war was concentrated on local authority housing (very often at high density) with little in the way of local community facilities and shops. Industrial development was basic and town centre renewal and redevelopment confined to a limited number of the more severely war-damaged cities. Planning control at this stage was not only negative it was also over-interventionist in the minutiae of control and an unnecessary interference in the liberty of the individual. It was administered by planning committees of lay members with limited experience and little appreciation of the need for continuity and consistency in decision-making. On the other hand, control of development through the restrictive covenant was exercised by professionals with both experience and an appreciation of the need for consistency and stability in the management of land and in particular the larger urban landed estates. It is little wonder, therefore, that those charged with the responsibility of handling applications for the discharge or modification of restrictive covenants should at this particular period have been sceptical of the town planning régime and protective of the well-tried and familiar control by way of restrictive covenant.

Matters of precedent and questions relating to its binding force came before the Lands Tribunal in this period. *Re Emery's Application,*[10] considered the question of what a local planning authority might do in the future and the possible precedent for further development presented by the 'thin end of the wedge' argument. Planning evidence that 'no houses would be allowed to be built on the back land' in the future was, in the eyes of the Tribunal, 'mere conjecture based apparently on the suburban ideas of the present planning officer...[A] great many houses [could] be built on the land either by the severance of the existing plots...or by the re-arrangement of boundaries'. The 'thin end of the wedge' argument (common to many of these applications and not always of great significance) was a relevant consideration to the decision to dismiss the application, although it is not clear how a modification (as applied for) to permit a second house on a plot restricted to one only, could invoke the 'thin end of the wedge' argument in respect of the back land which would still be protected by the restrictive covenant. Whilst, in *Re James T. Cook & Son's Application,*[11] an application to increase density to permit development of a type already allowed (following the necessary modification) on other land forming part of the same original estate, was dismissed on the grounds that the proposed development (as exemplified by that which had already taken place and in respect of which the approval of the planning authority had been obtained) would be out of keeping and 'an intrusion of inferior houses into a better class area'. Presumably it was the particular circumstances in the immediate area of the application that influenced the Lands Tribunal in what on the face of it appears to be a *contrary* decision and one that turned its back on following a precedent it had already set.

Re Potter's Application[12] appears on the face of it to be a case that was influenced by 'town planning arguments' to such an extent as to have resulted in a dubious decision. Briefly the facts were that a restrictive covenant (dating from 1851) prohibited 'any trade business process...which shall be noisy noxious dangerous or offensive to the neighbourhood'. The area was mainly residential with some commercial development and the application was to modify the restrictive covenant to allow light industrial user. Reference was made to the meaning assigned to 'light industrial building' in the Town & Country Planning (Use Classes) Order, 1950, namely that:

> it means an industrial building...in which the processes carried on or the machinery installed are such as could be carried on or installed in any residential area without detriment to the amenity of that area by reason of noise, vibration, smell, fumes, soot, ash, dust or grit.

It was held that whilst the restriction was not obsolete nor did it impede reasonable user, the objectors would not be injured by the use of a light industry and the restrictive covenant should be modified to allow such use. The question arises as to whether or not the Tribunal was over-influenced by a then quite commonly held but fallacious view of the effect of the meaning of 'light industrial building' in the Use Classes Order. That it is a use that *could* be carried on or installed in any residential area without detriment is no case for the argument that a light industrial building *should* be installed in a residential area - an argument often put in the simplistic form that as the application is for a light industrial building in a residential area it complies with the Use Classes Order and should *ipso facto* be approved. Could it be that the Lands Tribunal on this particular occasion fell into the trap of that argument?

A series of Lands Tribunal cases towards the end of the 1950's continues to show a degree of ambivalence. *Re Allnatt (London) Ltd's Application*[13] concerned an application to modify a restrictive covenant prohibiting other than industrial-related development in order to allow residential development, a planning application for permission to erect a factory having been refused and on appeal refusal having been upheld by the Minister who agreed 'with the local planning authority's policy to restrict...growth of industry in [the county]'. The land was not allocated for industry in the County Development Plan, planning consent for a factory or workshop was not likely to be granted, although planning approval for residential use was likely. The Tribunal held that 'the attitude of the planning authority, supported as it is by the Minister [is a] material circumstance which impedes the reasonable user of the land. Unless modified the restrictions in practice render the land sterile'. The Tribunal proceeded to modify the restrictive covenant to permit residential development (subject to conditions). In *Re Byrom's Application*[14] an application to modify a restrictive covenant to permit flats, on the ground that the existing restriction requiring the approval of plans by the covenantee or his assigns ought to be deemed obsolete 'bearing in mind the powers of the planning authority', was dismissed on the grounds that there was no basis for deciding the covenant ought to be deemed obsolete and 'any lessening of [the assignee's] rights would injure him'.

In *Re Carshalton Urban District Council's Application*[15] an application to modify a restrictive covenant in respect of six acres of land acquired for use as a park and open space, in order to permit half of the site to be developed by the erection of 26 bungalows, was refused on the grounds that use as a public open space was both possible and reasonable and that the restriction secured practical benefit to the objectors. The Tribunal, in criticising the absence of particulars of the proposed buildings, stated that 'the Tribunal cannot leave the rights of those entitled to the benefit of restrictions to be protected by the planning authority'. On the other hand in *Re Greaves' Application*[16] the Tribunal discharged covenants requiring some 10 acres of land to be used for allotments on an application by building contractors (apparently with no plans or other details of the development and in the absence of any indication that any form of development had, or would be likely to receive, planning permission) on the ground that there was now no demand for allotments and that most of the land was an uncultivated 'jungle'.

In *Re Shaw's Application*[17] an application to modify a restrictive covenant limiting development to a single house on each plot so as to permit higher density development, supported by planning evidence that 'because of the serious shortage of residential building land in the city and that the city council had adopted a much higher density of persons to the acre than currently existed on the estate', was dismissed on the grounds that the restrictions were still of benefit, had resulted in an estate of higher amenity value and that 'the applicant's evidence was preponderantly directed to planning matters, with which the Tribunal is only indirectly concerned, rather than to matters set out in section 84(1), which were not established'. But in *Re Hathway's Application*[18] an application to allow the erection of a three-storey block of flats on land subject to a restriction limiting development to detached and semi-detached houses, was 'modified as prayed', subject to conditions requiring that 'the building should comply with the planning permission which was before the Tribunal'.

Thus by the end of the 1960's, after 20 years experience of dealing with applications for the discharge or modification of restrictive covenants, the Lands Tribunal is still uncertain as to how to accommodate planning evidence. Its initial suspicion of planning control, as shown in the early 1950's, has been replaced by an acknowledgement that planning control exists but an inconsistency of approach as to how statutory plans and planning decisions should be embraced by the Lands Tribunal. How far this dilemma would be remedied by the amendments to section 84(1) to be made by the Law of Property Act, 1969 is a matter for the next period, after 1969.

Environmental and Amenity Issues

Whereas the overriding criterion in those cases decided by the Official Arbitrator in the period up to 1950 was that of 'effect on property values', by the 1950's, regardless of its attitude towards town planning, the Lands Tribunal began to concern itself with 'environmental effects'. Its concerns were twofold, being either matters of environmental pollution (noise, traffic, noxious emissions) or matters relating to environmental amenity (open spaces, nature conservation, privacy, views). From the reported cases it appears that issues relating to environmental pollution and in particular noise pollution surfaced in the early 1950's, whilst matters relating to environmental amenity came to the fore in the late 1950's and 1960's. The cases are examined under three headings, namely: (i) noise, (ii) amenity and (iii) the specific issue of 'views', because of their legal connotation (there being no right to a view) and their significance in planning and development.

Noise

A series of cases taken from the early 1950's illustrates how issues relating to potential 'injury' resulting from increased noise levels become the reasons for refusing to modify restrictive covenants, rather than as a matter relating to the level of compensation awarded as they might well have been in the 1930's. In *Re Solihull District Council's Application*[19] the noise and disturbance associated with a proposed community centre was held to be an altogether different matter from that associated with the small gatherings of the local youth club and the application was refused on the grounds that neighbours would be injured if the modification sought were granted. In *Re Hall & Co Ltd's Application*[20] a distinction was drawn as between noise levels which were acceptable and those which were not. On evidence that the process of winning gravel and ballast was much noisier than that of winning sand the Tribunal held that, as the applicants could consistently with the covenants build houses on the land and fell more trees on it, the extraction of sand would cause the objectors no injury but, owing to the greater noise of winning gravel and ballast, authority should be given for winning sand only. In *Re Reid's Application*[21] the Tribunal dismissed an application to modify a restrictive covenant to permit the continued keeping of pigs on land restricted to use as private gardens on the grounds that 'the noise and smell of the piggeries must depreciate the other plots'.

Questions of noise levels from the use of a church hall for dancing and the ringing of church bells arose in *Re Cowderoy's Application*.[22] Having decided there had been no change in the character of the neighbourhood the Tribunal refused an application for the erection of a church hall on the grounds that the noise from dancing might well depreciate the neighbouring properties but granted the application for the erection of a church on the grounds that it would not injure the persons (if any) entitled to the benefit of the restrictions, provided that no external bells were rung (and a limit imposed on the parking of cars). A rather different outcome resulted from *Re Jamelson Property Co Ltd's Application*.[23] An application for offices, a masonic suite, a restaurant and parking for 50 cars was held not to be objectionable in itself but, as there might well be excessive noise by the user of the car park at night and by music and dancing in the restaurant, restrictions to obviate these dangers must be imposed. It appears from the report of the case that these restrictions were confined to the siting of the car park and the restaurant within the development and did not control either the hours of use or the levels of noise.

This recognition by the Lands Tribunal of the potential damage and injury from noise came at a time when planning authorities were starting to deal with noise problems in earnest by the imposition of very specific and stringent conditions governing hours of operation and permissible noise levels, backed up by an enforcement procedure under the Town & Country Planning Acts. Non-observance of noise restrictions in a modified restrictive covenant could only be enforced by injunction through the courts and, although there is little evidence to substantiate the point, it would appear the more reasonable for the Lands Tribunal to refuse an application where problems of noise might arise rather than grant a modification subject to noise restrictions which could only be enforced by way of injunction. This raises the question as to whether it is equitable to impose such a 'burden' of enforcement on the person or persons entitled to the benefit of the restrictive covenant which, in its unmodified form, may well have been clear and unequivocal, as for example 'private dwelling houses only'. Furthermore, it raises the wider issue as to how far the Lands Tribunal is justified in attaching lists of general, specific and even elaborate conditions to its grant of a modification. If the modification is only acceptable if made subject to such a list of conditions there would appear to be a good *prima facie* argument that the modification should not be made at all. Is it right that a clear contract freely entered into by two parties should be complicated and made 'less certain' by a third party? Was the Lands Tribunal, like the Official Arbitrator before it, straying from the purport of section 84(1)?

Amenity

Towards the end of the 1950's and during the 1960's a number of Lands Tribunal decisions to refuse applications to modify restrictive covenants mention 'loss of amenity' as either the main ground for refusal or a significant contributory reason. In *Re Emery's Application*[24] the Tribunal accepted the submission that woodland retained in a building scheme had been regarded as a special feature and maintained as an amenity and refused to grant a modification to permit the erection of a dwelling house on land on the edge of the wood. It was a relevant consideration that the granting of such a modification would set an example which might lead to a deterioration in the character of the estate as a whole. Evidence that an open space (protected by a restrictive covenant limiting its use for sports or games) was an attraction to residential properties surrounding it, was accepted in *Re Cowderoy's Application*[25] and resulted in the application to modify being dismissed on the grounds that the owners of houses immediately adjoining and overlooking the open space would inevitably suffer some loss of amenity making those houses less readily saleable.

Generally the Lands Tribunal has taken great pains to distance itself from matters of aesthetics and design, claiming that it has neither the remit nor the expertise to assume the role of an arbiter of taste. It did, however, stray into this field in two cases in the early 1960's. In *Re K. & C. Bhavnani (Holdings) Ltd's Application,*[26] in dismissing an application on the grounds that the objectors would suffer injury by the proposed development and that any deterioration in the tone of the neighbourhood was to a considerable extent caused by the applicants, the Tribunal took the opportunity to refer to the design of a Regency chalet bungalow built by the applicants as follows:

> I can only think that it is a modern house likely to have been approved by the Prince Regent, reincarnate as a kind of town planning authority, if in the mean time he had studied domestic architecture first in Geneva and then in Bengal.

John Watson, presiding, then went on to emphasise that 'the Lands Tribunal is not a town planning authority; nor, in emulation of the Prince Regent, am I an arbiter of taste'.

By contrast, in *Re The Independent Television Authority's Application*[27] the Tribunal appears to have been 'overwhelmed' by the eminence of the 'aesthetic' witness. Planning permission had been given for the erection of a television tower on land restricted to use as a public park and pleasure ground. Sir Hugh Casson, on behalf of the applicant, expressed the opinion that the proposed tower was well designed and the site was appropriate for such a structure and that he did not consider it would harm the neighbourhood and that viewed from a distance it would be 'an attractive feature of the landscape'. The Tribunal held that the application ought to be granted having regard to the facts, *inter alia*, that the applicant was a public body and that the mast would be 'surprisingly unnoticeable'. Apart from the debatable issue of 'aesthetics' the case raises an important question concerning the status of a public body. If it be right to take that into account, surely the issue is whether or not the application is in the 'public interest' and not merely whether it is made by a 'public body'.

Arguments relating to amenity arose yet again in *Re Trollope's & Andrew's Application*.[28] Development having taken place on one side of a property it was argued that a restrictive covenant preventing development on the other side was obsolete. The Tribunal dismissed the application holding that 'the more [the property] was beset on other sides the more precious to it was the open outlook on one side secured by the covenant'.

The enjoyment of privacy as such has rarely been the subject of a Lands Tribunal hearing but it did arise in two cases in the 1960's. *Re Stephens' Application*[29] brought the conclusion from the Tribunal that 'a proposed development would injuriously affect the seclusion and privacy which [the objector's] property at present enjoys'. The Tribunal was satisfied that the proposed development would be visible from the objector's property and emphasised 'as this Tribunal has more than once pointed out, the benefits conferred by a restrictive covenant need not be financial'. *Contra*, in *Re Zopat Developments' Application*[30] the Tribunal modified a restrictive covenant in a case where the objector had opposed the application on the ground that the proposed house (which had received planning permission) would overlook his garden and that he valued his privacy. The Tribunal, having inspected the site, accepted that the occupier of the proposed new house would be as likely to secure his privacy as was the objector and went on to state that it could not believe that 'the occupants of the proposed house will spend their days looking out of the bedroom windows'. It is difficult to reconcile this latter decision in the light of previous pronouncements that an injury does not necessarily have to be a 'real injury' and that a 'perceived injury' may be none the less real.

Views

Turning now to a specific aspect of amenity, namely that of the 'protection of a view', because of the common law canon that there can be no right to a view, restrictive covenants (particularly relating to landed estates bordering on towns and other areas where development was likely) were essential as the only practicable means of protection.

Perhaps the most celebrated decision of the Lands Tribunal regarding 'a view' was that of *Re St Albans Investments Ltd's Application*[31] in which an application to modify a restrictive covenant forbidding the erection of any buildings, so as to enable development, was dismissed by the Tribunal on the grounds that 'modification would injuriously affect the view from Richmond Hill', the restrictive covenants having been imposed for 'the express purpose of preserving the well known view from Richmond Hill'. The Tribunal went on to add that 'even if the applicants had succeeded in making out a case under paragraphs (a) or (c) of the Law of Property Act, 1925, section 84(1) the Tribunal would not have been inclined to exercise its discretion in their favour; the view from Richmond Hill is one of outstanding beauty and the local authority's efforts to preserve it should not be frustrated in any way'. It is difficult to envisage a clearer statement of the Tribunal's assumed rôle as protector of nationally acknowledged sites of 'natural beauty'.

Its attitude is less clearcut when dealing with applications of a more local nature. In *Re Peyton's Application*[32] it granted an application in spite of the fact that an objector might lose the benefit of a view in that he will 'look out on a bungalow instead of a garden', whereas in *Re Collett's Application*[33] the Tribunal dismissed an application on the ground that the proposed modification would seriously obstruct the objector's view 'across the sea as far as Portland Bill' and depreciate the value of the objector's property. In *Re Saddington's Application*[34] the Tribunal dismissed an application on the grounds that the restrictive covenant secured practical benefits to the owners of the house which 'enjoyed extensive views across the field', the subject of the covenant forbidding any building, and in *Re Mawdit Harris's Application*[35] the Tribunal held that 'the change in the character of the neighbourhood since 1812, by countryside giving way to built up city, had not made the restrictions obsolete but more valuable, mainly by preserving the view to Plymouth Sound'.

One further example, namely *Re Margate Corporation's Application,*[36] illustrates the 'environmental' attitude the Lands Tribunal had adopted by the end of the 1960's. Margate Corporation sought a modification to enable it to reconstruct an amphitheatre to house a 'marineland' exhibition by the erection of a low dome rising to some 15 feet above the level of the surrounding land together with the erection of a lavatory block which would be visible above the surface of the restricted land. The amphitheatre, excavated in 1903 in breach of the restriction, was below the surface of the restricted land and consequently concealed from view. The Tribunal, in dismissing the application on the ground that the proposed change in the outlook from the premises of the objectors over the amphitheatre would be injurious to them, could not resist comparing 'the care and foresight of the corporation in 1903...with the insensible [sic] approach of the present day planners'. In doing so it reinforced the continuing distinct rôle that the restrictive covenant can play in the protection of private property interests (environmental as well as financial) which from time to time may be jeopardised by the actions of 'public bodies'.

The decisions of the Lands Tribunal regarding the 'protection of views' support the premise that where there is a view that is, in the eyes of the Tribunal, worth preserving and where the restrictive covenant has been expressly formulated to protect that view it will be less than sympathetic to an application affecting it. This appears to be the case regardless of whether the restrictive covenant was of some antiquity or more recently imposed and regardless of changes in the character of the neighbourhood which, in one case at least, appears to have been an added reason for retaining the restriction and protecting the view. The only exception in the cases here reported is that where a view over an adjoining plot of land was held to be an insufficient reason for refusing an application, but the case in question, although referring to a loss of view, could perhaps more realistically have been described as a potential loss of privacy.

Legal and Administrative Issues

In the course of its deliberations the Lands Tribunal has had to consider a wide range of both legal and administrative issues, including matters which are of particular relevance to aspects of land management and development. During its formative years in particular it provided much useful guidance on a number of practical issues, some of a quasi legal nature, and including: (i) the meaning of 'neighbourhood', (ii) the extent and nature of the Tribunal's 'discretion', (iii) the interpretation of certain 'words and phrases', and (iv) the Tribunal's attitude regarding 'compensation'.

Neighbourhood

In spite of its significance the term 'neighbourhood' had received little attention from the Official Arbitrator, apart from one or two instances where an area was held to be too large to be classified as a 'neighbourhood'.[37] The Lands Tribunal remedied this omission in its early days and considered the issue in the first reported case, *Re Davis' Application,*[38] holding that a map of a surrounding district half a mile square submitted by the applicant was too large to be regarded as a 'neighbourhood' but being of the opinion that provided 'a neighbourhood is sufficiently clearly defined to attract to itself and to maintain a reputation for quality or amenity, the size of that neighbourhood and what occurs outside it are of little consequence'. In this case the 'neighbourhood' was clearly shown by 'the area comprised in the 1914 deed and certain nearby land which was not comprised in that deed but was developed similarly'.

In *Re Knott's Application*[39] it was held that 'Berkeley Square is [for this purpose] a neighbourhood'. In *Re F. & H. Joyce Ltd's Application*[40] the Tribunal held that in considering whether changes had occurred in the character of the neighbourhood it was not bound to have regard only to the area which belonged to the trustees (in 1925) but might consider 'a much wider area', whereas in *Re Hedges' Application,*[41] where the Tribunal had already modified a restriction on the same site, it was held that the only changes which could be considered were such as had occurred in the neighbourhood since the modification.

Discretion

The degree of discretion afforded to the Lands Tribunal was the subject of a number of cases in the 1950's and 1960's. In *Re S. & K. Darvill Ltd's Application*[42] the Tribunal held that notwithstanding the doubt as to whether the covenant was enforceable by any person (save perhaps the original covenantee, who did not object) the application should be dealt with on its merits. Importantly, any doubt that there might have been that the power of the Tribunal under section 84 was discretionary was settled by the judgments of Denning and Morris, L JJ in the Court of Appeal in *Driscoll v Church Commissioners for England,*[43] by declaring unequivocally that the power of the Tribunal under section 84 is discretionary and not mandatory.

In *Re Wrighton's Application*[44] the Tribunal decided not to exercise its discretion to modify a restriction because 'the proposed flats would be inconsistent with the existing development of the neighbourhood and would have an injurious effect on the neighbouring owners', in spite of the fact that it had held that there was no one now entitled to the benefit of the restrictions and therefore no one entitled to such benefit who could be injured. Again, in *Re Wickin's Application,*[45] where the Tribunal found that no person having the benefit of the restriction would be injured and that the case fell within paragraph (c) of section 84(1), it nevertheless decided that it would be 'an abuse of the Tribunal's powers to grant a modification to the applicant, for he had bought his land only about two years ago and the restriction has very recently voluntarily been endorsed by him, though apparently without any intention of being bound by it'. The Tribunal's antipathy to modify covenants recently entered into was further demonstrated in *Re Wynyates Smith Ltd's Application*[46] where, although satisfied that the proposed modification would not injure the persons entitled to the benefit, nevertheless exercised its discretion by dismissing the application 'having regard to the facts that the covenant was very recently imposed, that the difficulty was owing to the original covenantor's own actions, and that the applicant was closely associated with the original covenantor'.

The exercise of its discretion caused the Lands Tribunal 'some heart searching' in *Re The Luton Trade Unionist Club & Institute Ltd's*

Application.[47] Having decided that the object of the covenant was no longer capable of fulfilment, and that any injury which would be caused to the objectors as a result of the proposed development and its use was co-incidental and should not prevent the Tribunal from being satisfied that the covenant was obsolete, the Tribunal in granting the application as drafted went on to say that 'we do not think it would be right to refuse to exercise our discretion because of the injury we have mentioned, for we think that that would be to import purely town planning considerations into our decision'.

Interpretation

In its early years the Lands Tribunal took the opportunity to clarify a number of 'legal' points and matters of legal interpretation. For example in *Re Hobbs' & Marshall's Application*[48] it made it clear that 'it is for the Court and not for the Tribunal to determine the validity of the restriction or the parties entitled to the benefit of it. The Tribunal's Order is made on the assumption that the restriction brought before it is enforceable in the courts, but without making any determination on the point'.

Two cases in 1954 clarified the status of objectors claiming that they were 'other persons' within the contemplation of section 84(1)(a) enjoying 'practical benefits' from the restriction. In *Re Winship's Application*[49] it was held that 'the other persons in paragraph (a) must be other persons who are entitled to the benefit of the restriction' and in *Re Fisher's Application*[50] it was held that the objectors' failure to establish their titles 'would not exclude them when assessing the practical benefit of the covenants to 'other persons' within the second limb of paragraph (a)'. Presumably, the Tribunal for the purposes of its deliberations is assuming 'proper title', leaving it to the Courts to resolve any dispute if it should arise in the future.

The conduct of the covenantee was a deciding issue in two cases in 1962. In *Re Murray's Application*[51] the Tribunal accepted that the covenantee had in the past 'paid strict attention to his obligations, perhaps in the main moral obligations, towards the covenantors and consequently that the part of the restriction which required his blessing on plans of development has not been an empty or valueless one'. The evidence showed that the whole area had been very well developed and maintained and that the covenantee would be injured 'if his control of development, exercised with skill and discretion in the past, were to be weakened by the grant of this application for what I find to be inconsistent development'. Again, in *Re Teagle's & Sparks' Application,*[52] it having found that 'the system of covenants was either wholly or substantially intact', the Tribunal went on to hold that 'the applicant had to show that the proposed discharge or modification would not be injurious to [the covenantee]. The very making of an Order for modification would injure the covenantee, as it would show that the system of restrictions had become vulnerable, and the application therefore must be dismissed'.

Very few cases succeeded on the grounds of 'other circumstances', i.e. circumstances other than changes in the character of the property or the neighbourhood as laid down in section 84(1)(a). An exception was *Re Associated Property Owners Ltd's Application.*[53] The facts were that in December 1963 the Minister of Housing & Local Government, acting under the planning legislation, had approved the development of 51 acres of land to the west of the application site by the erection of council houses at a density of 80 persons per acre and the development of 108 acres immediately to the south of the application site by private housing development of a like density. The Tribunal held that these ministerial decisions amounted to 'other circumstances of the case' which should be deemed material within the wording of paragraph (a) of section 84(1) of the Law of Property Act, 1925 and that they had the effect of rendering obsolete the restrictions on the application site.

Generally, these decisions, taken together with those relating to the exercise of the discretion of the Lands Tribunal, showed, in contrast to some of the decisions of the Official Arbitrator, that the Tribunal considered itself very much a 'court of equity' (using the word 'equity' in its broadest sense as importing 'discretion') and that persons seeking the modification or discharge of restrictive covenants must act in both a responsible and moral manner if they hoped to succeed in the Lands Tribunal.

Compensation

The decisions of the Official Arbitrator were often accompanied by the award of compensation which led to the criticism that modification was a question of the 'buying out of private property rights', sometimes with scant regard for the proper interpretation of section 84(1). This criticism could not be laid at the door of the Lands Tribunal in the period up to 1970 and in the cases reported there are few examples of the award of compensation. From the first reported case, *Re Davis' Application,*[54] the Lands Tribunal made its position very clear. Holding that the case was not one for granting the application with compensation it went on to observe that the compensation provisions appeared to be directed only to such cases as those where the covenant is set aside under the 'other circumstances' provision, for example where a future change of character is inevitable and an Order is made to enable the development to conform.

In *Re Watson's Application,*[55] having found that the restriction would impede reasonable user and that its discharge would 'not injure the objector except to the extent that he would be deprived of the opportunity of obtaining damages *ex contractu* for its breach', the Tribunal proceeded to discharge the restriction subject to the payment of compensation to the objector. This is apparently an exceptional case and in general the Lands Tribunal seems to have gone out of its way to avoid the criticisms levelled against the Official Arbitrator in respect of the award of compensation in cases where the application would have more properly been dismissed.

At the end of chapter 3, dealing with the decisions of the Official Arbitrator, some major points of critisism were identified, namely:

(a) a frequent failure to have due regard to the legal interpretation and purport of section 84(1);

(b) a bias towards the granting of a modification on the basis that compensation would recompense for any loss, i.e. a financial rather than an environmental approach, and

(c) a tendency towards accepting the decisions of planning authorities and current planning policies and principles uncritically as evidence of obsolescence and of themselves a ground for modification.

From the evidence of reported decisions the Lands Tribunal (no doubt by reason of its judicious mix of lawyers and valuation surveyors) was successful in meeting the first-named criticism. Regarding the second criticism, namely the compensation issue, it may well have overreacted and, in an effort to show that it was not concerned with the 'buying out of private property rights', have in certain cases refused to modify where modification with a degree of compensation might have been more appropriate. Regarding the third criticism, namely the attitude it should take to town planning matters, the cases examined force the conclusion that it replaced the previous embrace of the Official Arbitrator with a degree of both scepticism and ambivalence to the extent at times of seeing itself as a

Tribunal whose duty it was to correct and remedy the indiscretions of local planning authorities and at other times (perhaps less frequently) as having to accept and adopt town planning decisions as an inevitable *fait accompli.*

That it had not been entirely successful in dealing with the issue of compensation and the role of town planning in its decisions lay behind the amendments to section 84 introduced by the Law of Property Act, 1969. But the amendments made by the 1969 Act and how far they would be instrumental in reconciling the private property law of the restrictive covenant with the public law of planning control are a matter for the next chapter.

Notes

1   (1950) 7 P & CR 1.
2   (1951) 7 P & CR 33.
3   (1956) 7 P & CR 219.
4   (1956) 7 P & CR 270.
5   (1956) 7 P & CR 359.
6   Report of the Royal Commission on *The Distribution of the Industrial Population,* Cmd. 6153.
7   Report of the Committee on *Land Utilisation in Rural Areas,* Cmd. 6378.
8   Final Report of the Expert Committee on *Compensation & Betterment,* Cmd. 6386.
9   White Paper on *The Control of Land Use,* Cmd. 6537.
10   (1956) 8 P & CR 113.
11   (1957) 8 P & CR 460.
12   (1958) 10 P & CR 68.
13   (1959) 12 P & CR 256.
14   (1960) 12 P & CR 273.
15   (1963) 16 P & CR 68.
16   (1965) 17 P & CR 57.
17   (1966) 18 P & CR 144.
18   (1968) 20 P & CR 505.
19   (1953) 7 P & CR 97.
20   (1955) 7 P & CR 159.
21   (1955) 7 P & CR 165.
22   (1955) 7 P & CR 184.
23   (1956) 7 P & CR 253.
24   (1956) 8 P & CR 113.
25   (1957) 9 P & CR 522.
26   (1960) 12 P & CR 269.
27   (1961) 13 P & CR 222.
28   (1962) 14 P & CR 80.
29   (1962) 14 P & CR 59.
30   (1966) 18 P & CR 156.

31 (1958) 9 P & CR 536.
32 (1959) 12 P & CR 263.
33 (1963) 15 P & CR 106.
34 (1964) 16 P & CR 81.
35 (1966) 18 P & CR 138.
36 (1969) 21 P & CR 669.
37 Compare the concept of the urban 'neighbourhood' in town planning terms (derived from the Report of the Study Group of the Ministry of Town & Country Planning, published as an appendix to the Dudley Report on the *Design of Dwellings,* 1944) as a social unit of between 5,000 and 10,000 population, with a range of facilities including, in addition to a diversity of housing types, a primary school, open spaces, local shops, public buildings, service industry and workshops, and contained within defined boundaries, either natural (rivers and open spaces) or man-made (railways and main roads).
38 (1950) 7 P & CR 1.
39 (1953) 7 P & CR 100.
40 (1956) 7 P & CR 245.
41 (1956) 7 P & CR 270.
42 (1955) 7 P & CR 212. The Tribunal's stance in *Darvill's Application* regarding 'absence of objection' has recently been endorsed by a Court of Appeal decision which, additionally, has emphasised the need for a clear, unequivocal notice of application. In *Re University of Westminster, University of Westminster v President of the Lands Tribunal* [1998] 3 All ER 1014 (CA) it was held that: 'On an application for the discharge or modification of a restrictive covenant, the burden was on the applicant to satisfy the Lands Tribunal, as a matter of fact, that one or more of the grounds in section 84(1) of the 1925 Act was made out...In the instant case, having regard to the wording of the notice, the Tribunal had been entitled to find that recipients of it might have been misled and not appreciated the true effect of an order for discharge, and to conclude that it was not right to infer agreement from absence of objection'.
43 (1956) 7 P & CR 371.
44 (1961) 13 P & CR 189.
45 (1961) 13 P & CR 227.
46 (1963) 15 P & CR 85.
47 (1969) 20 P & CR 1131.
48 (1951) 7 P & CR 25.
49 (1954) 7 P & CR 151.
50 (1954) 7 P & CR 153.
51 (1962) 14 P & CR 63.
52 (1962) 14 P & CR 68.
53 (1964) 16 P & CR 89.
54 (1950) 7 P & CR 1.
55 (1966) 17 P & CR 176.

5 Discharge or Modification and the Lands Tribunal after 1969

The Law of Property Act, 1969, which came into operation on 1 January 1970, made significant changes to section 84(1) of the Law of Property Act, 1925. That some amendment, or at the least clarification, was needed has already been demonstrated through the decisions of the Lands Tribunal in the period 1950-1969. The 1960's had witnessed a resurgence in the building construction industry, particularly in private house building, the redevelopment of town centre shopping areas and the construction of major high-rise office developments. The Lands Tribunal had shown a reluctance to modify restrictive covenants which still retained an element of value to the beneficiary but which impeded some reasonable user of the land for public or private purposes and where the award of compensation would have been an adequate recompense. The aspirations of developers in the 1960's demanded an approach to the issue of compensation more in line with that adopted by the Official Arbitrator in the inter-war period. The reaction to the 'buying out' of restrictive covenants and the apparent determination of the Lands Tribunal not to place itself in the position of being similarly criticised had led to a situation where restrictive covenants with little residual value were in danger of frustrating the development or use of land in the wider public interest.

When the Lands Tribunal in 1950 took over the jurisdiction previously exercised by the Official Arbitrator, the new town and country planning régime ushered in by the Town & Country Planning Act, 1947 had been in operation for just 18 months. By 1969 development planning and planning control had become an accepted (if not always an acceptable) way of life. The Lands Tribunal, in the absence of any statutory guidance in section 84(1) of the Law of Property Act, 1925, and consisting as it did of eminent lawyers and valuation surveyors drawn from the senior echelons of their professions, was never sure as to how it should deal with, and what its attitude should be towards, this new public planning régime controlling the use and development of land.

The Law of Property Act, 1969 addressed both of the issues of 'compensation' and 'planning'. Before considering the decisions of the Lands Tribunal (post 1969) it is necessary to examine the amendments, which were to have a marked effect on the decisions of the Tribunal. The 1925 Act in the second limb of paragraph 84(1)(a) had provided for discharge or modification where the continued existence of the restrictive covenant would 'impede the reasonable user of the land for public or private purposes without securing practical benefits to other persons'. In essence this was replaced in the 1969 Act by sections 84(1)(aa) and (1A) and their effect may be summarised as follows:

(a) The benefits must be benefits to 'persons entitled to the benefit', thus making it clear that it is only those persons who can show a legal entitlement to the benefit of the restrictive covenant that have any locus.

(b) The practical benefits claimed must be of 'substantial value or advantage' to the beneficiary to counter successfully the contention of the applicant that the restriction is impeding 'some reasonable user of the land'.

(c) That, in impeding some reasonable user of the land for public or private purposes, the restriction is 'contrary to the public interest', thus inviting the inference that there may be cases where 'public interest' may be prayed in aid of modifying or discharging a restrictive covenant impeding some reasonable user of the land for purely private purposes.

(d) That money will be adequate compensation for the loss or disadvantage (if any) suffered by any person legally entitled to the benefit of the restrictive covenant.

The amended section 84(1) makes clear that when compensation is to be awarded it shall be assessed as either a sum representing the loss or disadvantage suffered as a result of the discharge or modification, or a sum to recompense for the reduced consideration received on the disposition of the land when the restrictive covenant was imposed. Thus, as will be seen later, attempts to obtain a share of 'developers' profit' realisable on the modification or discharge of a restrictive covenant cannot (or at least should not) succeed, being outside the limits laid down in section 84(1) governing compensation awards.

The 1969 Act dealt also with the position that the Tribunal should adopt in respect of town planning matters. In section 84(1B) it states that in determining whether a case is one falling within sub-section (1A) the Tribunal shall take into account 'the development plan and any declared or ascertained pattern for the grant or refusal of planning permissions'. Although sub-section (1A) relates to sub-section (1)(aa) it seems clear that the inclusion of the words 'in any such case or otherwise' in parenthesis in sub-section (1B) implies that the Tribunal shall take this planning advice into account when considering applications under the other headings of section 84(1), namely (a), (b) and (c). Furthermore, the opportunity is taken to widen the view that the Tribunal should take in dealing with applications for discharge or modification by drawing attention to the relevance of 'the period at which and context in which the restriction was created or imposed and any other material circumstances'.

Finally, under sub-section (1C) it declared that the power conferred to modify a restrictive covenant included a power to add 'such further provisions restricting the user of or the building on the land affected as appear to the Lands Tribunal to be reasonable in view of the relaxation of the existing provisions'. In declaring such a power it was giving statutory recognition to a practice that had been in operation since 1925, first by the Official Arbitrator and later by the Lands Tribunal itself.

To assist the frequent reference to the amendments and their effect on the decisions of the Lands Tribunal (post 1969), the amended text of section 84 of the Law of Property Act, 1925 is reproduced in Appendix 2.

Against this background of the important changes made by the Law of Property Act, 1969 the decisions of the Lands Tribunal can now be considered to see how far they were affected by the amended objectives of 'freeing' land from restrictions which, although not obsolete, were nevertheless an unnecessary 'clog' on the freedom of use and development, and how far the operation of section 84(1) could be made relevant to the planning system and the changing economic and social structure.

For purposes of comparison the cases are examined chronologically (in order better to discern trends) under the general headings previously adopted of dealing first with planning issues, secondly with environment issues and thirdly with legal and administrative issues. Two further issues, arising partly from the amendments introduced by the Law of Property Act, 1969 and partly as a result of the increasing use of planning agreements, necessitate two further sub-divisions dealing with first, compensation matters and secondly, the rôle of the Lands Tribunal in the discharge or modification of 'restrictive conditions' in planning agreements made under the Town & Country Planning Acts.[1]

Town Planning Issues

One of the first cases to be heard under the amended code introduced by the Law of Property Act, 1969 was that of *Re Henman's Application.*[2] The Wentworth Estate, Virginia Water had been 'systematically developed' under a building scheme providing, *inter alia,* for one dwelling house per plot. One plot having been sub-divided and the Planning Authority having given permission for a second house on the undeveloped sub-plot, the applicant sought the modification of the covenant so as to enable implementation of the planning permission. The Tribunal, whilst acknowledging that planning permission was from the Planning Authority's point of view quite proper, was of the opinion that the Tribunal had to take a 'rather wider view' and after reviewing the history of the planning of, and the restrictions affecting, the Wentworth Estate, concluded that 'the continuance of the scheme of covenants secured practical benefits' to the Estate Company and to the Roads Committee as the elected representatives of the owners, and proceeded to dismiss the application.

Furthermore it was of the opinion that 'the thin end of the wedge' argument had some real force in this case as 'in these days' owners might be tempted to use the 'infilling' arguments and to grant the application would give them encouragement, thereby ultimately wrecking the whole of a 'carefully worked out development'. The policy of the Local Planning Authority was to increase density and to encourage infilling where appropriate, as it was with many planning authorities at that time (and indeed today) in line with general policies relating to the safeguarding of agricultural land and the preservation of green field sites. The Tribunal, having as the 1969 Act required, considered the materiality of the development plan and planning control criteria, quite properly drew a distinction between the objectives of statutory planning control and private estate management; a distinction which, as will be demonstrated, it has pursued to this day in spite of occasional 'lapses'.

Questions relating to planning and 'the public interest' arose in *Re Davies' Application.*[3] The Tribunal considered the application to modify under sub-sections 84(1)(a), (aa) and (c). Having decided that there was no case under para (a), there being no change such as to render the restriction obsolete, nor under para (c), as the objectors would be injured if the application were granted, it proceeded to deal with the application under para (aa) and by reference to sub-section (1A). In this regard the Tribunal was of the opinion that although the proposed user would be a reasonable one within section 84(1)(aa), the restriction still secured practical benefits of substantial value and advantage to the objectors. Turning then to the question of whether the restriction was 'contrary to the public interest' it proceeded to put into context the relationship between a planning permission and the public interest in the following terms:

> It could not be said that this restriction, in preventing development for which planning permission had been given, was operating against the public interest. When planning permission is granted the authority granting it is merely saying that the permitted development would not be contrary to the public interest; it is not saying that it would be contrary to the public interest if such development did not take place. The planning permission is therefore relevant to the point of public interest but is in no way decisive.

The case, not being within section 84(1A), modification could not be granted under para (aa). The application was dismissed as failing on all three grounds.

The question of 'public interest' arose again in *Re Beardsley's Application*,[4] in which the Tribunal was of the opinion that it did not follow that 'because there is an acute shortage of building land in a given locality, that any restriction which prevents development of land is *ipso facto* contrary to the public interest'. The public interest has to be considered in a broad context having regard to the meaning of the words in section 84(1B) to 'consider not only the ascertainable pattern for the grant or refusal of planning permissions but also the context in which the restriction was imposed, and any other material circumstances'. From which it may be inferred that a general statement of an acute shortage of building land in a given locality is not sufficient to establish a case based on public interest.

A contrary decision was arrived at in *Re S.J.C. Construction Co. Ltd's Application*[5] in which the Tribunal held that the restriction ought to be modified, under para (b) of sub-section (1A), on the ground that in impeding the reasonable user of the burdened land the restrictions were contrary to the public interest, there being 'a scarcity of land available for building in the whole of southeast England, including Cheam'. The Tribunal was influenced by the fact that planning permission had been granted; that in its view the adverse effect was not serious; that building work so far done would be wasted; that the applicants had acted in good faith, and that, on the assumption that a substantial amount of compensation can be awarded, although there would be a loss to the public interest insofar as publicly owned land would suffer some disadvantage, yet some other public interest could be furthered. The Tribunal held that the application must fail under all of the other provisions of section 84(1), save under para (b) of sub-section (1A). In this respect it may be argued that the Tribunal was influenced by the fact that the 'dominant land' was 'publicly owned land' and that by the award of substantial compensation to the local authority 'some other public interest could be furthered'.[6]

The provision in section 84(1A) under which the Lands Tribunal is required to consider whether a restrictive covenant is impeding some reasonable user of land 'contrary to the public interest' seems to have caused the Tribunal some problems in the interpretation of what is meant by 'public interest' and how it should deal with varying degrees of public interest and the conflicts between differing public interests arising in the same case. In *Re Collins' & Others' Application*[7] the Tribunal was of the view that:

> for an application to succeed on the ground of public interest it must be shown that that interest is so important and immediate as to justify the serious interference with private rights and the sanctity of contract.

The case is also important in the clear distinction that the Tribunal drew between its jurisdiction and that of a Town Planning Inquiry. Having heard arguments for the admission of 'a large number of documents issued at various times by public authorities concerned with planning, either in the immediate vicinity of the property of the applicants or in various wider areas in which that property was comprised', it held that under the new sub-section (1B) of section 84 the 'only admissible documents are those which, like an approved town map or development plan, have been published, subjected to a public inquiry and then approved by the Minister'. To avoid all doubt as to the view it took the Tribunal added, *per curiam*:

> It would seem most inappropriate for a hearing under this jurisdiction before the Lands Tribunal to become something in the nature of a town planning inquiry.

This clear statement of principle concerning 'public interest' and the jurisdiction of the Lands Tribunal *vis a vis* a Town Planning Inquiry appears not always to have found favour with the Tribunal in subsequent cases. In *Re Patten Limited's Application*[8] the Tribunal arrived at what, on the face of it, can only be described as a contrived and 'precious' decision. The restrictive covenant prevented any building on a piece of back land; the applicants sought authority to build ten houses on the land; the Tribunal found that the proposals of the applicants were reasonable but that in impeding them the restriction was not contrary to the public interest. Noting that it had power under section 84(1C) to grant a modification permitting a smaller number of houses it stated that if seven houses (rather than ten) were built in reasonable positions they would not cause serious loss of amenity and furthermore if only seven houses were built, to prevent such a development would be contrary to the public interest. Thus, the Tribunal appears to be saying that while the building of ten houses (although reasonable) would cause a serious loss of amenity, the building of seven would not and that to prevent the building of ten would not be contrary to the public interest but to prevent the building of seven would. Fortuitously, and for reasons unstated, the modification was unacceptable to the applicants and, having no power to impose new restrictions unless accepted by the applicant, the Tribunal was later forced to refuse the application, thereby (it is suggested) saving itself from an embarrassing decision.

Conflict between competing 'public interests' and the rôle of town planning arose in *Re Mansfield District Council's Application*.[9] The application was for the total discharge of a restrictive covenant limiting the use of land 'for the purpose of markets and fairs generally and especially of a cattle market', in order to enable the District Council who owned the land subject to the restrictive covenant to develop it as a leisure centre for which they had granted themselves planning permission. The Tribunal, in considering the question as to whether the covenant in impeding the leisure centre use was contrary to the public interest and, noting that in doing so it was compelled to make a decision between two conflicting public interests (a cattle market especially or a leisure centre) quite properly had to have regard to 'the development plan and any declared or ascertainable pattern for the grant or refusal of planning permissions in the area...and any other material considerations'.

Having reviewed the relevant planning documentation, the Tribunal then proceeded to consider such issues as (i) the need for a cattle market, (ii) alternative sites for a cattle market and (iii) the intention of the council as to the provision of another cattle market on an alternative site. Furthermore, it was of the opinion (iv) that the grant of planning permission by the District Council to themselves as planning authority could not be regarded as being at all persuasive on town planning grounds as that Council were 'judges in their own cause' and (v) that the proposed use as a leisure centre, contrary to the Development Plan and without providing an alternative site for a cattle market, was in conflict with the Development Plan, and that that aspect should have been drawn to the attention of the Secretary of State who should have held a Public Inquiry.

That the Tribunal should have regard to the Development Plan and planning permissions is quite proper. That it should go behind those decisions to the extent of questioning both their integrity and their effect would seem to be quite improper and outside the scope of section 84(1B). That indeed may have been in the mind of the Tribunal for, having commented on the decisions themselves and the manner in which they were taken, Douglas Frank, QC, presiding, in dismissing the application then went on to say:

> It is not for me to make [the] planning judgment, and in the absence of it the burden seems to be fairly and squarely on the applicants to show that, notwithstanding the planning position, it would be contrary to the public interest to allow the covenant to stand in the way of the leisure centre. I think the applicants would at least have to show first that there is no suitable alternative site for the leisure centre and secondly that it was either wholly impractical or uneconomic to continue the cattle market at the present site or on another site.

In this case the Tribunal, by introducing its own views regarding the planning merits, clouded the issue which, even if the resolution of it was difficult, was of itself quite straightforward. The restrictive covenant prevented the building of a leisure centre, which had a valid planning permission, was a reasonable user of the land and the development of which was *prima facie* in the public interest. The restrictive covenant safeguarded the use of the land as a cattle market, being an established use which, again *prima facie,* was in the public interest. It can be argued that it is not within the jurisdiction of the Lands Tribunal to adjudicate as between conflicting public interests. Section 84 (1A) requires the Lands Tribunal to satisfy itself that the restriction in impeding some reasonable user of land is contrary to the public interest. Having accepted that the use of land as a leisure centre was a reasonable user in the public interest, it was not called upon to consider whether the present user was one in the public interest let alone whether that be a greater or lesser public interest than use as a leisure centre. The Local Planning Authority, being the authority charged with the duty of considering applications 'in the public interest' had already decided that issue in favour of the leisure centre. Being satisfied that the use as a leisure centre was a reasonable user and that its impediment was contrary to the public interest the Lands Tribunal had the option of either granting the modification (subject to the payment of compensation if appropriate) or, because its decisions are always discretionary, refusing the application on some ground based in equity or on ethics. The Tribunal appears not to have addressed the real issues, namely: (i) does the public interest (a leisure centre) outweigh the benefit of the restrictive covenant to the owner of the dominant land and (ii) is the value of that restrictive covenant (limiting use especially to a cattle market) of substantial benefit to the dominant owner? Even by the mid 1970's the Tribunal cannot resist, despite frequent protestations to the contrary, espousing (and contesting) planning argument.

Two further cases in the latter half of the 1970's show a hardening of attitude by the Lands Tribunal to the question of 'the public interest'. In *Re Brierfield's Application*[10] the Tribunal held that the 'fact that planning permission had been granted did not of itself come near to establishing the proposition that the restriction, in impeding the proposed user, was contrary to the public interest'. To make this submission good it must be shown that the public interest is such that it overrides all other objections. Later, *Re Osborn's & Easton's Application*[11] dealt with the status of Government policy in the consideration of questions of public interest. The applicants having received planning permission (granted on appeal by the Minister) for the erection of blocks of flats, sought to have restrictive covenants limiting development to one house per plot modified to enable them to implement those permissions. The Tribunal, refusing the application, held that the proposed buildings would be substantially different in scale from the existing buildings on the plots and the other houses on the estate and that the proposed development would substantially increase noise, the covenants having been imposed to avoid the kind of development now proposed. On the question of public interest the Lands Tribunal held that, while declared Government policy is that when redevelopment takes place advantage should be taken of such opportunities that occur for redeveloping at higher densities, it does not follow that redevelopment by single dwellings would be contrary to the public interest. The Tribunal is now on much firmer ground by distinguishing very clearly between the public and the private interests and its rôle as distinct from that of planning.

The 'thin end of the wedge' argument which featured so prominently in the early days of the Lands Tribunal has been viewed with a greater degree of scepticism since the early 1980's. In *Re Chapman's Application*[12] the argument that if the application were granted a similar application to build on an adjoining site would be likely to succeed, drew from the Tribunal the response that qualified objectors could then oppose any such application and that it would be 'wrong for the Tribunal now to discuss or pre-judge any such future case'. Again, in *Re Farmiloe's Application*[13] the Tribunal, commenting on the 'thin end of the wedge' argument, said that each future application would have to be decided on its own merits, uninfluenced by the present decision. Thus, the Lands Tribunal is borrowing from the town planning régime the criterion that each case must be considered on its merits, without acknowledging that the decision in the instant case will influence, if not be a precedent for, like decisions in similar cases. Nevertheless in a recent case, *Re Page's Application*,[14] the 'thin end of the wedge' argument was accepted by the Lands Tribunal as relevant as 'the proposed modification would make it easier to seek further modification'.

We conclude this section dealing with town planning issues[15] by referring to some recent cases to illustrate the current attitude of the Lands Tribunal to town planning. *Re Love's & Love's Application*[16] concerned an application to build a garage (with the benefit of planning permission obtained on appeal) on land the subject of a restrictive covenant imposed on the sale of a council house in pursuance of the statutory right to buy under provisions of the Housing Act, 1985. The Council objected on grounds including detriment to visual amenity, creation of a traffic hazard, and that it would be the 'thin end of the wedge' in that it would destroy the Council's control over the estate by means of the covenants. The Council was considered to be a custodian of the public interest by reason both of its retention of substantial parts of the estate and the provisions of the Housing Act, 1985, section 609. The Tribunal holding, *inter alia,* that the estate was of no special architectural merit, that on the evidence the garage would not create a traffic hazard and that few buildings on the estate could accommodate a garage in the same manner, granted such limited modification as that sought as it would not 'inhibit the Council from enforcing similar covenants affecting its houses on the estate'. The Tribunal added a proviso to the relevant covenant to the effect that 'the erection of a garage, in accordance with planning permission, should not be deemed to be in breach of any covenant therein, thus leaving the full benefit and protection of the covenant in the hands of the Council'. This raises the question as to whether the Tribunal was in fact modifying the covenant or was it merely allowing the garage as a specific exception to the covenant, the wording of which remained unchanged.

On the other hand, in *Re Solarfilms (Sales) Limited's Application*[17] the Tribunal dismissed an application to modify a restrictive covenant to permit use as a children's day care nursery - a reasonable user for which planning permission had been granted on appeal - there not being such a degree of urgency as to justify the modification on the grounds of public interest. The Tribunal was apparently influenced by the fact that although it was accepted that property values would not be affected, the objectors' aims in insisting on the observance of the covenant to maintain their estate as strictly residential were 'sincere and not tinged with any ulterior motive'. The outcome of the decision of the Lands Tribunal in this case resulted in the restrictive covenant not only effectively protecting the rights of the beneficiaries but also upholding the planning decision of the Local Planning Authority as against that of the Secretary of State for the Environment.

The argument and decision in *Re Severn Trent Water Limited's Application*[18] are important as illustrating the extent to which the Tribunal is prepared to go in order to accommodate the 'town planning climate' within which it operates. The case concerned an application for the discharge or modification of restrictive covenants imposed in 1939, which prevented land from being used other than as a sewage disposal works, for agricultural purposes, or as a cemetery, so as to enable the land to be used as a leisure centre, for which the Local Planning Authority had resolved to grant conditional planning permission, subject to the making of an agreement under the Town & Country Planning Act 1990, section 106. The objector, who had the benefit of the restrictions, owned five acres of land to the south of the application land and considered that the possibility that he might obtain planning permission in the future to build upon that land would be prejudiced if the leisure centre as proposed should go ahead. Although it had been planning policy to maintain the five acres as open space to provide a buffer zone, the objector considered that the need to provide more housing than already allocated in the current Structure Plan would lead to the need to identify further 'green field sites' of which his was one of those most suitably located for release for housing development. The emerging Structure Plan for the area identified the application site for leisure use and the objector's site as an open buffer zone and the applicants contended that there was thus no reasonable likelihood of development being permitted on the objector's land and even if it were permitted the proposed use of the application site as a leisure centre would have no adverse effect upon it.

The Lands Tribunal, modifying the covenants so as to permit the proposed leisure use, held that such use of the application site was a reasonable user impeded by the restrictions without securing any practical benefit to the objector, that the evidence supported the contention that the possibility of obtaining planning permission for the objector's site was 'so remote as to be negligible', and that in any event the proposed development of the application site would not hinder the obtaining of such a permission, nor would it prejudicially affect any residential development carried out in accordance with such a permission.

It would seem quite proper for the Lands Tribunal to hold that the proposed leisure use was a reasonable use and that the restrictions impeded such a use without securing any practical benefit to the objectors. It would have been quite proper for it to conclude that the restriction preventing the use as a leisure centre was contrary to the public interest and any residual benefit to the objectors could be adequately recompensed by the award of compensation. It is questionable, however, as to whether it was necessary or prudent for it to have concluded that 'the possibility of obtaining planning permission for the objector's site was so remote as to be negligible', and that the proposed development of the application site would not hinder the obtaining of such a permission, nor would it prejudicially affect any residential development carried out in accordance with such a permission.

The Tribunal's view may well have been a fair interpretation of what might happen in the future, but it is surely not for the Tribunal, any more than it is for a planning authority, to forecast the outcome of future planning applications and, in particular, to make a subjective value judgment that the leisure centre use would not 'prejudicially affect any residential development' if such were to be permitted on the objector's land. The Tribunal had earlier ruled that references to the 'planning background' in section 84(1), as modified by the Law of Property Act, 1969, should include only statutory development plans and any discernible pattern of planning control decisions in the locality, that other documentation of an 'informal' nature should be excluded, and that future applications would be considered on their merits as and when they were made.

The planning comments in the instant case would appear to be both gratuitous and, it may be argued, outside the jurisdiction of the Lands Tribunal. Nonetheless this is an instructive case on which to conclude an examination of the way in which the Lands Tribunal handles town planning issues. It illustrates the Lands Tribunal's distinct and individual approach to the modification or discharge of restrictive covenants within the realm of 'private land law' whilst at the same time recognising that it takes such decisions within the context of an established planning régime statutorily empowered and mandated to control the use and development of land in the public interest. That it chose in this case to comment further than may have been thought necessary in arriving at its decision does not in itself question the correctness of that decision but, unless such comment is considered as *obiter*, the practice of attaching planning reasons for its decision would be one to be treated with concern. Section 84(1B) requires the Lands Tribunal to take into account 'planning matters' in determining whether a case is one falling within section 84(1A). Having so decided that it does, the Tribunal then proceeds under this section as authorised by section 84(1)(aa) in the context of the planning background but not by reason of it.

Environmental and Amenity Issues

In at least three cases in the 1970's the Lands Tribunal decisions embraced in one form or another a kind of environmental evaluation. In *Re Mercian Housing Society Limited's Application*[19] a modification of a restrictive covenant, limiting development to one private dwelling house to each quarter of an acre plot, was sought in order to permit the erection of six blocks of flats. The Tribunal, in granting the modification so as to permit five of the blocks (excluding the sixth on the ground that it would have a 'devastating' effect on one house and a 'serious' effect on another), then went on to compare the scheme submitted by the applicant with proposals put forward by the objectors for the development of the site in accordance with the restrictions. Apparently, it was not contended that the proposals put forward by the objectors for the development of the site in accordance with the restrictions (being part of a 'scheme of development') were not 'some reasonable user of the land' nor was evidence adduced that such proposals would be uneconomic. The Tribunal (as reported) took its decision solely on the basis of a comparison between the applicant's scheme and the objectors' proposals, founded on environmental preference and in particular the preservation of trees. The applicant had negotiated with the Local Planning Authority a scheme which preserved 'over 99% of the trees and the most important part of the landscaping' as a result of which planning permission had been obtained. Commenting that it 'would be a crying shame if the glade was destroyed and the [applicant's] scheme avoids this and preserves many more trees elsewhere, whereas [the objectors' scheme] would inevitably fragment the glade and involve much more destruction of trees', the Tribunal proceeded to 'set aside' the objectors' scheme of development, contrary to the wishes of some 100 residents on the estate, without any evidence of any change in the character of the neighbourhood and solely on the ground that development of the site of 2.685 acres by the erection of nine houses would be unlikely to receive planning permission and that such development would result in the destruction of many mature trees and much landscaping. By the introduction of an alien form of development (three-storey blocks of flats in an area of low density housing) it must be a debatable point as to whether the 'wider environmental character' of the estate was not being sacrificed in the interests of the 'narrower environmental landscape' of the immediate arboreal locality. In the event the decision of the Lands Tribunal appears to have been based entirely on a selective and subjective 'value judgment', without apparently any attempt to weigh *all* the environmental issues, and with scant regard for the provisions of s.84(1).

In *Re Wards Construction (Medway) Limited's Application*[20] an application failed despite the fact that the proposed user was a reasonable one and that the unmodified restriction impeded it, on the grounds that it 'secured the objectors practical benefits of substantial value'. Among other things 'they valued space, quiet and light, while the proposed building would blot out the sky and some of the valuable sunlight'. Whilst in *Re Forestmere Properties Limited's Application*[21] the Tribunal, in exercising its discretion to discharge parts of a restrictive covenant, were not prepared to do so without the imposition of new restrictions to preserve the trustees' control of development over the application land, requiring the trustees' approval to the plans of any new building or subsequent alteration thereto. The Tribunal emphasised the importance of restrictive covenants (in this case imposed in 999 year leases made in 1931, 1935 and 1943) to 'good estate management' and the need to preserve the trustees' control of development which the trustees had, either by ownership or powers of management, exercised in respect of such matters as density and plot ratio in a reasonable and generous manner.

In the former case the Tribunal recognised the rights of an individual to secure 'living standards' over and above those that might be protected at common law or under the law relating to town and country planning. Whereas in the latter case it recognised the value of restrictive covenants controlling design matters as part of the practice of good estate management, whilst accepting at the same time that the modification of restrictive covenants is needed to meet changed circumstances, albeit still retaining the power of the trustees to control design, density, plot ratio and use through the submission of plans for the trustees' approval.

In the 1980's a number of cases were heard wherein the question of a 'right to a view' was a paramount consideration. The scene was set by two Court of Appeal cases, the first being by way of an appeal from the County Court and the second by way of appeal from the Lands Tribunal itself. In *Wakeham v Wood*[22] the Court of Appeal held that the judge in the County Court was in error in awarding damages in lieu of a mandatory injunction, having found that the defendant (in the instant case) had acted in flagrant disregard of the plaintiff's rights under the restrictive covenant, there having been a 'serious interference with the plaintiff's legal right to a view of the sea and that interference was incapable of being estimated in money terms'. On these grounds the appeal was allowed.

In *Gilbert v Spoor*[23] the appellant contended, *inter alia,* that the enjoyment of the landscape view could not in law be of practical benefit to the objectors under the restrictive covenant because it was not a benefit annexed to the land owned by the objectors, since the view was not one obtainable from their land. In dismissing the appeal the Court held that 'the Tribunal was entitled to hold that a view was a benefit whether or not that benefit could be said to touch and concern the land' but in any event 'the land of the objectors in this case was touched and concerned by the covenant, since the covenant was intended to preserve the amenity of the neighbourhood generally, and loss of a view just round the corner could well affect the estate detrimentally'. Per Waller, LJ:

> If a building estate contains a pleasant approach with restrictions upon it and some building is done contrary to those restrictions which spoils the approach, if then the owner of a plot complains about breach, the fact that he does not see it until he drives along the road, in my opinion does not affect the matter... A view is not something which can be valued in money terms; indeed it may be and perhaps I would say in this case is, priceless.

These two Court of Appeal cases provided a firm foundation for the deliberations of the Lands Tribunal over the next decade. Thus, for instance, in *Re Bushell's Application*[24] the Tribunal dismissed an application on the ground that 'the intrusion of the roof-line of the proposed house into the unusual view enjoyed by one objector' was sufficient to defeat the application. The proposed new house would interfere significantly with the 'high quality landscape view southeastwards across the roofs and houses and trees towards St Mary's Church', that it was unusual to find such a landscape view so close to the centre of London (Wimbledon) and money could not be an adequate compensation.

The other aspect of environmental amenity which exercised the Lands Tribunal in this period was that relating to noise and disturbance. In *Re William's Application*,[25] having accepted that the proposed development would constitute a reasonable user of the application land and would be impeded by the continued existence of the restrictions, the Tribunal dismissed the application on the ground that at least two of the objectors would suffer serious detriment to their amenities in a loss of spaciousness, nuisance from building works and diminution in the value of their properties, for which compensation would not provide adequate recompense. Thus, even short term nuisance arising from building works is seen, at least in part, as a reason for refusing modification. On the other hand in *Re Shah & Shah's Application*[26] objections relating to noise and other possible disturbance resulting from the use of a private dwelling house as a nursing home were countered by the Tribunal making its decision subject to a condition that the applicants should not permit 'anything amounting to a nuisance, annoyance or disturbance to the neighbours' and that the objectors would be adequately protected by the remedies available to them at law in respect of nuisance, annoyance and disturbance, should these problems arise.

A recent Lands Tribunal case, *Re Lloyd's & Lloyd's Application*,[27] raises the question that first appeared in 1955[28] as to how far the perception of possible nuisance or disturbance should be taken into account when considering applications under section 84(1). The application in the instant case was for the use of a private house as a community care home for ten psychiatric patients. The objectors contended that mental patients in the area would be disruptive and that their presence would inevitably detract from the value of neighbouring properties. Having held that there had been no change in the character of the neighbourhood such as to render the restrictions obsolete, as the essential character of the neighbourhood as a high class residential area had been preserved by them, the Tribunal held that the restrictions, in impeding what was accepted as a reasonable use of the property, were contrary to the public interest, in that Government Policy in regard to mental illness required the provision of care homes in the community; that the need for such a facility in this area was desperate; that the present premises were well located to answer that need, and that the owners were well qualified and able and willing to adapt the premises for that use. Being of the opinion also that there was no evidence that the proposed use would be more or less objectionable than a school or boarding house both of which were permitted under the covenants, the Tribunal proceeded to modify the restrictions so as to permit the proposed use as a community care home for psychiatric patients. This decision may, on the face of it, seem harsh to the beneficiaries of a restrictive covenant which had been successful (on the admission of the Lands Tribunal itself) in maintaining the 'essential character of the neighbourhood as a high class residential area'.

Legal and Administrative Issues

In recent times the Lands Tribunal has found it necessary to readdress the issues of the use of its discretion and the interpretation of certain aspects of section 84 in the discharge or modification of restrictive covenants.

Discretion

Decisions of the Lands Tribunal to grant or refuse applications for the modification or discharge of restrictive covenants are, as the Courts and the Lands Tribunal have made clear, discretionary. The way it exercises that discretion has been a matter for comment and explanation on a number of occasions by the Tribunal. Where the evidence and conclusions of the Tribunal lead inexorably to a particular decision and in the exercise of its discretion the Tribunal holds to the contrary, it should give reasons for exercising its discretion against the run of evidence and conclusions of fact.

A number of cases in the 1970's throw light on the way in which the Lands Tribunal then sought to exercise its discretion.[29] In *Re Goodman's Application*[30] Sir Michael Rowe, QC, President, referring to the exercise of the Tribunal's discretion where there were no objectors stated that 'even if there are no objections the Tribunal still has a discretion not to make any Order without requiring an applicant to prove his case or to satisfy the Tribunal by other means that the application should succeed'. Three years later, the same learned President, in *Re Saviker's Application (No.2),*[31] where an estate owner had sold plots forbidding the erection of more than one house per plot and the applicant had sought modification to enable the building of a second house on one of the plots, dismissed the application noting, *inter alia,* that the estate owners had 'a moral obligation to honour their bargain with their purchasers' and that the Tribunal ought to exercise its discretion against the application.

The exercise of the Lands Tribunal's discretion came before the courts in 1974 in *Jones & Another v Rhys-Jones.*[32] The Lands Tribunal had held that, in line with a general principle laid down in *Cresswell v Proctor*[33] in 1968, it was not right that purchasers should agree to be bound by a covenant and then seek to modify it within a matter of months. In that case Harman and Danckwerts, LJJ, dismissing an appeal, had held that the Lands Tribunal had acted rightly in refusing to exercise its discretion in favour of an application made within so short a time (four years) of covenants having been voluntarily entered into, as to do so would be contrary to public policy and an abuse of the Tribunal's powers. However, in *Jones & Another v Rhys-Jones,* the Court of Appeal, following dismissal of the application by the Lands Tribunal, held that:

> there was no general principle that the shortness of the time between the imposition of the burden of the restrictive covenant...and an application for its modification was a decisive factor forbidding the grant of the application [and that] modification of a restrictive covenant was a matter of discretion for the tribunal and each case must be considered on its merits; that the time which had elapsed might be a factor to be taken into consideration as were also the nature of the covenant, the relationship of the parties to the original covenantors and changes in the property benefited by the covenant or in the neighbourhood; and that the matter should be remitted to the tribunal for reconsideration accordingly.

The admonition administered by the Court of Appeal in *Jones & Another v Rhys-Jones*[34] registered with the Lands Tribunal for, in *Re Pearson's Application,*[35] in granting a modification of the restrictions 'imposed only in 1970', the Tribunal held that 'it would not be right to exercise the discretion of the Tribunal by refusing the application' adding that but for the decision of the Court of Appeal in *Jones & Another v Rhys-*

Jones it might have adopted a stricter view and followed the observations of Harman and Danckwerts, LJJ in *Cresswell v Proctor.* In fact, some 20 years later in *Re Page's Application,*[36] the Lands Tribunal followed *Cresswell v Proctor* intimating that the *recent* date of imposition of the covenant was relevant since 'the sanctity of contract must have some relevance'.

In exercising its discretion the Lands Tribunal must always be aware that the manner in which that discretion is exercised is a matter that may become the concern of the Court of Appeal. Appeal against any decision of the Lands Tribunal is by way of case stated on a question of law, but to bring the 'exercise of a discretion' before the Court of Appeal the appellant may have to do no more than show that the rules of natural justice were not followed in the exercise of that discretion. Matters of fact are for the Lands Tribunal but as the exercise of its discretion will almost inevitably mean that it is deciding 'against the facts', it follows that wherever the Tribunal exercises its discretion it will *prima facie* lay itself open to an appeal against such decision.

Interpretation

The meaning of 'obsolescence' within the context of s.84(1) has been considered from the very early days of the operation of the Act and many Orders of the Official Arbitrator and Decisions of the Lands Tribunal on the issue have already been noted and commented upon, but two recent cases add to the 'case law' on the subject.

In *Re Quaffers Limited's Application*[37] the Tribunal discharged restrictions imposed in 1972 and 1974 absolutely. Whilst accepting that there had been no change in the character of the neighbourhood since 1974, it considered that the restrictions were obsolete when imposed as the land retained was not capable of being benefited by the restrictions 'on account of the motorway round the...site' and furthermore that no compensation would be awarded 'as there would be no detriment to amenity'. That 'obsolescence' is not merely a question of the passage of time is further illustrated by *Re Barclays Bank plc's Application.*[38] This case concerned an application to discharge a restrictive covenant imposed by an agreement under section 52 of the Town & Country Planning Act, 1971. The Lands Tribunal's jurisdiction regarding planning agreements and obligations is referred to later but this case is important for the general principle that it establishes. The restriction, being part of a section 52 agreement, was entered into in 1977 on the sale of land and provided that the use of the dwelling for which planning permission was being granted was subject to an 'agricultural occupancy condition'. Because most of the land held with the dwelling at the date of the section 52 agreement had since been disposed of for non-agricultural purposes the Tribunal held that it was not possible for any prospective purchaser to achieve the original object of the restrictions imposed by the agreement and consequently the restrictions must be deemed obsolete. Thus obsolescence, as in the former case, can be built in and, as in the latter case, ensue within a few years of its imposition through changed circumstances which could not necessarily have been foreseen.

Further assistance has been given by the Lands Tribunal on the question of obsolescence in two recent cases. In *Re Kennet Properties' Application*[39] it took the opportunity to differentiate between section 84(1)(a) and (aa):

> Paragraph (a) is concerned with whether the restriction itself is obsolete, that is to say is now out of date compared to when it was imposed, as to which its original purpose must be the touchstone, whereas paragraph (aa) is concerned with the benefit which the restriction is conferring at the time of the application which may well be different from its original purpose.

Even more recently in *Re North's Application*[40] the Tribunal, following the format of considering the application by means of a series of questions (on lines first adopted in *Re Bass's Application*),[41] again took the opportunity, the application having been made under section 84(1)(a) and (aa), to distinguish the two paragraphs. Considering first para (a) it found that, there having been no material changes in the neighbourhood since the restriction was imposed, the restriction could not be deemed obsolete and the application must fail under section 84(1)(a). It then considered the matter under para (aa). Having decided (i) that the proposed use was a reasonable user for the land and (ii) that it was impeded by the restriction, it then proceeded to decide (iii) that the restriction secured practical benefits of substantial value or advantage to the objectors and, noting (iv) that the parties had agreed that the restriction was not contrary to the public interest, found that the application must fail under section 84(1)(aa).

On a separate point, but nevertheless one coming within the category of 'interpretation', the special significance of the building scheme has once again been recognised and endorsed by the Lands Tribunal. In *Re Lee's Application*[42] the Tribunal held that:

[A] building scheme establishes a system of local law and its effect is that there is a greater presumption that restrictions imposed under it will be upheld and a greater burden of proof on the applicant to show that the requirements of section 84 have been met.

In *Re Hunt's Application*[43] the Tribunal observed that:

The [building] scheme...had the primary intention of securing a relatively low density residential development which had so far been achieved without any deviation from it and the maintenance of that scheme of covenants provided the objectors with substantial and practical benefit.

Nor was the Tribunal satisfied that to prevent the erection of a house or, if necessary, to pull a house down was contrary to the public interest.

From these cases it seems that the Tribunal is affording the building scheme a 'higher status' than it gives to the generality of restrictive covenants as such. First, it appears to imply a 'greater presumption' in favour of restrictive covenants in a scheme. Secondly, it recognises the advantages that a scheme achieves in environmental and management terms.

Reference has already been made to two further issues that need to be addressed, namely the award of compensation and the modification of planning agreements. The former is as a direct result of the changes made by the Law of Property Act, 1969 to section 84(1) of the Law of Property Act, 1925 'encouraging' the award of compensation which, as has been demonstrated, was discouraged following the 'enthusiasm' of the Official Arbitrator for this method of resolving competing interests. The Lands Tribunal's involvement in applications for the modification or discharge of restrictions in planning agreements came about indirectly through the Town & Country Planning Act, 1968. The power to make planning agreements had been introduced in the Town & Country Planning Act, 1947, section 25 and later re-enacted in the Town & Country Planning Act, 1962 section 37, but until 1968 that power had only been exercisable with the approval of the Secretary of State and as a result very few local planning authorities had availed themselves of it. In the 1970's and in particular following Local Government reorganisation in 1974, Local Planning Authorities made great use of planning agreements first under section 37 of the 1962 Town & Country Planning Act, later under section

52 of the 1971 Town & Country Planning Act, and now under section 106 (as amended) of the 1990 Town & Country Planning Act. Both the increasing award of compensation (and its assessment) and the greatly increased use of planning agreements (and the attitude of the Lands Tribunal to the modification of restrictions contained in such planning based documents) are important to the practice of estate management and development, the implementation of planning policy and environmental protection generally. The main implications are now considered by reference to Lands Tribunal decisions taken since 1969.

The Award and Basis of Assessment of Compensation

The Law of Property Act, 1969 in its amendment to section 84(1) made it very clear as to when compensation should be considered an adequate remedy and the basis for its assessment. It is surprising therefore that the Lands Tribunal and the Court of Appeal seem to have had so much trouble in coming to terms with it.

The Act provides that in awarding compensation the basis shall be either (i) a sum to make up for any loss or disadvantage suffered by the beneficiary as a result of the discharge or modification, or (ii) a sum representing the reduction in the purchase price attributable to the effect of the imposition of the restrictive covenant. The wording of the amended section 84(1) clearly excludes, on any interpretation, an allowance for possible 'development value' although it will be seen that in a few cases the Lands Tribunal (sometimes with the acquiescence of the Court of Appeal) has found means of awarding increased compensation, wrongly it is suggested, to reflect a share of the 'development value' released by the discharge or modification of the restriction.

Under section 84(1A), in its decision to award compensation as being adequate for the loss or disadvantage, the Tribunal is called on to determine whether benefits are of 'substantial value' and what constitutes 'public interest'. Both of these criteria have from time to time exercised the judgment of the Tribunal. What is or is not 'substantial value' in the eyes of the beneficiary often does not equate with the view of what constitutes 'practical benefits of substantial value' to those who may be able to adopt a more objective stance. Similarly, what constitutes 'public interest' is influenced by prevailing public perception and varies through time and circumstance and as between areas of differing social and economic structure.

Compensation as an Adequate Remedy

Turning now to an examination of the cases dealing with compensation issues it is instructive to start with one which attempted to set down for the benefit of the Tribunal the questions that had to be asked in coming to a decision as to whether or not compensation was an adequate remedy for the loss of the benefit of the restrictive covenant. In *Re Bass Limited's Application*[44] Counsel for the applicants submitted that in arriving at a decision under section 84(1)(aa) the Tribunal had to consider a number of questions. This approach commended itself to the Tribunal in that case and indeed has been adopted as a format in subsequent cases by the Tribunal. The approach may be summarised[45] as follows:

(a) Is the proposed user reasonable under sub-section (1)(aa)?

(b) Do the covenants impede that user?

(c) Does impeding the proposed user secure practical benefit to the objectors under sub-section (1A)?

(d) If so, are those benefits of substantial value or advantage? If not, would money be an adequate compensation?

(e) Is impeding the proposed user contrary to the public interest? If so, would money be an adequate compensation?

It was further submitted by Counsel that in questions arising under sub-section (1A) regard should be had to the planning context as required by sub-section (1B). Having found that the proposed user was reasonable and that the covenants impeded that user, the Tribunal, being in no doubt that the impeding of the proposed user secured practical benefits of substantial advantage to the objectors and that it was not satisfied that impeding the proposed user was contrary to the public interest, held in the instant case that the application must be refused. The discipline imposed on the Tribunal by the adoption of a logical approach of this nature does much to assist the Tribunal in coming to a decision which both parties can understand even though the decision goes against one of them.

Practical Benefits of Substantial Value

One of the key questions concerns an assessment of whether the proposed user impedes 'practical benefits of substantial value or advantage'. In *Re John Twiname Limited's Application*,[46] one of the earlier cases to be decided under the amended section 84(1), the Tribunal held that although the advantages were not of 'substantial value' the removal of the restriction would entail some loss or disadvantage to the objectors but that money would be an adequate compensation. In *Re Gaffney's Application*[47] the Tribunal concluded that the 'true measure of substantiality lies in the degree of depreciation in the value of the enjoyment of the property of the objector which would result from the application being granted', thereby asserting that it is the value of the benefit as seen through the eyes of the beneficiary.

In *Re Da Costa's Application*[48] the Tribunal, whilst finding that the restriction did secure 'practical benefits of substantial value or advantage', nevertheless held that money would be sufficient compensation since the objector's interest was in effect reversionary. It is difficult to understand why a freeholder not in possession should be adequately compensated by a money payment whereas if he had been in possession he would not, the Tribunal having found that the benefit was of substantial value. Presumably the Tribunal considered that any practical benefit from the restriction, though substantial, would be limited to the effect on the value of the reversionary interest, which could be calculated in purely financial terms and that, therefore, the payment of money by way of compensation would be both appropriate and adequate, there being no question of any 'personal enjoyment' of the benefit as such in, for example, 'environmental terms', which a beneficiary in possession might enjoy.

Development Value, Hope Value and Market Value

Although the modified section 84(1) makes clear the basis on which compensation is to be awarded the Lands Tribunal and the Court of Appeal have experienced difficulty in dealing with 'hope' value and claims for a share in 'development' value. The dilemma is well illustrated in *Re S.J.C. Construction Co. Limited's Application*[49] in which the Tribunal held that though the restriction secured 'practical benefits of substantial advantage' the restrictions ought to be modified on the ground that in impeding the proposed user the restrictions were contrary to the public interest. Having stated that the relevant basis for the award of compensation was 'a sum to make up for any loss or disadvantage suffered by [the person entitled] in consequence of the discharge or modification', the Tribunal then went on to consider the effect of the judgment in *Stokes v Cambridge*[50] and concluded that, although it was arguable that the only loss or disadvantage which could be considered is that affecting the dominant land as such, the construction which it regarded as equitable was one which involved the sharing of the development value flowing from the modification of the restriction. Douglas Frank, QC (presiding) said:

> In *Stokes v Cambridge* the Tribunal would have split equally the development value, but for the fact that they considered that the owner of the 'dominant' land would have obtained some advantage or some potential advantage from the development and therefore decided that the 'dominant' owner would have accepted one third of the development value. In the instant case no such consideration arises and I think that the most likely outcome of friendly negotiations would have been an agreement to split the development value equally and I so decide.

The decision of the Lands Tribunal was contested in the Court of Appeal in *S.J.C. Construction Co. Limited v Sutton London Borough Council*[51] on the ground that the Tribunal had erred in principle in awarding compensation on the basis of 50% of the development value. In dismissing the appeal the Court held that the 'loss or disadvantage' for which compensation was to be awarded was 'an intangible matter incapable of exact calculation in money...and that the Tribunal had adopted a fair and reasonable way of assessing the loss or disadvantage and had not erred in law in taking 50% of the realisable development value of the site'. The reluctance of the Court of Appeal to involve itself in valuation matters is understandable, but to contend that the assessment of compensation is 'an intangible matter incapable of exact calculation in money' is an inadequate reason for accepting a 50:50 division of development value as a basis for complying with the requirement of section 84(1) para (i) to assess a sum representing 'any loss or disadvantage suffered...in consequence of the discharge or modification' of a restrictive covenant. The appellants contended that section 84(1) as amended required assessment 'by reference to any depreciation in value of the respondent's land consequent upon the modification' and that the Tribunal wrongly declined to adopt that method of assessment. The decision of the Lands Tribunal, supported as it was by the Court of Appeal, in the assessment of compensation is believed to be not only arbitrary but wrong in law as the basis is clearly laid down in section 84(1) as amended. Furthermore, the art and practice of valuation is not so 'intangible' as to justify such a crude approach.

The decision of the Court of Appeal in the *S.J.C. Construction case* has been criticised in a number of quarters. Perhaps the most useful commentary is to be found in a probing article in the Journal of Planning Law[52] published shortly after the decision of the Court of Appeal. The comments are particularly important as they were made by a leading Chartered Surveyor with extensive practical valuation experience and the author of standard works on Valuation and Estate Management.

The award in the *S.J.C. Construction case* was made under para (i) of the amended section 84(1), i.e. based on 'loss or disadvantage' flowing from the discharge or modification, and as Leach points out the power of the Tribunal to award 'such compensation as it thinks just' means as is just within the rules and does not extend to 'loss of bargaining power'. Moreover 'there is no basis of relationship between the loss and disadvantage sustained by the objector and the value of the gain of the applicant. The Act does not provide for an applicant's gain to be brought into account as a means of compensation to an objector'.[53]

Claims for a 'share in the development value' had a chequered history throughout this period. Following shortly after the decision in *Re S.J.C. Construction Co. Limited's Application*[54] and before the Court of Appeal's affirmation of that decision in *S.J.C. Construction Co. Limited v Sutton LBC*,[55] the Lands Tribunal in *Re Vaizey's Application*[56] held in that case that the 'correct measure for compensation was not to give the objector a share in the development value of the burdened land released...and that since the objector would suffer no substantial damage the compensation should be £75'. The Tribunal sought to distinguish the *S.J.C. Construction case* on a number of grounds including, *inter alia,* that in that case modification was granted on the ground of public interest and that the applicant had been a 'wrongdoer', whereas in *Vaizey's case* he was not. A stronger and more relevant ground, it is suggested, was that the decision in *Stokes v Cambridge Corporation*[57] was inapplicable in that it related to a case of compensation for the compulsory purchase of land to enable the development of an area which was landlocked. The 'ransom strip' valuation approach, however applicable it may be to a matter of compulsory purchase, has no relevance in a case involving the modification of a restrictive covenant. V.G. Wellings, QC (presiding) declined to make any award on the basis of *Stokes v Cambridge* as it would be 'quite unjust if I were to award to [the objector] a share of the development value' resulting from the modification.

In *Re Kershaw's Application*[58] Douglas Frank, QC (presiding) held that although the houses of the objectors might sustain some loss in market value, 'market value would not be the correct measure for compensation, since it would not allow for the loss peculiar to the occupier of a house...the correct test would be what the objectors, being reasonable persons would have accepted in friendly negotiations'. There appears in this statement to be a contradiction in that what 'reasonable persons in friendly negotiations' would have accepted is precisely 'market value' which is based on the assumption of a 'willing buyer and a willing seller'. The objectors are not 'willing sellers' of their rights under the restrictive covenants and a more appropriate basis would appear to be the loss in 'market value' plus some additional sum to represent the 'peculiar' loss that the objectors would suffer, i.e. to compensate for the element of compulsion in the loss of their particular (and personal) enjoyment of their property.

A return to the assessment of compensation in accordance with the Act occurred in *Re New Ideal Homes Limited's Application*[59] in which, having decided that there was 'no real detriment to objectors' the Tribunal awarded under para (ii) by way of compensation 'the sum of £51,000, being a sum to make up for any effect which the restriction had, at the time it was imposed, in reducing the consideration then received for the land affected by it'.[60] An attempt to claim compensation on the basis of a 'reasonable' proportion of the value of the site failed in *Re Briarwood Estates Limited's Application*[61] as the Tribunal did not consider that the objectors would suffer any loss in consequence of the proposed modification, it appearing that their main purpose in objecting was to claim compensation.

That the Lands Tribunal was still not at ease with the question of the assessment of compensation is illustrated by *Re Edwards' Application*[62] in which V.G. Wellings, QC (presiding) awarded £500 for the objector's loss of amenity adding that it 'is a sum which I calculated by a form of intelligent guesswork, not in any way related to what might be assumed to be diminution in value of the property as a result of the change'. Whereas in *Re Richards' Application*[63] and *Re Harper's Application*[64] the Tribunal awarded compensation on the basis of a sum representing the reduction of the original purchase price due to the imposition of the restrictions.

In some of its more recent decisions the Lands Tribunal has again had to consider the issue of 'development value'. In *Re Bradley Clare Estates Limited's Application*[65] where the objectors claimed compensation of £30,000 (one third of the agreed development value which the discharge or modification of the restrictions would release) the Tribunal, in granting the application, refused to award any compensation on the ground that the restrictions were obsolete by reason of changes in the character of the neighbourhood and the proposed development was in the public interest. *Contra*, in *Re Fisher & Gimson (Builders) Limited's Application*[66] the Tribunal, having held that 'the practical benefits were not of substantial value to the objectors' and that 'the restriction in impeding reasonable user was contrary to the public interest' then proceeded to award compensation of £6,000 as 'a share in the development value of the application land released by the modification'.

A recent case, namely *Re Cornick's Application*[67] should, if it is followed in subsequent decisions, have provided much needed guidance as to the limited relevance of 'development value' in any award of compensation. In that case Judge Bernard Marder, QC, President, held that although the discharge of the restriction would not affect the market value of the objector's property he would have asked a higher price for the land without the restriction thus reflecting any potential development value it possessed, and proceeded to award £5,000 as compensation.

This last case would seem to hold the key in that 'development value', which, as has been asserted, should never feature in an assessment of compensation under section 84(1) para (i), should only feature under section 84(1) para (ii) when an element of 'hope' value could have been foreseen at the time the restriction was imposed and it can be shown that the consideration then received for the land was discounted on that account.

There is, however, a case for the proposition that it is never appropriate for compensation under section 84(1) to include any element of 'hope' value, let alone 'development value', by reference to the objective of a restrictive covenant. A landowner imposes a restrictive covenant on the sale of land because he wants to control the use or development of the land sold in the interest of preserving or even enhancing the value, be it financial or environmental, of the land he retains, by either restricting all development, the density of development or some specified kind of development or use. The object is to 'prevent' all or some specific use or development.

Should an owner of land want at the time he disposes of land to safeguard a share in any future increase in value of the land sold resulting from development of that land he will not do so by way of a restrictive covenant. His motive is entirely different. Far from wishing to restrict development or use he is 'hoping' to participate in the fruits of some future development. In such case the sale will be subject to an agreement in terms providing that as and when planning permission is obtained for development he will be entitled either to a fixed sum or a percentage share in the 'development value' released by the planning permission.

If he proceeds by way of restrictive covenant he is not contemplating, far from encouraging, development of the land sold. He is entitled, under the Act, to compensation for either loss or disadvantage attributable to the removal of the restriction or a sum reflecting the reduced consideration he received at the time the restriction was entered into. The former excludes compensation based on any gain to the person relieved of the restrictive covenant; the latter excludes 'hope' value, or it should, as the restrictive covenant is not in contemplation of development, but rather the opposite, and therefore the reduced consideration was not in respect of any loss of future development value but reflected the increase in value of the retained land resulting from the reduced value of the land disposed of by reason of the restriction placed on its use or development.

Discharge or Modification and Compulsory Purchase

The Lands Tribunal seems to have had difficulty in at least one case involving a restrictive covenant and the assessment of compensation for compulsory acquisition, despite the fact that the effect of a restrictive covenant on the basis of assessment of compensation for compulsory acquisition is comparatively clear.[68] The saga of *Abbey Homesteads and Northamptonshire County Council* illustrates the need to keep a clear distinction between consideration of the two issues. The matter started in the Lands Tribunal in *Re Abbey Homesteads (Developments) Limited's Application*[69] where, upon preliminary issues, the Tribunal held that a condition requiring some 1.23 hectares to be 'made available for educational purposes' out of a larger area of some 13 to 14 hectares with planning consents for residential development, was 'a positive covenant'. On appeal, in *Abbey Homesteads (Developments) Ltd v Northamptonshire County Council*[70] the Court of Appeal reversed the decision of the Lands Tribunal holding that the 'covenant was just as restrictive as the seminal one in *Tulk v Moxhay*' and the compensation payable on the compulsory purchase of the 1.23 hectacres of land must be determined on the basis that such land was affected by the restrictive covenant.

Having determined the legal basis for the assessment of compensation the matter came before the Lands Tribunal again in *Re Abbey Homesteads*

(Developments) Ltd v Northamptonshire County Council[71] for determination of the award of compensation for the compulsory purchase. In awarding compensation of £300,000 the Tribunal held that 'the diminution in the value of the land caused by the restrictive covenant must be disregarded under the Pointe-Gourde Principle'[72] and that 'the Court of Appeal was dealing with the real world when determining that the land must be valued for compensation purposes subject to the restrictive covenant, but the Lands Tribunal, in assessing compensation, was not concerned with the real world, and so was unfettered by that decision'. Nonetheless it made an alternative award of £255,000 (£300,000 less 15% to cover diminution caused by the existence of the covenant) in case its findings were incorrect. The matter was again considered by the Court of Appeal in *Abbey Homesteads (Developments) Ltd v Northamptonshire C.C.*[73] Allowing the appeal, the Court held that 'the interest to be valued was the freehold of the site subject to the restrictive covenant...and that neither the Pointe Gourde Principle nor the Land Compensation Act, 1961, section 9 [74] could apply so as to remove that restriction or require it to be disregarded'.[75]

The Court of Appeal accepted the alternative valuation of £255,000 (full market value less 15%) arrived at in the Lands Tribunal on the making of 'various assumptions based on the position in the no-scheme world' adding that 'the Lands Tribunal, as we were reminded, is a specialist Tribunal, specifically charged with dealing, amongst other matters, with problems of compensation. There is no material upon which we could disagree with that judgment of the President'. Put bluntly, law is for the Court of Appeal, assessment of compensation is for the Lands Tribunal. Provided that in assessing compensation the Lands Tribunal follows the law the Court will not challenge the quantum of the assessment.

The restriction in the *Abbey Homesteads case* was enshrined in an agreement made under section 52 of the Town & Country Planning Act, 1971 and attention must now be directed to the way in which the Lands Tribunal has exercised its jurisdiction in applications for the discharge or modification of restrictions in planning agreements.

The Lands Tribunal and Planning Agreements

Although the power to deal with applications for the discharge or modification of restrictions in planning agreements made under the Town

& Country Planning Acts had been with the Lands Tribunal from its inception in 1950 it appears that the first occasion on which it was called upon to consider such an application was in *Re Beecham Groups Limited's Application.*[76] The Local Planning Authority had entered into an agreement under section 37 of the Town & Country Planning Act, 1962, as part of a planning permission, with the applicant that certain land be kept free of development in line with its declared planning policy to retain open land between two distinct settlements. The applicant had obtained planning permission on appeal to the Secretary of State for the Environment in spite of the fact that his Inspector, after an Inquiry, had recommended otherwise. The Lands Tribunal allowed the modification on grounds including, *inter alia,* that the application site was the only piece of land available and suitable for the proposed building; that the Tribunal had jurisdiction to modify or discharge restrictions imposed by planning agreements; that important factors in the case were the decision of the Secretary of State, and that the Council did not own any land in the area and had not put forward any objection on aesthetic grounds.

Apart from the fact that the Tribunal appears not to have indicated the sub-section of section 84(1) under which it arrived at its decision, its reasoning that one of the important factors in the case was that 'the Council did not own any land in the area' demonstrates a confusion as to the purpose of town and country planning law and practice under which decisions are taken in the public interest and not for the 'benefit of the Council'.

Fortunately the reasoning and apparent perversity of the decision in *Beecham's case* was not repeated later in 1986 in *Re Martin's Application.*[77] The Local Planning Authority had refused a planning application for development on a site, protected under a section 37 agreement restricting its use to that of a private open space only. The decision was reversed by the Minister on appeal but the Council nevertheless insisted on its rights under the agreement. The Tribunal, dismissing the application, held that the restriction was 'taken to protect the amenities of the area and that the provisions of section 37, under which the Council was to be treated as if it owned adjacent land, were intended to give the covenant the validity of a normal restrictive covenant'. The Tribunal added:

Decisions of the Secretary of State on planning questions do not necessarily determine whether the restriction ought to be deemed obsolete or whether, in impeding reasonable user, it is a practical benefit to the Local Authority or is contrary to the public interest. These questions have to be determined on their merits.

This view was upheld two years later in the Court of Appeal in *Re Martin's Application*[78] when the Court held, in dismissing an appeal, that 'a grant of planning permission was merely a circumstance that the Lands Tribunal should take into account' and 'did not necessarily require that the Lands Tribunal discharge the covenant'. It found on the facts that there was no ground to interfere with the conclusion of the Lands Tribunal that the purpose of the covenant was not obsolete, notwithstanding the existence of the planning permission, and that the covenant should not be discharged. Similarly, in *Re Houdret & Company's Application*[79] the Lands Tribunal dismissed an application on the ground that 'the Council would be injured in its capacity as custodian of the public interest if the modification sought was allowed and that this was of substantial value and advantage to it', adding that money would be no adequate compensation for the loss.

In *Re Towner's & Goddard's Application*[80] the Tribunal allowed an application to modify a restriction in a section 52 agreement made under the Town & Country Planning Act, 1971 holding that, 'although the Council was right to guard the Green Belt jealously, the Council, as custodian of the public interest, would suffer no injury in this case'. *Contra* in *Re Whiting's Application*[81] the Tribunal refused to modify a restriction entered into in a section 52 agreement on the ground that 'the National Trust in its capacity as custodian of the natural beauty of the land would be seriously injured by the modification sought, suffering a loss or disadvantage, aesthetic in character, for which money would provide no adequate compensation'.

The appropriateness of compensation in cases concerning the discharge or modification of restrictions in planning agreements has been a matter of comment and opinion in two recent articles in the Journal of Planning and Environment Law. In the one, the author[82] states that ' money will never be adequate compensation for a local authority or other public body acting in the public interest' and in the other[83] that 'planning and similar agreements taken for public purposes cannot generally be released by the payment of money'.

Most recently, in *Re Willis's Application*,[84] the Tribunal has confirmed the general view, adding that:

> although it is accepted that money could never be adequate compensation for insubstantial loss arising from the discharge or modification of a restriction

where the restriction was held by a public body acting as custodian of the public interest, so that an application in such cases must fail, this would not be the position where such a body had suffered no loss...as the question of compensation would not arise to defeat the application.

These views emphasise the clear distinction that has to be drawn between those matters where the local authority or other public body is acting as custodian or guardian of the public interest and those matters which are in furtherance of the interests of public bodies and private individuals.

An important gloss on these decisions was provided by *Re Jones' & White & Co's Application*.[85] In that case the District Council sought to oppose an application to modify a restriction in a section 52 agreement where it had itself been responsible for granting planning permission for the proposed development. The Tribunal held that the section 52 agreement 'enabled the District Council to consider matters from a subjective point of view, whereas when exercising its functions in relation to planning permission, it had to be objective. The District Council had in submission drawn a clear distinction between the general powers to control development under the Town & Country Planning Acts and those flowing from the benefit of a restriction upon the use of land in a specific agreement or deed'. For this proposition the District Council relied on the decision of the Court of Appeal in *Re Martin's Application*[86] in which Fox, LJ said 'it seems to me that, while the two régimes impinge upon each other to some extent, they constitute different systems of control and each has, and retains an independent existence'. This persuasive argument influenced the Lands Tribunal in dismissing the application, regardless of the fact that a restriction imposed in a section 52 or any other planning agreement (or obligation) is attached to the planning permission and is part of it and is therefore not in the category of a free-standing restrictive covenant, where the distinction so clearly drawn by Fox, LJ would apply.

Two recent cases show how far the Lands Tribunal has moved from the position it first adopted in *Beecham's case* back in 1980. In *Re Wallace & Co's. Application*[87] the Lands Tribunal dismissed an application on the ground that 'the object of the section 52 agreement...was to keep restricted land open' and although impeding a reasonable user it 'secured a practical benefit of substantial value to the Local Authority as custodian of the public interest'. Even though the Local Authority possessed no land in the area it could in any event under section 52 enforce the restriction as if it possessed adjoining land. Similarly in *Re Hopcraft's Application*[88] the

Lands Tribunal dismissed an application on the ground that 'the proposed development would be damaging to visual amenity and would bring about intrusion on a significant scale of an urban form of commercial development into a pleasant open area which should remain open ...the public interest required that the application land be kept free from development'.

Finally in *Re Williamson's Application*[89] the Lands Tribunal, in modifying a restriction in a section 52 agreement so as to allow a use in accordance with a planning permission obtained on appeal, concluded that the 'fact that planning permission had been granted for the proposed use was taken into account by the Tribunal but was held not to be binding, as the planning régime was separate from the restrictive covenant régime'. Thereby, yet again, compounding the confusion as the restriction in a planning agreement attached to a planning permission is part of the 'planning régime', not part of the 'restrictive covenant régime'.

This anomalous situation has at last been recognised by Parliament and, following the amendment to section 106 of the Town & Country Planning Act, 1990 by the Planning & Compensation Act, 1991, applications for the discharge or modification of restrictions in planning agreements or obligations (entered into after 25 October 1991) will be determined on appeal by the Secretary of State for the Environment and not by the Lands Tribunal, although agreements entered into before the coming into operation of the Act will still only be capable of discharge or modification under section 84(1) and will remain within the jurisdiction of the Lands Tribunal.

We commenced our commentary on the Discharge or Modification of Restrictive Covenants with a quote from G.H. Newsom and it is appropriate to end with another,[90] taken from the last of a long and valuable series of articles contributed by him to the Journal of Planning & Environment Law on the jurisdiction and practice of the Lands Tribunal in the matter of restrictive covenants:

> [T]he jurisdiction [of the Lands Tribunal], as increased by the provisions of the Law of Property Act 1969, and the procedure as re-arranged by the amendments to the Lands Tribunal rules..., is operating in a business-like way along lines that are becoming well understood.

Satisfaction with the procedure and more pertinently the resulting decisions of the Lands Tribunal has never been universal and there appears to have been times in the past when its decisions have been unsound on matters of fact and questionable in matters of law even though supported by the Court of Appeal.

It is over 70 years since section 84(1) of the Law of Property Act, 1925 came into operation. The varying interpretations of meaning of s. 84(1) and the perceived inconsistencies of decisions, first by the Official Arbitrator and later by the Lands Tribunal itself, have already been the subject of comment, which it would be tedious and unnecessary to repeat here.

The period of most vociferous criticism probably occurred in the mid 1960's and was expressed in measured terms in the Law Commission Report on Restrictive Covenants[91] which, although dealing primarily with the creation of a new interest in land called a 'Restrictive Land Obligation', made specific recommendations for widening the powers of the Lands Tribunal to enable it to consider 'all the existing circumstances including the age of the restriction, the circumstances in which it was imposed, the planning position and the development policy for the area'.

More forthright criticism appeared at this time in the law journals and the professional press and found probably its most trenchant expression in an article by A.R. Mellows in the Conveyancer and Property Lawyer, of which the following is an extract from the author's[92] conclusion:

> There is an uneasy compromise between planning restrictions and restrictive covenants. If the whole basis of the planning legislation is to secure that land is put to the use which is best from the point of view of the community, why should that object be frustrated by privately imposed covenants when most private property rights are overridden. [The] position would be improved if it were clearly recognised that the grant of planning permission should be taken into account when dealing with section 84 applications. At present, one mentions the planning aspect of the matter and hopes the Tribunal will not be incensed: if he is a lawyer, he is far more likely to be than if he is a surveyor. Planning has had a striking impact on English real property law; perhaps it is a pity that more effort has not been made to dovetail it into the previous law so that a coherent result could be produced.

Few surveyors, and it is suggested even fewer lawyers, charged with the task of advising property owners contesting applications for the discharge or modification of restrictive covenants would have supported then (or, for that matter, now) the proposition that implies the universal supremacy of planning law. The premise that private property interests should be subservient to public administrative decisions is contrary not only to English land law - an exception being compulsory acquisition which carries with it the right to compensation - but also to planning law itself. Planning legislation, through the instrument of the planning permission, restores to the individual property owner (or occupier) rights which the same planning legislation had denied him. To follow the line of reasoning whereby a planning permission frustrated by a restrictive covenant should override that restrictive covenant would result in the effective transfer without compensation of a right which the applicant for planning permission had not previously enjoyed and which, in law, 'belonged' to another.

As has been pointed out many times, both in the Lands Tribunal and in the Court of Appeal, the two régimes exist side by side. There is no more justification or support now for a proposition implying the supremacy of planning law than when it was first mooted 30 years ago. The two régimes are distinct, fulfilling different purposes, although at times they may have similar objectives. All the evidence supports the view that they should remain distinct.

The reference to the attitude of the Lands Tribunal to planning matters, however, had substance and was largely remedied by the amendments to section 84(1) made by the Law of Property Act, 1969, embracing the suggestions made in general terms by the Law Commission in its 1967 Report. Mellows had expressed a commonly held view, borne out it is suggested by an examination of the reported cases of the Lands Tribunal in the Planning and Compensation Reports of the time, and the legislature responded.

The 'dovetailing' of planning into English land law raises many issues. If by 'dovetailing' is meant no more than a recognition by each that the other exists and that the two systems have to be cognisant of the other's effect in land transactions this has been achieved. If by 'dovetailing' is meant 'fusion', in the sense that where the two conflict one, presumably (according to Mellows) planning, should prevail, that is a proposition which would make the 'equality of the law' as between private landed interests subservient to the vagaries of decision-making in the 'public arena'.

It might be argued that in the operation of section 84(1) in particular (and probably in the area of restrictive covenant control in general) a distinction should be drawn between planning decisions taken in the wider public interest, as for example the regeneration of a town centre, the development of a major industrial or business park or a 'free-standing' shopping centre or mall, where the 'public interest' may (and perhaps even should) prevail, and planning permissions for narrower and essentially private purposes, as for example a house or house extension or a change of use from a house to a shop or office, where the planning permission of itself would rarely justify the discharge or modification of a restrictive covenant (taken to protect the property of a neighbouring landowner) on the grounds that the restriction frustrated the implementation of the planning permission.

That there is a conflict is to an extent demonstrated by the many attempts of the Law Commission to address such issues as the relationship between restrictive covenants and positive covenants, and between restrictive covenants and planning (agreements), the creation of new forms of land obligation and the automatic lapse of 'old' restrictive covenants. The virtually complete lack of any action on the Reports of the Law Commission may be attributed to the absence of parliamentary time or that, in respect of discharge or modification under section 84(1), the adaptability of the Lands Tribunal has resulted in the jurisdiction 'operating in a business-like way along lines that are becoming well understood' and so rendering change unnecessary.

We conclude this part with two general propositions:

(1) The Restrictive Covenant, through the mechanism for discharge or modification under the Law of Property Act,1925, section 84(1), is adaptable to changing circumstances whilst at the same time providing for the protection of private property interests where still relevant. Such relevance could be enhanced in practice if conveyancers were more often prepared to 'weed out' spent, anachronistic and patently obsolete restrictive covenants, thereby reducing the need for recourse to section 84(1).

(2) The Restrictive Covenant is complementary to planning control but essentially separate and distinct therefrom. It is an important, and arguably an indispensable, 'tool' in estate management and development control by private individuals, particularly in those cases where planning control may be supine, anachronistic or occasionally perverse. Furthermore, it is enforceable by the 'beneficiary' in and at his own discretion, whereas the enforcement of planning control is in the hands of another, namely the Local Planning Authority, exercisable, or not as the case may be, at its discretion and by its choice.

Meanwhile, two issues continue to confront the restrictive covenant, namely (i) the possible reform of the law as it might affect the restrictive covenant itself and its relationship with other interests and (ii) its future interface with planning and environmental law and control. These issues are the subject-matter for the final two chapters.

Notes

1 Town & Country Planning Act, 1947, section 25; Town & Country Planning Act, 1962, section 37; Town & Country Planning Act, 1971, s.52, and Town & Country Planning Act, 1990, section 106.
2 (1970) 23 P & CR 102.
3 (1971) 25 P & CR 115.
4 (1972) 25 P & CR 233.
5 (1974) 28 P & CR 200.
6 This case is considered again later together with other cases dealing with compensation.
7 (1974) 30 P & CR 527.
8 (1975) 31 P & CR 180.
9 (1976) 33 P & CR 141.
10 (1976) 35 P & CR 124.
11 (1978) 38 P & CR 251.
12 (1980) 42 P & CR 114.
13 (1983) 48 P & CR 317.
14 (1996) 71 P & CR 440.
15 Planning agreements are dealt with later as a separate item.
16 (1993) 67 P & CR 101.
17 (1993) 67 P & CR 110.
18 (1993) 67 P & CR 236.
19 (1971) 23 P & CR 116.
20 (1973) 25 P & CR 223.
21 (1980) 41 P & CR 390.
22 (1981) 43 P & CR 40.
23 (1982) 44 P & CR 239.
24 (1987) 54 P & CR 386.
25 (1987) 55 P & CR 400.
26 (1991) 62 P & CR 450.
27 (1993) 66 P & CR 112.
28 *Re Dr Barnardo's Homes National Incorporated Association's Application* (1955) 7 P & CR 176.
29 Cases concerning discretion decided before 1970 have already been commented on in chapter 4.
30 (1970) 23 P & CR 110.
31 (1973) 26 P & CR 441.
32 (1974) 30 P & CR 451.
33 (1968) 19 P & CR 516.

34 (1974) 30 P & CR 451.
35 (1978) 36 P & CR 285.
36 (1966) 71 P & CR 440.
37 (1988) 56 P & CR 142.
38 (1990) 60 P & CR 354.
39 (1996) 72 P & CR 353.
40 (1998) 75 P & CR 117.
41 (1973) 26 P & CR 156.
42 (1996) 72 P & CR 439.
43 (1997) 73 P & CR 126.
44 (1973) 26 P & CR 156.
45 A comprehensive account of the operation of this approach is given in Preston and Newsom's *Restrictive Covenants Affecting Freehold Land*, 9th edition by G.L. Newsom, Sweet & Maxwell, 1998, pp. 248-259.
46 (1971) 23 P & CR 413.
47 (1974) 35 P & CR 440.
48 (1986) 52 P & CR 99.
49 (1974) 28 P & CR 200.
50 (1962) 13 P & CR 77.
51 (1975) 29 P & CR 322.
52 W.A. Leach, FRICS, *Compensation under section 84 of the Law of Property Act 1925*, (1976) JPL 18-30.
53 *Ibid*, (1976) JPL 18, at 27.
54 (1974) 28 P & CR 200.
55 (1975) 29 P & CR 322.
56 (1974) 28 P & CR 517.
57 (1962) 13 P & CR 77.
58 (1975) 31 P & CR 187.
59 (1978) 36 P & CR 476.
60 A not inconsiderable sum in 1978, particularly as the loss occasioned 'no real detriment'. This case is an example of where it is advantageous to substantiate a claim under para (ii) of section 84(1) based on reduced consideration rather than under para (i) based on resulting loss.
61 (1979) 39 P & CR 419.
62 (1983) 47 P & CR 458.
63 (1983) 47 P & CR 467.
64 (1986) 52 P & CR 104.
65 (1987) 55 P & CR 126.
66 (1992) 65 P & CR 312.
67 (1994) 68 P & CR 372. Two years previously it had been held in *Surrey CC v Bredero Homes* [1992] 3 All ER 302, that the basis of compensation was the loss suffered by reason of the breach and not a share of the profits. This view has been reinforced in a recent case, viz. *Jaggard v Sawyer and Another* [1995] 1 WLR 269, in which it was held that 'in assessing damages to compensate the plaintiff for the continuing invasions of her rights the court would value those rights, not at a ransom price, but on the price which might reasonably be demanded by the plaintiff for relaxing the covenant'.
68 Where land with the *benefit* of a restrictive covenant is compulsorily acquired the increase in value resulting from the benefit will be reflected in the (higher) price paid

for the land. Where land with the *burden* of a restrictive covenant is compulsorily acquired the reduction in value resulting from the burden will be reflected in the (lower) price paid for the land. It may be noted that in the latter case the covenantee's claim to compensation is limited to 'injurious affection', namely the diminution in the value of his land resulting from the acquisition of the 'servient land' with the consequential loss of the benefit of the restrictive covenant, and with no 'ransom' element recoverable.

69 (1984) 49 P & CR 263.

70 (1986) 53 P & CR 1.

71 (1990) 61 P & CR 295.

72 In essence, the Pointe-Gourde principle (originating in the decision of the House of Lords in *Pointe Gourde Quarrying and Transport Co. Ltd. v Sub-Intendent of Crown Lands* [1947] AC 565 PC and expanded in later statute and case law) provides that in the assessment of compensation for land following compulsory purchase, any increase or decrease in value arising as a result of the 'scheme' necessitating the compulsory acquisition is to be disregarded.

73 (1992) 64 P & CR 377.

74 This section, which is an extension of the Pointe-Gourde principle, requires depreciation in the value of land to be ignored in the assessment of compulsory purchase compensation where such depreciation is attributable to an indication of future compulsory acquisition having been given in a development plan or 'by any other means'.

75 Notwithstanding that the restrictive covenant arose from a planning agreement, with the beneficiary being the local authority concerned, it was essentially part of the 'interest' itself and not just part of a scheme or project for compulsory acquisition.

76 (1980) 41 P & CR 369.

77 (1986) 53 P & CR 146.

78 (1988) 57 P & CR 119.

79 (1989) 58 P & CR 310.

80 (1989) 58 P & CR 316.

81 (1988) 58 P & CR 321.

82 H.C. Abraham, *The Local Authority as Objector to Applications for Modification or Discharge of Restrictive Covenants,* (1994) JPL 792, at 796.

83 G. Chesman, *Restrictive Covenants - An Update,* (1994) JPL 783, at 786.

84 (1998) 76 P & CR 97.

85 (1989) 58 P & CR 512.

86 (1988) 57 P & CR 119.

87 (1993) 66 P & CR 124.

88 (1993) 66 P & CR 475.

89 (1994) 68 P & CR 384.

90 G.H. Newsom, QC, *Restrictive Covenants* (1984) JPL 847, at 852.

91 Law Commission, *Transfer of Land - Report on Restrictive Covenants,* Law Com. No. 11, 1967.

92 A.R. Mellows, Solicitor, *Planning and Restrictive Covenants,* (1964) 28 Conv. (NS) 190, at 204.

PART III

THE FUTURE FOR RESTRICTIVE COVENANTS

6 The Restrictive Covenant and Law Reform

The restrictive covenant has retained a degree of utility for 150 years. For over 70 years this has been due, in no small measure, to the existence and operation of section 84 of the Law of Property Act, 1925 and for the last 50 years in spite of (and some would say because of) the advent of comprehensive planning control in the public interest. But what are the prospects for the future? There have, since the Wilberforce Committee[1] reported in 1965, been numerous suggestions for reform but virtually nothing has changed. The issues appear to fall into three main categories, namely:

(1) Some form of unification of the law relating to restrictive covenants and positive covenants.

(2) Some more radical reform embracing all servitudes.

(3) Some clarification/reform vis-a-vis restrictive covenant control and planning control whereby either restrictive covenant control is subsumed in, or made subservient to planning control or, more rarely, whether some of the elements of planning control could not be transferred to private restrictive covenant control.[2]

The Wilberforce Committee in 1965 was not the first to recommend reform of the law of covenants. Official committees have been considering reform of the law of servitudes since the early 19th century and the Real Property Commissioners in their Third Report in 1832[3] recommended that for restrictive covenants outside of leases equitable remedies be available except against a purchaser for value without notice of the covenant - the view taken by the courts 16 years later in *Tulk v Moxhay* [4] - and went on to suggest the same treatment for positive covenants, but Parliament still has not implemented this recommendation.

Reporting on the desirability of amending the law relating to *positive* covenants, the Wilberforce Committee argued for a fundamental reform of the existing position and for the the assignability and enforcement of positive covenants to be, as far as possible. assimilated with that of negative covenants. The view was taken that 'broadly speaking, and subject to certain necessary qualifications, in the case of positive covenants as in that of negative covenants, the burden should run with the land encumbered, and the benefit should run with the land advantaged'.[5]

Concerning the question of the extent of the sphere of enforceability, the Committee could see 'no reason why a covenant…should continue to be enforceable by the original covenantee when he had parted with his land, or against the original covenantor when he no longer [owned] the servient land'.[6] Believing the obligations to be 'of concern only to owners and occupiers for the time being of the land affected',[7] it recommended that the benefit should inure for the benefit of all owners and occupiers of the land but that the burden 'should fall only upon persons having for the time being an interest in the servient land'.[8] The opinion being that, were this so, the effect would be an assimilation, in this respect, to the situation regarding easements 'which are enforceable only as between the dominant and servient owners for the time being'.[9]

In 1967 the Law Commission reported on a study which it had made of *restrictive* covenants.[10] Finding the current law defective, the Commission thought there was an urgent need for 'a clear code of law governing the creation and enforcement of covenants'.[11] A reformulation of the law was proposed which involved the creation of a new interest in land called a 'Land Obligation'. Imposed on specified land for the benefit of other specified land, so that the burden and benefit would run automatically, such obligations would 'be enforceable only by and against the persons currently concerned with the land as owners of interests in it or occupiers of it', and they would be 'more akin to easements than to covenants'.[12] Moreover the Report noted that the substance of the proposals 'was applicable to positive as well as to restrictive obligations'.[13]

A few years later the Law Commission reviewed the subject of appurtenant rights as a whole, it being considered that various earlier efforts had suffered the disadvantage of a piecemeal approach.[14] Desirous of giving the whole subject a coherent structure, the Commission proposed a reformulation of the law in which, *inter alia*, there would be an assimilation of easements, profits à prendre, restrictive covenants and positive covenants under a new classification of 'Land Obligations'.

With the aim of overcoming the illogicalities and uncertainties of the existing law, the Commission's Working Paper recommended eliminating most of the distinctions among the existing categories of servitudes. All land obligations could exist as either legal or equitable interests; all would be subject to similar registration requirements; all could run with both servient and dominant land, binding only those with an interest in the former and enforceable only by those with an interest in the latter, and all would be subject to the jurisdiction of the Lands Tribunal. The Working Paper also included a recommendation to increase the power of the Lands Tribunal to allow it to impose land obligations as well as to discharge or modify them.

Having recommended eliminating most of the distinctions, the Working Paper recognised that there are fundamental differences among servitudes and proposed a classification system similar to the current categories. The new system would comprise:

(1) Obligations which restrict the use of the servient land for the advantage of the dominant land - thus including restrictive covenants and negative easements.[15]

(2) & (3) Obligations to execute or maintain any works on the servient land or to pay or contribute to the cost of works on the dominant land - thus including positive covenants and the (anomalous) easement of a right to have fences maintained.

(4) Positive easements.[16]

(5) Appurtenant profits à prendre.

In 1977 the Law Commission announced a resumption of work on appurtenant rights, nothing having come to fruition from the 1971 Working Paper. An intention was expressed to consider certain distinct issues in the arena of appurtenant rights, with the law reform of positive and restrictive covenants seen as a priority.[17]

The Commission's proposals appeared in 1984,[18] it being made clear in the introduction to the Report that the mainspring for the work was the unsatisfactory state of the law regarding the inability to impose a positive covenant in such a way as to bind successive owners of the burdened land. The broader efforts of 1971 were believed in retrospect to have been over ambitious, and it was thought that reform should concentrate on welding positive and restrictive covenants into a unified system.

With regard to the perceived need to weld positive and restrictive covenants into a unified system, the question was whether it would be possible to overcome the main problem of the burden of a positive covenant not running simply by saying that the law for positive covenants should be the same as for restrictive covenants.[19] The answer to the question was that it would not be possible, inasmuch as the existing law of restrictive covenants was felt not to be suitable for positive covenants.

Two main reasons for this unsuitability were given and it is necessary to examine them in some detail because of the way in which they highlight the difference between positive and restrictive covenants and, consequently, the particular nature of the latter.

The first reason related to the 'character' of the person upon whom the burden of observing a covenant might properly be laid. Subject to notice and registration rules, the owner of any interest in the burdened land, albeit a very small one, was obliged to observe the restrictive covenant. This, it was thought, was 'as it should be, because the restrictive covenant requires people merely to refrain from doing something'.[20] By contrast, positive covenants required of a person that they actually do something, which might indeed be burdensome and expensive. It was believed that it would be wrong if, for example, a weekly tenant was made personally liable to perform a positive covenant such as one 'to erect and maintain a costly sea wall'.[21] Accordingly, 'liability to perform a positive covenant [could] not rest on all those interested in the burdened land'.[22]

The second reason concerned the appropriateness of available remedies. With the burden of a restrictive covenant running only in equity, equitable remedies were alone available for its enforcement. This might be of little consequence with restrictive covenants where injunctions would be the most frequently sought remedy.[23] However, for positive covenants a legal remedy had to be available. The notion of enforcing a covenant to pay money via an equitable remedy was 'wholly artificial' and, furthermore, 'the normal remedy for breach of a covenant to carry out works [had to] be legal damages'.[24] In the view of the Commission this point went 'to the heart of the conceptual nature of the covenant'.[25] Unless the burden ran at law a legal remedy could not be available and the burden could not run at law unless the benefit amounted to a legal rather than an equitable interest in land. Thus the law of restrictive covenants was fundamentally unsuitable.

Having reached the view that the existing restrictive covenant régime could not simply be extended to positive covenants and that the creation of a new régime was called for, it was imperative that faults which currently beset the control of restrictive covenants should not be reproduced. For instance, it would not be appropriate to incorporate the rule that as between the original contracting parties the covenant remained enforceable even after they had disposed of their respective lands.[26]

In contemplating the creation of a new régime the Commission were of the view that the existing law on restrictive covenants could not properly be left in place alongside and that the only way forward was to include both positive and restrictive covenants in the reforms and to establish a unified system.[27]

Recommending a comprehensive reform and using the law of easements as a model the Commission envisaged the creation of a new interest in land, namely a 'Land Obligation'. Under the system it would be possible for positive or negative obligations to be imposed on one piece of land for the benefit of another and they would 'be enforceable by...the owner for the time being of the one piece of land against the owner for the time being of the other'.[28] Further, as with an easement, the new interest would 'normally subsist as a legal interest in land and be enforceable by legal remedies'.[29] However, a Land Obligation (again as with an easement) would be able to exist either at law or in equity.

The Commission saw Land Obligations as falling into two categories, being either *neighbour obligations* 'to be used where the obligation is imposed on one plot for the benefit of another plot'[30] or *development obligations* 'to be used where an area of land is to be divided into separately owned but inter-dependent units such as a housing development or a block of flats'.[31] The former the Commission envisaged as taking the shape of either a restrictive obligation, or a positive obligation (calling for the execution of works or services), or a reciprocal payment obligation (requiring payment for expenses incurred by a person fulfilling a positive covenant). The latter the Commission envisaged as able not only to take such forms but also to 'require servient land to be used in a particular way which benefits the whole or part of the development...and to require payment to a manager for expenditure incurred'.[32]

Finally, three further points from the Law Commission's Report of 1984 are of note. First, the Commission took care to deal with the view that because positive covenants involve expenditure it is inappropriate for all those with interests in the servient land, however small, to become personally responsible for their observance and in this regard made special recommendations.[33] Secondly, as a happy prospect for many law students, 'the highly technical rules determining whether the benefit and burden of restrictive covenant may pass to new owners of the land [would] disappear'.[34] Thirdly, the introduction of two new remedies were suggested, namely self-help in the event of failure to execute works, and the creation of a charge over the servient land where performance of the obligation was vital.[35]

Despite the extent of the endeavour leading to the Report and its recommendations no new régime has materialised. In 1991, however, the Law Commission produced a further Report in the sphere of covenants recommending the phasing out of most restrictive covenants after the introduction of a Land Obligation scheme. It went on to propose that all restrictive covenants should lapse after 80 years from their creation but, where a covenant was not obsolete, the person having the benefit of it would be able to seek its replacement with a Land Obligation having similar effect.[36]

Given the length and intensity of the reform programme the lack of legislative advance calls for comment. It is true that the concept of the Land Obligation has been applied in the field of planning law, substituting for the Planning Agreement the Planning Obligation[37] but this is a matter of distinct particularity in the general context. There may be a number of reasons why there is not yet in existence a new régime. One which immediately springs to mind is that there may be neither parliamentary time nor inclination. As Lord Denning once observed in another context, '[Parliament] were not interested in reform in the law. There were no votes in it'.[38] So to suggest, however, is too simplistic.

The idea of giving a coherent structure to the whole arena of servitudes could indeed have been a step too far. The notion of bringing more closely together the law relating to positive and negative covenants and thereby in particular enabling the running of the burden of the former might well lack the degree of unanimity that would ensure its advance.

Undoubtedly there is a powerful body of thought which sees wisdom in drawing together positive and negative covenants. It is in no sense fleeting as the length of the reform process gives witness. In particular the rule denying the running of the burden of a positive covenant, even though capable of circumvention,[39] can often result in a covenant being without remedy, a situation which cannot be satisfactory.

On the other hand, when it comes to any change in the issue at the heart of the matter, i.e. the inability of the burden of the positive covenant to run, the judiciary, at the highest level, shows no enthusiasm for change. The lack of support for reform was prominently displayed not long ago in *Rhone v Stevens*,[40] where the House of Lords refused to allow the running of the burden of a positive covenant to keep a roof in wind and water tight condition.

In refusing to overrule the principle of *Austerberry v Corporation of Oldham*,[41] Lord Templeman (with the concurrence of all their Lordships) adverted to the fact that:[42]

[F]or over 100 years it [had] been clear and accepted law that Equity [would] enforce negative covenants against freehold land, but [had] no power to enforce positive covenants against successors in title of the land.

Considering whether or not to overrule the *Austerberry* principle, the learned judge believed that this would create 'difficulties, anomalies and uncertainties'.[43]

To Lord Templeman, mindful of the fact that equity must always follow the law, compelling an owner to comply with a positive covenant entered into by his predecessors in title would flatly contradict 'the common law rule that a person cannot be made liable upon a contract unless he was a party to it'. Whereas, enjoining a successor from acting in breach of a restrictive covenant is only to prevent that successor 'from exercising a right which he never acquired'.[44] In his Lordship's opinion 'to enforce a positive covenant would be to enforce a personal obligation against a person who has not covenanted, [whereas] to enforce negative covenants is only to treat land as subject to a restriction'.[45]

Nevertheless, there is much force in a criticism made of this stance on the lines that 'a covenant, whether positive or negative, is in essence a contract and, as the rules in *Spencer's case*[46] show, there is no reason why the burden of positive and negative covenants cannot run in similar fashion'.[47] By contrast, it can be equally well argued that positive and negative covenants differ in too many respects for comfortable assimilation, as for example in their thrust, in the range of persons who might properly be thought the appropriate subject of obligatory observance, and in the type of remedy most suitable to meet the need of a person aggrieved by breach. Indeed, they are different creatures, the positive covenant being directed to the performance of acts, whilst the essence of the restrictive covenant is the control of use, a characteristic which brings in its train a kinship with planning control.

In consequence it may be best to recognise their respective rôles, to preserve the distinction, and to resist the law reformers' predeliction for 'tidying the law'. If, however, reform is to take place it may perhaps be better pursued in another direction. It could be that it would be more helpful if attention were directed to strengthening the rôle of the restrictive covenant (rather than confusing and possibly weakening it through amalgamation with the positive covenant, which is not an instrument of control) by considering whether, in certain circumstances, defined restrictive covenants could exist as legal interests, for example those specifying main categories of use (residential, commercial and industrial) and those safeguarding amenity (density, open space provision and the protection of views by means of restrictions on building within a defined 'envelope'). At present, easements and covenants are complementary in that easements deal with the major issues of 'enjoyment' - way (access), air, light, support and water - and as such can exist as 'legal interests', whereas restrictive covenants deal with the more 'intimate' and 'qualitative' issues of 'enjoyment' - use, density, design, amenity, freedom from noxious and noisome activities, namely what are today generally described as 'environmental' matters - and as such can only exist as 'equitable interests'. From an estate management viewpoint however they provide equally the basic tools for the private control of the use and development of the land of another. There could be a certain value and logic in the elevation of the more significant restrictive covenants such that they had the capacity to exist at law, albeit the full implications of such a concept and the ensuing practical consequences would need to be the subject of detailed examination before any legislative changes were contemplated.

Notes

1   Report of the Committee on *Positive Covenants Affecting Land,* Cmnd. 2719, 1965.
2   Categories (1) and (2) are the subject matter of this chapter; (3) is considered in chapter 7 - The Restrictive Covenant and Planning Control.
3   An Inquiry into the Law of England respecting Real Property, 44-58, 71-73.
4   (1848) 2 Ph 774.
5   Cmnd. 2719, 1965, para 10.
6   *Ibid,* para 18.
7   *Ibid.*
8   *Ibid,* para 19.
9   *Ibid,* para 18.
10 Law Commission, Report No. 11, *Transfer of Land: Report on Restrictive Covenants,* 1967.
11 *Ibid,* para 24.
12 *Ibid,* para 27.
13 *Ibid,* para 30.
14 Law Commission, Working Paper No. 36, *Transfer of Land: Appurtenant Rights,* 1971.
15 A negative easement is one which 'gives the owner of the dominant tenement a right to stop his neighbour doing something on his (the neighbour's) own land...long recognised in the cases of the easements of light and support (Cheshire & Burn, *Modern Law of Real Property,* 1994, p. 527).
16 A positive easement is one which allows the owner of the dominant tenement to do or place something, or make use of some facility, on the servient land, for example

easements of way and water.

17 Law Commission, Report No. 78, Eleventh Annual Report, 1975-76 (1977).
18 Law Commission, Report No. 127 (HC201), *Transfer of Land: The Law of Positive and Restrictive Covenants,* 1984.
19 *Ibid,* para 4.14 ff.
20 *Ibid,* para 4.17.
21 *Ibid.*
22 *Ibid.*
23 With damages in lieu.
24 Law Commission, Report No. 127 (HC 201), para 4.17.
25 *Ibid.*
26 *Ibid,* para 4.18.
27 *Ibid,* paras 4.19, 4.20.
28 *Ibid,* para 4.21. Moreover, because the new interest would be regarded as essentially one attaching to the ownership of particular areas of land, it would not (unlike restrictive covenants) 'remain enforceable between the original parties after they had parted with the land' (see para 4.22).
29 *Ibid,* para 4.22.
30 Cheshire & Burn, *Modern Law of Real Property,* 1994, p.641.
31 *Ibid.*
32 *Ibid.*
33 Law Commission, Report No. 127 (HC 201), para 4.25.
34 Ibid, para 4.22.
35 In Maudsley & Burn's *Land Law Cases and Materials,* 6th edition at p. 913 it is pointed out that self-help 'would be useful not only for emergencies such as an over-flowing gutter but also for things such as a decaying fence'. There would have to have been reserved a right to enter on the land before such a remedy could be exercised.
36 Law Commission, Report No. 201 (HC 546), *Transfer of Land: Obsolete Restrictive Covenants,* 1991.
37 Town & Country Planning Act, 1990 section 106 (as amended by the Planning & Compensation Act, 1991) which enables a developer to enter into a 'planning obligation', either by agreement with the authority or by the developer giving a unilateral undertaking. Such agreements or obligations may include positive as well as negative obligations
38 Denning, *The Discipline of Law,* 1979, p. 287.
39 A number of ways are available, including for example, chains of indemnity covenants or the creation of an estate rentcharge.
40 [1994] 2 All ER 65.
41 (1885) 29 ChD 750.
42 [1994] 2 All ER 65, at 71.
43 *Ibid,* at 72.
44 Thus, Lord Templeman continued (at p. 68): 'Equity did not allow (in *Tulk v Moxhay*) the owner of Leicester Square to build because the owner never acquired the right to build without the consent of the person...from time to time entitled to the covenant against building'. For his Lordship, the enforcement of negative covenants lay in the law of property, while positive covenants were part of the law of contract.
45 [1994] 2 All ER 65, at 71.
46 (1583) 5 Co Rep 16a [1558-1774] 4 All ER Rep 68.

47 P.J. Clarke, *Freehold Covenants: the triumph of orthodoxy,* All ER Rev 1994, 245-248, at 246. Professor Clarke is also of the view that the opinions of the authors of the various reform documents are sufficiently weighty to persuade Government that there should be change (see p. 248).

7 The Restrictive Covenant and Planning Control

Introduction

In the chapters dealing with the discharge or modification of restrictive covenants continual reference has been made to the relationship between restrictive covenant control and planning control. Some consideration has now to be given as to how the relationship between the two forms of control may develop in the future.

For long the relationship between the two has been considered by many as unsatisfactory. For instance, in 1964, A.R. Mellows[1] posed the question:

> If the whole basis of the planning legislation is to secure that land is put to the use which is best from the point of view of the community, why should that object be frustrated by privately imposed covenants when most private property rights are overridden?

Clearly he was inferring, if not stating specifically, that restrictive covenants should be subservient to and either subsumed in or overridden by planning control - an extreme view which found little favour with either lawyers or landowners.

More recently a view has been expressed that some of the 'controls' within the remit of the Planning Acts could, certainly insofar as 'neighbour' developments are concerned, be transferred (over time) to restrictive covenant control. For example, B.J. Pearce[2] has observed that:

> Town planners have traditionally used the instrument of development control to restrain the location of land uses and land users which would impose heavy external diseconomies on adjoining activities and people.

He has gone on to suggest that, as development control often denies individuals the chance of reaching positions of mutual benefit with

193

neighbours by negotiation, since it requires the local authority to assess the public interest involved in each development rather than allowing private agreement, what is required is a 'private property rights alternative' solution. His solution would be to expand greatly the private rights and obligations associated with real property, thereby providing a legal remedy whereby 'landholders' could protect those 'rights' from 'harm' by other persons. Such an extension of the law of nuisance (and trespass) has already occurred in the United States where 'un-neighbourly acts' (uses and development) are not embraced by their 'zoning and building codes'. An extension of private property rights, particularly if enshrined in a written code, would be analogous to, and constitute a kind of universal set of restrictive covenants.

At the 'community planning' level the demarcation between those issues that can be left to private control and those which should be made subject to public control has never been satisfactorily resolved. Planning control has been seen as a means of protecting private property interests 'on the cheap', by avoiding the more 'costly' remedy available to the landowner through recourse to the courts in respect of nuisance, and by placing less reliance on the use and enforcement of the restrictive covenant. The situation was well summarised by J. Boynton[3] as long ago as 1979:

> There is one area where the courts could play a bigger role than they do [with respect to town planning]. We could revise and update the law of nuisance. We could set down in statutory form the rights which an owner of property should have and which courts should protect. It puts planning authorities under unreasonable pressure if they are expected to safeguard the interests of adjoining owners, and have to take the place which the law could surely take.

Those 'statutory rights' could well be founded on, *inter alia*, the major issues which restrictive covenant control has embraced. The loosening of planning control, particularly at the 'community' level, and the greater reliance on private property rights (in which the restrictive covenant has an important rôle) are matters to which later we return.

The Limitations of Planning Control and Restrictive Covenant Control

The real power of control (as the word necessarily implies) is to prevent unacceptable (in land use planning terms) uses and development. In this the planning control system has been reasonably successful; it has in general prevented the worst 'excesses', except where 'political' intervention has occurred at the local or national level. Although such perverse decisions can be challenged in the courts this is inevitably at the expense of time and money and for a result which, even when successful, may do little to restore the *status quo*.

The control power, linked as it is to the development plan, is slow to respond to changed circumstances and new demands and its reputation for fairness and even-handedness suffers when it is required to provide solutions to problems outside its remit, as for example the provision of 'affordable housing' and other instances of 'social engineering', to solve a socio-economic problem.[4]

Planning control is at its least effective and most unpopular when it intervenes at the domestic level and concerns itself overly with detail and minutiae. Many of these matters are best left to resolution (or even continuing dispute) between the neighbouring parties concerned. Planning control also operates less successfully at the other end of the scale in dealing with major installations (e.g. power stations) and 'energy-based' industries, primarily due to lack of any national planning guidance and the incidence of political interference and vested interest pressures.[5] It works best at the intermediate level, from quite small scale up to large scale developments, where local decision-making (in the context of local plans) can be seen to be arrived at (even if not welcomed) by an accountable elected body, after public consultation.[6]

Any attempt to draw a comparison between the effectiveness of planning control powers and restrictive covenant powers must be prefaced by the obvious but important *caveat* that their exercise is for very different reasons, albeit similar objectives. The extent of the restrictive covenant control power has been the subject matter of many of the cases already considered. The only legal limits to the exercise of the power are those arising from the fundamental rules of contract and those imposed by Parliament in such Acts as the Race Relations Acts; however, actual enforcement may be difficult where 'current issues of political correctness' are present.[7] The only practical limits to the exercise of the power are those which the covenantee is willing to accept as deviations from, or exceptions to, the benefit of the restrictive covenant to which he is entitled.

Restrictive covenant control is potentially wide in scope, whereas planning control is circumscribed by law, regulation and policy. However, in each instance the *real* measure of power lies in the respective ability to enforce the control and the efficiency and efficacy of enforcement procedures.

The Enforcement of Planning Control and Restrictive Covenant Control

The main remedies open to a local planning authority for the enforcement of breaches of planning control are Enforcement Notices, Stop Notices and Injunctions. The more common form of action is the Enforcement Notice; the much rarer is the Stop Notice (which may result in the payment of compensation), and even more rarely (but increasingly) resort to the courts for an Injunction, particularly in the case of major breaches.

Enforcement action by the issue of an enforcement notice or by the service of a breach of condition notice, may be taken in respect of a breach of planning control, defined as carrying out development without the required planning permission, or failing to comply with any condition subject to which planning permission has been granted.[8] Action by the local planning authority is discretionary, subject to certain time limits for the bringing of enforcement action and to the local planning authority being of the opinion that there has been a breach of planning control and that it is expedient to issue the notice, having regard to the provisions of the development plan and to any other material considerations.[9] The effect of this last requirement has assumed a greater significance through the introduction of section 54A into the Town & Country Planning Act, 1990, giving the development plan a status of primacy. Most importantly however is the element of discretion which lies entirely within the hands of the local planning authority, so that 'other' persons who are adversely affected by the breach in their use and enjoyment of their own lands have no more than a persuasive power to require the local planning authority to take action. The only avenues open to them, in dealing with a recalcitrant local authority, are 'peripheral', being either an application for Judicial Review (expensive and of limited application and scope) or reference to the Ombudsman where, if it can be shown that there has been mal-administration on the part of the local planning authority, compensation (but not action to stop the breach) may ensue.

In cases where development is in the process of being carried out, either without planning permission or in contravention of planning permission, the local planning authority has the additional power of serving a stop notice 'prohibiting the carrying out of that activity on the land to which the enforcement notice relates, or any part of that land specified in the stop notice'.[10] The purpose of the stop notice is to overcome the problems that could be associated with delay in the enforcement notice procedure occasioned by appeal and other delaying tactics. The Secretary of State on appeal is less likely to require the demolition of a building which has been completed than one in the early stages of erection. Whilst being undoubtedly an effective control measure, taking effect within three days of it being served, if the enforcement notice which it supplements is quashed or varied on appeal, compensation may become payable. In major construction projects a stop notice can cause considerable loss even if only a few months pass between the issue of the stop notice and the quashing or variation of the enforcement notice. The fear that compensation may be payable and the possibility of local councillors being surcharged has deterred local planning authorities from issuing stop notices.

Victor Moore[11] claims that in fact the liability to pay compensation is much restricted as it is only payable if the enforcement notice is quashed on grounds other than that planning permission ought to be granted for the development to which the notice relates, or where the authority decide to withdraw the stop notice, or it is varied on appeal so that the matter alleged to constitute a breach of planning control is no longer included in the notice. The circumstances in which compensation is not to be payable are clarified by section 186(5), incorporated in the 1990 Act by the Planning & Compensation Act, 1991, which now provides that no compensation is payable in respect of any prohibition in a stop notice of any activity which, at any time when the notice is in force, constitutes or contributes to a breach of planning control. Nevertheless local planning authorities will still be reluctant to use the stop notice so long as there is a 'perceived' fear of compensation, no matter how little in reality.

Thus, enforcement notices and stop notices are subject to statutory limitations, procedural constraints, the 'possibility' of compensation, and most significantly lie firmly in the discretion of the local planning authority.

Local planning authorities have in the past resorted to injunctions to enforce planning control. Prior to 1991 local planning authorities operated under section 222 of the Local Government Act, 1972, which gave a general power to local authorities who considered it expedient for the promotion or protection of the interests of the inhabitants of their area to 'prosecute or defend or appear in any legal proceedings and, in the case of civil proceedings, institute them in their own name'.[12] Since 1991, local planning authorities have, through the introduction of section 187B into the 1990 Act, by the 1991 Planning & Compensation Act, an express right in planning law to obtain from the High Court or a County Court an injunction. The section applies to any actual or apprehended breach of control and is available to the local planning authority whether or not it has exercised or proposes to exercise any of its other powers as, for example, enforcement and stop notices. Few cases have as yet been brought under the new section, although it has already been held that it is much wider than the power previously available in that it is no longer necessary to show that criminal penalties are not enough to deter the defendant from infringing planning law.[13]

Again, as with the other remedies, instituting action to enforce planning control by means of an injunction is at the discretion of the local planning authority, with all the consequences that flow from the use or non-use of a discretionary power.[14]

Having looked at the 'limitations' associated with the enforcement of planning control, attention is now transferred to considering those in relation to restrictive covenant control. As noted earlier only equitable remedies are available and, furthermore, the only equitable remedy appropriate to a negative covenant is that of injunction. Although since 1858[15] the court has power to award damages in any case where an injunction could have been awarded, they are rarely a satisfactory remedy for the breach of a covenant intended to preserve the value of land. Mandatory injunctions may be granted[16] but, as with all applications for injunctions, grant lies within the discretion of the court. The rules of Equity apply and an injunction will be refused if it would be 'inequitable' to grant it because of, for example, acquiescence in the breach, overt acceptance of breaches of the covenant such as to indicate an intention not to enforce, or where the character of the neighbourhood has been so completely changed that the covenant has become valueless.[17] As in other areas of Equity there is seen here, as noted earlier, both a desire to 'do Equity' for the defendant and also an unwillingness to act in vain.

As with planning control, the enforcement of restrictive covenants by means of injunction is subject to the discretion of the courts, with the inevitable inconsistencies (and reluctance) that they have from time to time exhibited.[18] Unlike planning control, however, procedure for the enforcement of a breach is entirely within the hands of the beneficiary of the covenant. It is the covenantee or his successors who have the power to institute proceedings, at their discretion, though they may well be deterred by the cost of court proceedings and the element of chance for success. Nonetheless, despite the potential inhibition of cost, restrictive covenants have, subject to the limitations of acquiescence and obsolescence, a degree of permanence and endurability.[19] Furthermore, the discharge or modification mechanism has ensured a continuing relevance whereby a particular control, which might otherwise have failed entirely, has been resuscitated in a modified form, and thereby enabled to continue to give at least a measure of regulation where otherwise none may have survived.

All the planning control powers that are necessary are, it is submitted, already available.[20] Local planning authorities have in the Town & Country Planning Acts a comprehensive package of controls. They need to make better use of them and to show better 'foresight' of problems and future requirements. Enforcement action should be relegated to the category of 'last resort'. Planning control (through permissions, conditions and obligations) should aim to be self-enforcing and self-regulatory. This may best be achieved through a partnership between local planning authorities, developers and the public[21] leading to better appreciation of the rôle of planning control and its wider environmental objectives and to local planning authorities framing planning conditions and obligations in clear language and confined to those essential to the proposed use or development.

With the facility provided by the restrictive covenant in the private arena and the planning condition and obligation in the public sphere, the law has afforded generally effective mechanisms for the enforcement of burdens related to land use and development. As is the case with any mechanism, however, there are occasions when their furtherance by the courts and the Lands Tribunal is vulnerable to criticism.

Instances of such perceived vulnerability include the problems (already noted) experienced under section 84 with the issue of the basis of assessment of compensation upon the discharge or modification of a restrictive covenant. Similarly, in the context of the same section, attention has been drawn to the way in which, when faced with covenants in planning agreements, there has on occasion been a tendency to deal with them as if they were distinct from the planning permission to which they were attached.[22]

Reference may also be made to the decision reached in the case of *Wrotham Park,*[23] the outcome of which was at the least debatable and, though not a subject explored here, to the Courts' approach to the admittedly contentious problem of 'planning gain'.[24] In certain cases the courts have approached the relevant statutory machinery, namely the planning agreement/obligation régime,[25] as if it existed independently of the planning statute of which it forms part and have thereby extended to it a much wider interpretation than the legislature surely intended.[26]

From matters such as these the question may follow as to whether they and other issues of like kind might benefit were they to be resolved within a structure infused by a broad 'environmental based' philosophy. Could they for instance be more advantageously addressed in the atmosphere of an Environmental Court or an Environmental Tribunal?

An Environmental Court or Tribunal

For a number of reasons, including the spate of environmental law and regulation, the highly specialist and technical issues involved and the growing public interest and concern in environmental matters, the need for a body or bodies devoted to the resolution of environmental questions has been increasingly canvassed. Noting the way in which environmental disputes may be heard by a range of courts or determined at different levels within the administrative system, Professor Malcolm Grant has expressed the belief that there 'would be advantages in drawing these jurisdictions together so as to ensure consistency and the development of an environmental jurisprudence'.[27]

Existing bodies are not always the most appropriate vehicles for the determination of environmental disputes[28] and in the courts there is the further problem of a protracted time-scale for hearings. The adversarial approach can militate against 'compromise' solutions which can only flow from a less formal consideration of technical, scientific and aesthetic issues.[29] Furthermore, a 'strict' interpretation of the letter of the law may not always result in socially acceptable solutions to environmental and planning matters - the province of administrative decision-making with acknowledged (although circumscribed) political, social and economic influences.

Were there to be introduced a specialist body or bodies - a change of such major significance as to be worthy of a Royal Commision - it is suggested that such should 'flow' naturally from existing institutions and embrace criminal, civil and administrative jurisdictions.[30] Necessarily, there would need to be provision for different 'levels' of hearing and one possible approach would be a system involving an Environmental Court and an Environmental Tribunal, each functioning (though obviously variously) both at 'first instance' and as an 'appellate' body. Without entering into any depth of detail such a régime could assume a basic form as now described.

First, there would be the Environmental Tribunal, acting (as noted) as both a 'first instance' and an 'appellate' institution, embracing much of the current jurisdiction of the Lands Tribunal with added jurisdiction in respect of 'environmental' and 'planning' issues. Powers might be bestowed upon it, *inter alia*, to adjudicate environmental disputes between parties who saw advantage in compromise or mediation, to decide minor breaches of environmental codes,[31] and to determine appeals from the decisions of the Environment Agency, Local Authorities and Local Planning Authorities.[32]

Second, there would be the Environmental Court, again with both first instance and appellate jurisdictions. Regarding the former, it could act in respect of defined major breaches of the criminal code and of the commission of the 'established' land-based environmental torts of, for example, nuisance and strict liability. Its jurisdiction could be extended to the protection of property rights such as restrictive covenants and easements. Regarding the appellate jurisdiction, it could hear appeals from the decisions of the Environmental Tribunal on matters of law and the proper interpretation of fact. All the necessary enforcement powers would have to be conferred upon it,[33] with criminal and civil matters best kept distinct.[34]

Of the two bodies it is conceived that it is at the level of the Tribunal that 'grass roots' issues would be the better resolved and, in consequence, the Tribunal should deal with the majority of issues, save the most serious and politically sensitive. A Tribunal modelled on the Lands Tribunal but with a broader remit,[35] functioning at different levels, performing a variety of rôles, and much enhanced both in composition and powers, could bring together the inter-régime conflicts which environmental issues raise. In so doing it would import greater transparency and clarity to the issues involved.

From the wider perspective a good case can be made for the creation of both an Environmetal Court and an Environmental Tribunal in terms of

202 The Restrictive Covenant in the Control of Land Use

facilitating the resolution of the often delicate balance between competing interests, between public good and private property rights, between differing environmental objectives and between development and the conservation of resources.

From the more precise aspect of enforceable land-related obligations it could be that the discharge or modification of such obligations under section 84 of the Law of Property Act, 1925 would be aided by being conducted under the larger 'umbrella' of an Environmental Tribunal. Furthermore, on a somewhat different note, it might be that through the development of an environment-related institutional structure, working practices and a 'jurisprudence', the relationship between restrictive covenant control and planning control could at least be clarified, if not finally resolved.

That which has been outlined is but one view of a possible development. It is, however, not without interest to consider such a development as eventually constituting a landmark in the progress of the restrictive covenant. As the *Tulk v Moxhay* doctrine grew it had in due course to be seen in the context of the wider régime of public planning control. Now, restrictive covenant control and planning control have to be seen against the still more expansive backdrop of environmental regulation. Where this will lead for the doctrine and whether, as surely not unlikely, an Environmental Court and/or Tribunal features in the scene, is for the future.

Before coming to any conclusions as to the future relationship between restrictive covenant control and planning (environmental) control it is instructive to consider how the matter of the control of land use and development has progressed in that country which received and based much of its real property law on our English system, namely the United States of America.

The American Approach

While the control of land use in the United States has involved such legislative intervention as zoning and building codes,[36] it has placed particular emphasis on the imposition of servitudes. Adverting to their importance, Uriel Reichman, writing in the early 1980's, observed that:[37]

Servitudes provide the legal foundation of many of today's comprehensive private planning schemes that determine the physical layout regulation and operation of large residential and commercial developments.

Not long before, he had pointed out in similar vein that:[38]

[From the late 1960's onwards] several new towns and hundreds of large communities in the United States were planned and constructed almost exclusively by private enterprise. By structuring comprehensive regulatory schemes, private developers were able to exercise land use controls and supply services traditionally provided by municipalities and Government agencies. Primarily facilitated by the extensive use of both regular and 'discretionary' servitudes, the introduction of these so-called residential private governments resulted in a substantial restriction of landowner's liberties.

And a particularly graphic account of the significance of servitudes was provided by Professor Winokur writing at the end of the 1980's:[39]

Neighborhood uniformity is preserved by a complex battery of restrictions on everything from permitted uses to permissible colors of garden accessories to storage of personal belongings visible from other lots or the street. Even minor aesthetic changes are often prohibited without advance approval of a neighborhood architectural review committee. Often called conditions, covenants and restrictions, such residential restrictions typically take the form of real covenants and equitable servitudes that bind for several decades, or even permanently, not only the original creating parties but their successors in interest. They are usually reciprocally enforceable among residence owners within a subdivision or condominium project and also by the homeowners or condominium association. These restrictions serve the significant salutary purpose of maintaining a desirable character and quality in many residential areas. Reciprocally enforceable promissory servitudes preserve neighborhood characteristics important to residents who value quiet, privacy and status; who prefer car transportation to walking or public transit; and who favour supermarkets and shopping center department stores over ethnic or esoteric neighborhood shops. Consistency of aesthetic design throughout a neighborhood can produce residential areas of striking beauty.

Those parts of the American law of servitudes which concern 'running covenants' share both the ancestry and complexity of their English counterparts but not the precise pattern of the current principles. A distinction is drawn between covenants which run at law and those which run under the doctrine of *Tulk v Moxhay*. While the former are called 'real covenants' and today mostly comprise landlord and tenant covenants, the latter are called 'equitable restrictions' and, most interestingly, include both negative *and* affirmative covenants.

To the modern importance of the equitable doctrine of *Tulk v Moxhay*, Cunningham, Stoebuck and Whitman, the authors of *The Law of Property*,[40] bear implicit witness. They point out that 'plaintiffs can usually employ equitable-restriction theory [and that] recent court decisions rarely turn upon real covenant doctrine'.[41] The widespread application of equitable-restriction theory has cause it 'to eclipse real covenant theory'.[42] They explain that the commonest form of 'notice' in American cases is 'constructive notice' through the operation of Recording Acts and that it is the recognition of this form of notice which has facilitated the eclipsing of real covenant theory by the equitable doctrine.

The emphasis which has been placed on servitudes, and in particular on equitable restrictions, reflects the fact that the control of land use through the public mechanism of planning has not been so effectively or comprehensively deployed as in the United Kingdom. To the distinction, in terms of effectiveness, between resort to servitudes and to zoning, Winokur draws attention in the following words:[43]

> Calls for liberalized promissory servitude enforcement sometimes reflect critics' concerns that modern zoning is of limited effectiveness as a planning and allocation tool. These critics see zoning as particularly ineffective in its role of segregating land uses. In comparison with private systems such as a regime of promissory servitudes, zoning has been criticised as an ineffective land use allocator.

Traditionally the argument ran in favour of unencumbered titles but the attitude gradually changed. It became apparent that 'in many ways permanency of development of land [was] desirable',[44] witness 'the prevalence of equitable restrictions and the tendency towards zoning laws and towards building line restrictions'.[45]

As Winokur intimates, support for control by means of servitudes has been founded both on economic and segregational (environmental) arguments. As to the former he observes:[46]

> The stability of land development and use promised by regimes of servitudes enforceable between successors has persuaded both courts and scholars that servitudes tend to enhance the very land values they were once thought to diminish.

Regarding the latter he comments:[47]

> Whether servitude goals are cast in terms of preserving land values, maintaining neighborhood aesthetics, or expressing a community character and style, a substantial proportion of homeowners want to restrict the use of the land adjacent to their homes without having to rely on Government initiatives.

The inherent worth of servitudes pervades these observations but even so they are not without their difficulties. Probably the most significant, namely their inflexibility over time, is highlighted by Winokur in an observation he makes regarding the need to update or recast older servitudes:[48]

> By creatively addressing the most troublesome problem of promissory servitudes - their inflexibility over time, especially in large servitude regimes - a structural recasting of the enforcement relationships for older servitudes can simplify the current morass of rules, and substantially improve the overall impacts of promissory servitudes on land utility, individual liberty, and personal identity.

The heightened importance of the American equitable promissory servitude, relative to the English counterpart of the restrictive covenant, was vivdly reflected in the description (already quoted) that Winokur gives of a typically low-density suburban neighbourhood of single-family residences built in a virtually uniform design.

No suggestion is made that such an extreme scenario could occur under English law. Nevertheless a loosening of public control, particularly at the 'community' level, and the reform of the law whereby positive covenants would run so as to bind and benefit in the same manner as restrictive covenants, might well encourage movement in that direction.

The United States planning system, based primarily on zoning and building codes, needs imperatively to be supplemented by a comprehensive range of 'servitudes' to achieve environmental and aesthetic protection and enhancement. If nothing else, an appreciation of the law of servitudes as operating in the States testifies to their importance, and in particular that of the 'restrictive covenant', in the control of the development and use of land alongside a public planning régime.

Conclusion

We commented in chapter 6 on the proposals for reform that have from time to time been considered. Whether or not any reform of the law ever takes place, the rôle of the restrictive covenant (independently of planning control) will remain an important land management 'tool'. Its worth is plain, even where planning control has become advanced, and was highlighted by the American academic, Susan French, when referring to the English situation:[49]

> The advent of comprehensive governmental land use regulation in the twentieth century actually increased the incidence of private land use arrangements for two reasons: public regulation itself often uses private servitudes as tools of regulation; and the inherent shortcomings in public regulation encourage private arrangements.

Likewise, nearer home, the Law Commission has reinforced the continuimg value of the restrictive covenant in the following terms:[50]

> Planning law may overlap to some extent with restrictive covenants, but we do not believe that it has removed the need for them. Perhaps especially in residential property developments, restrictive covenants commonly regulate many things for which planning law would not cater - and do so for the mutual benefit of the residents and with the aim of preserving the character and standard of the development as a whole.

> It might perhaps be argued that the answer lies not in preserving the power to impose private restrictions, but in extending the ambit of planning law. We think it unrealistic, however, to expect planning authorities to concern themselves with all the detailed matter for which restrictive covenants now commonly make provision...It must also be remembered that restrictive covenants may be used to serve purposes which are private and individual and for which planning law would not cater however far it were extended.

The restrictive covenant has survived, with varying degrees of fortune, for 150 years. It will continue to be not only relevant but necessary and, for the following reasons, its use is likely to increase as also will its range, significance and complexity:
(1) The number of households in England is projected to grow by 4.4 million between 1991 and 2016.[51] Not all of this increase will require new dwellings but a significant proportion of it will. Housing development will

generally take place in new settlements (small towns and villages), urban villages, suburban estates, and on reclaimed land in towns and cities.

(2) The great majority of new development will be undertaken by private developers and housing associations who will rely on some form of restrictive covenant control. In particular, new types of development, for example in parkland settings or as part of recreational complexes (golf courses, marinas), will necessitate 'novel' control régimes for their successful implementation and future maintenance.

(3) The public demand for greater environmental protection of the home and the work place, embracing both matters of amenity and design on the one hand and security for both person and property (from crime and vandalism) on the other hand, will increase the need for some form of 'extended' restrictive covenant control.

(4) The relaxation of 'public' planning control (by for example the extension of permitted development rights under the General Development Order Consolidation or the simplification of use classes in the Use Classes Order) and the vagaries of the implementation of planning control would mean increasingly that new generations of residents in particular would demand the additional safeguard provided by private control.

(5) Regardless of whether planning control will be loosened, the 'ability to enforce', which is in the hands of the 'property owner' will continue to be the most telling reason for restrictive covenant control to a landowner or occupier who doubts the ability or will of a local planning authority to exercise control in his interest. As earlier indicated the case for taking some planning control at the 'community' level out of the hands of public planning authorities and placing it within the ambit of private landowners is a proposition that may well come to fruition. Whether or not it does, the fear of relaxation of planning control at the 'community' or local level will be sufficient to bolster the clamour for private control.

On the question as to whether the restrictive covenant will survive for another 150 years it would be imprudent to conjecture. What is more certain is that public demand, particularly in new housing, for greater control by residents means that some form of control will be needed for the foreseeable future, be it in the form of the basic restrictive covenant, an 'improved' development or building scheme, an extension of maintenance agreements and charges, or some other specific form of control, as for example the 'estate rentcharge'.[52]

Having made the case for the future of some form of restrictive covenant control perhaps we should conclude on a more cautionary note provided for us by Susan French[53] and which itself encapsulates the case for, if not full scale reform, at least some rationalisation, clarification and simplification of the law:

> Among the most complicated and confusing of all legal rules are those which concern enforceability of promises on behalf of and against successors of the original parties to the agreement...Since the first English case interpreting the first English statute on the subject, commentators have doubted that the courts understood the law, and a study of judicial opinions from *Spencer's Case* on, is bewildering at best.

Therein, at least for some, lies the fascination.

Notes

1 A.R. Mellows, *Planning and Restrictive Covenants*, (1964) 28 Conv (NS) 190, at 203.
2 B.J. Pearce, *Property Rights vs. Development Control*, (1981) 52 Town Planning Review, 47, at 48.
3 J. Boynton, *Planning Policy - Its Formulation and Implementation*, Report of Proceedings of Town and Country Planning Summer School, RTPI, 1979, p.71.
4 Although planning control is directed to 'the use of the land', the courts have held that planning authorities may in certain circumstances take into account such matters as personal need and hardship, the commercial viability of small businesses, local needs, the needs of agricultural occupation and affordable housing. Nearly all these exceptions fall within the category of what may be termed 'social engineering' and whilst not necessarily contrary to the proper planning control of the use of land and buildings may, unless strictly circumscribed, jeopardise the 'fairness' of the planning system, as for example, by the granting of planning permission for 'affordable housing' on sites outside the village boundary or 'envelope', the development of such sites being denied to all others.
5 But also as a result of an inadequate 'democratic' process whereby local communities and environmental groups are disadvantaged.
6 Even here it is dependent on up-to-date advice and guidance by Circular and PPG, *vide* the tardy advice on superstores (PPG6) which came too late to control their number and size, to the detriment of town centre renewal.
7 As long ago as 1972, J.F. Garner in an article entitled *Racial Restrictive Covenants in England and the United States* (1972) MLR 478, suggested that a restrictive covenant of a form providing that 'the premises shall be used and occupied by persons of the white or Caucasian race' might be invalid as being contrary to public policy. An injunction or damages might be refused on grounds, *inter alia*, that the benefit did not touch and concern the dominant land; that it would be unlawful under the Race Relations Acts to comply with the covenant by refusing 'prohibited' persons thus rendering the covenant void; or that simply the covenant was void as being contrary to public policy. Whether or not a particular restriction is or is not invalid the practical

question is whether or not it is enforceable. The enforcement issue has been clearly demonstrated in a judgment of the U.S. Supreme Court. In *Shelley v Kraemer* (1948) 334 US 1, 62 SCt 836, 92:1161 the court held that, although racially restrictive covenants are valid between private persons, they may not be enforced by state courts as to do so makes the state a party to the action in violation of the 14th Amendment's Guarantee of Equal Protection of the Laws.

8 Town & Country Planning Act, 1990, section 171A (1).

9 *Ibid*, section 172 (1).

10 *Ibid*, section 183 (1).

11 *A Practical Approach to Planning Law*, 6th edition, 1997, p. 357.

12 See, for example, *Westminster City Council v Jones* [1981] JPL 750, where the local authority acted to prevent the operation of an amusement arcade causing nuisance and disturbance in a residential area.

13 *Runnymede DC v Harwood* [1994] JPL 724.

14 It is to be noted that damages in lieu of an injunction are rarely if ever appropriate in breaches of planning control.

15 The Chancery Amendment Act, section 2.

16 See, for example, *Wakeham v Wood* (1981) 43 P&CR 40.

17 The chapters on Discharge or Modification cite many examples of where applications have been refused on one or other of these grounds.

18 See, for example, *Wrotham Park Estate Company v Parkside Homes Ltd. and others* [1974] 2 All ER 321.

19 They are, it may also be noted, unaffected by perpetuity rules: *Mackenzie v Childers* (1889) 43 ChD 265, at 279.

20 Some might argue for the right of third parties to intervene but, apart from the inevitable delay this might cause and the threat of capricious action, the rights of third parties are (or should be) protected by the democratically elected members of the local planning authority, responsible for both the decision and its enforcement in the public interest.

21 As, for example, the very successful liaison committees set up to monitor the implementation of mineral planning permissions, often under a specific requirement in a section 106 obligation.

22 This problem has been obviated for the future by the transfer of jurisdiction from the Lands Tribunal to the Secretary of State for the Environment on appeal.

23 *Wrotham Park Estate Company v Parkside Homes Ltd and others* [1974] 2 All ER 321.

24 Although 'planning gain' is nowhere defined and has no statutory significance, it is generally understood to embrace those situations where a local planning authority requires, or an applicant offers, some additional benefit as an enhancement or pre-condition to the grant of planning permission.

25 See Sections 106, 106A and 106B of the Town & Country Planning Act, 1990 (as amended by the Planning & Compensation Act, 1991).

26 See, for example, *R v Plymouth City Council (ex parte Plymouth & South Devon Co-operative Society)* [1993] JPL 1099 and *Tesco Stores Ltd. v Secretary of State for the Environment and Others* [1995] 1 WLR 759.

27 *Arguments for an Environmental Court* - Paper presented to '*Environmental Litigation - Towards an Environmental Court*' Conference, Royal Institute of Public Administration, 1992. More specifically, Professor Grant pointed out that: '[A]n environmental dispute may come before a bench of lay magistrates (such as on a

prosecution or a statutory nuisance complaint under the Environmental Protection Act 1990, or a prosecution under planning legislation); or it may go to the Crown Court (for major cases or not-guilty pleas), or to the County Court (civil injunctions) or the High Court (civil injunctions and judicial review of decision-making by officials). Other disputes (sometimes even the same dispute), may be determined within the administrative system, such as on a planning appeal to a planning inspector, or an appeal to the Secretary of State for the Environment against refusal of an authorisation under the new system of integrated pollution control. There would be advantages in drawing these jurisdictions together so as to ensure consistency and the development of an environmental jurisprudence.'

28 Consider the technical complexity and often inter-disciplinary nature of the questions involved and such issues as the irreversibility of damage, the collective interest in the resolution of problems, the absence of environmental absolutes and the difficulty of anticipating environmental damage.

29 Furthermore, the courts themselves have always been reluctant to become involved in matters relating to subjective issues, as for example aesthetics, amenity and design, which many environmental disputes display.

30 One of the earliest Environment Courts was the New South Wales Land & Environment Court, a 'specialist one-stop supreme court with mixed personnel', established by the Land & Environment Court Act, 1979 (NSW).

31 With power to secure enforcement, impose penalties and award damages, etc.

32 With certain exceptions such as, for example, retaining the right of the Secretary of State to intervene in matters of political, national or international inportance or sensitivity.

33 A panoply powers, including (to take the most obvious instances) fines, imprisonment, injunctions and the award of damages.

34 It has to be recognised that some argue the case for an Environmental Court on the ground that, *inter alia,* it would present the opportunity to overcome the rigid distinction between civil and criminal jurisdictions, thereby enabling consideration of alternative *remedies* (as well as alternative forms of *decision-making*). Bell, in Ball & Bell on *Environmental Law* (4th. edition, 1997, at pp. 17 & 22), observes that, by giving consideration to the 'decriminalisation' of whole areas of environmental law, not only would a clear distinction be drawn between infringements that are properly administrative in nature and truly criminal breaches such as blatant environmental vandalism, but also the whole range of alternative remedies (for example, revocation of licences, closure of plants, levying of clean-up costs, imposition of damages) would be available in cases where at the moment a fine or imprisonment is the only (and often inappropriate) remedy. Nonetheless, it is suggested that it is an essential element of English Jurisprudence that the individual (or corporate body) should be made aware of whether he (or it) is in breach of a criminal offence, rather than a civil tort or an administrative regulation.

35 Embracing environmental, planning and possibly a range of other property-based matters.

36 And in addition, extensive judicial involvement, principally in the form of nuisance actions.

37 *Toward a Unified Concept of Servitudes,* 55 S Cal LR 1179 (1982).
38 *Judicial Supervision of Servitudes,* 7 J Legal Studies 139 (1978).
39 *The Mixed Blessings of Promissory Servitudes,* (1989) Wisc L Rev 1, at 3.

40 Second edition, West Publishing Co., 1993.

41 *Ibid*, at 486.

42 *Ibid*, at 492.

43 *The Mixed Blessings of Promissory Servitudes*, (1989) Wisc L Rev 1, at 21.

44 *Ibid*, at 17. (Referring to a comment by Judge Charles Clark when he was Dean of the Yale Law School).

45 *Ibid*.

46 *Ibid*, at 15.

47 *Ibid*, at 96. It is, of course, acknowledged that the supporting arguments are inter-related.

48 *Ibid*, at 97. In the context of 'old' servitudes there does not appear to have developed the like of the sophisticated discharge or modification régime fostered by section 84 of the Law of Property Act, 1925. However, if conditions have changed to the extent that enforcement would provide no substantial benefit to the plaintiff and would be inequitable to the defendant the court will refuse an injunction and may declare the restriction terminated.

49 *Toward a Modern Law of Servitudes*, 55 S Cal LR 1261, at 1262 (1982).

50 Law Commission, Report No. 127 (HC 201), *Transfer of Land: The Law of Positive and Restrictive Covenants,* 1984, paras 2.5, 2.6.

51 Projections of Households in England to 2016, HMSO, 1995 and *Household Growth: where shall we live?,* Cm. 3471, 1996. Although the projection of 4.4 million has recently (March 1999) been revised to a lower figure of 4.1 million the effect in substance will be the same.

52 The Rentcharges Act, 1977, which generally prohibited the creation of new rentcharges and provided for the ultimate 'abolition' of existing rentcharges, excepted an 'estate rentcharge' created for the purpose, *inter alia*, of making covenants to be performed by the owner of the land affected by the rentcharge enforceable by the rent owner against the owner for the time being of the land (s.2(4)). By this means 'positive' (as well as restrictive) covenants can be enforced on freehold land against successors in title. Although the positive covenants in themselves will not 'run', the right of entry exercisable on breach of the positive covenant will 'run'. The effect of this is that although right of entry under section 121, Law of Property Act, 1925, is exercisable generally to recover arrears of rentcharge only, the estate rentcharge deed may provide for a wider right of entry, exercisable following breach of a number of positive covenants, under which the rent owner can carry out the covenant and recover the expense of so doing. The position of the rent owner can be further strengthened if the estate rentcharge deed incorporates a right of *re-entry* providing in effect for forfeiture of the land on breach of any covenant, whether positive or negative. For a fuller explanation see S. Bright, *Estate Rentcharges and the Enforcement of Positive Covenants,* [1988] Conv 99.

53 In 55 S Cal LR 1261 (1982) footnote 1, quoting G. Lefcoe, *Land Development Law,* (1974), 768-9.

Appendices

Appendix 1

Law of Property Act, 1925, Section 84(1)
(as first enacted)

Power to discharge or modify restrictive covenants affecting land
84.–(1) The Authority hereinafter defined shall (without prejudice to any concurrent jurisdiction of the court) have power from time to time, on the application of any person interested in any freehold land affected by any restriction arising under covenant or otherwise as to the user thereof or the building theron, by order wholly or partially to discharge or modify any such restriction (subject or not to the payment by the applicant of compensation to any person suffering loss in consequence of the order) on being satisfied –
(a) that by reason of changes in the character of the property or the neighbourhood or other circumstances of the case which the Authority may deem material, the restriction ought to be deemed obsolete, or that the continued existence thereof would impede the reasonable user of the land for public or private purposes without securing practical benefits to other persons, or, as the case may be,would unless modified so impede such user; or
(b) that the persons of full age and capacity for the time being or from time to time entitled to the benefit of the restriction, whether in respect of estates in fee simple or any lesser estates or interests in the property to which the benefit of the restriction is annexed, have agreed, either expressly or by implication, by their acts or omissions, to the same being discharged or modified; or
(c) that the proposed discharge or modification will not injure the persons entitled to the benefit of the restriction:
Provided that no compensation shall be payable in respect of the discharge or modification of a restriction by reason of any advantage thereby accruing to the owner of the land affected by the restriction, unless the person entitled to the benefit of the restriction also suffers loss in consequence of the discharge or modification, nor shall any compensation be payable in excess of such loss; but this provision shall not affect any right to compensation where the person claiming the compensation proves that by reason of the imposition of the restriction, the amount of the consideration paid for the acquisition of the land was reduced.

Appendix 2

Law of Property Act, 1925, Section 84(1)
(as amended by the Law of Property Act, 1969 - major changes in **bold**)

Power to discharge or modify restrictive covenants affecting land
84.–(1) The Lands Tribunal shall (without prejudice to any concurrent jurisdiction of the court) have power from time to time, on the application of any person interested in any freehold land affected by any restriction arising under covenant or otherwise as to the user thereof or the building thereon, by order wholly or partially to discharge or modify any such restriction on being satisfied–
(a) that by reason of changes in the character of the property or the neighbourhood or other circumstances of the case which the Lands Tribunal may deem material, the restriction ought to be deemed obsolete; or
(aa) that (in a case falling within sub-section (1A) below) the continued existence thereof would impede some reasonable user of the land for public or private purposes or, as the case may be, would unless modified so impede such user; or
(b) that the persons of full age and capacity for the time being or from time to time entitled to the benefit of the restriction, whether in respect of estates in fee simple or any lesser estates or interest in the property to which the benefit of the restriction is annexed, have agreed, either expressly or by implication, by their acts or omissions, to the same being discharged or modified; or
(c) that the proposed discharge or modification will not injure the persons entitled to the benefit of the restriction;
and an order discharging or modifying a restriction under this sub-section may direct the applicant to pay to any person entitled to the benefit of the restriction such sum by way of consideration as the Tribunal may think it just to award under one, but not both, of the following heads, that is to say, either–
(i) a sum to make up for the loss or disadvantage suffered by that person in consequence of the discharge or modification; or
(ii) a sum to make up for any effect which the restriction had, at the time when it was imposed, in reducing the consideration then received for the land affected by it.

(1A) Sub-section (1) (aa) above authorises the discharge or modification of a restriction by reference to its impeding some reasonable user of land in any case in which the Lands Tribunal is satisfied that the restriction, in impeding that user, either–
(a) does not secure to persons entitled to the benefit of it any practical benefits of substantial value or advantage to them; or
(b) is contrary to the public interest;
and that money will be an adequate compensation for the loss or disadvantage (if any) which any such person will suffer from the discharge or modification.
(1B) In determining whether a case is one falling within sub-section (1A) above, and in determining whether (in any such case or otherwise) a restriction ought to be discharged or modified, the Lands Tribunal shall take into account the development plan and any declared or ascertainable pattern for the grant or refusal of planning permissions in the relevant areas, as well as the period at which and context in which the restriction was created or imposed and any other material circumstances.
(1C) It is hereby declared that the power conferred by this section to modify a restriction includes the power to add such further provisions restricting the user of or the building on the land affected as appear to the Lands Tribunal to be reasonable in view of the relaxation of the existing provisions, and as may be accepted by the applicant; and the Lands Tribunal may accordingly refuse to modify without some such addition.

The Law of Property Act, 1925, section 84(1) as first enacted and as amended by the Law of Property Act, 1969 is reproduced with the permission of the Controller of Her Majesty's Stationery Office.